PROFILES IN INTERNATIONAL SOCIAL WORK

PROFILES IN INTERNATIONAL SOCIAL WORK

M. C. Hokenstad • S. K. Khinduka • James Midgley
Editors

NASW PRESS

National Association of Social Workers
Washington, DC

Barbara W. White, PhD, ACSW, *President*
Mark G. Battle, ACSW, *Executive Director*

Library of Congress Cataloging-in-Publication Data

Profiles in international social work / M.C. Hokenstad, S.K. Khinduka, and James Midgley, editors.
p. cm.
Includes bibliographical references and index.
ISBN 0-87101-215-4 (acid-free paper)
1. Social service—Cross-cultural studies. I. Hokenstad, Merl C. II. Khinduka, S. K. III. Midgley, James.
HV40.P715 1992
361—dc20 92-11051
CIP

Printed in the United States of America
Cover and interior design by Janice Mauroschadt Design

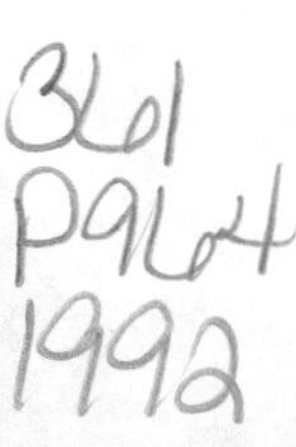

DEDICATION

This book is dedicated to the memory of Dr. Daniel Sanders in recognition of his leadership in the field of international social work. At the time of his untimely death in 1989, Dr. Sanders was Dean of the School of Social Work at the University of Illinois (Urbana-Champaign) and President of the Inter-University Consortium for International Social Development. He was also active in many other international organizations and events. He was a man of ideas and energy whose mission and approach transcended national boundaries. His scholarship and organizational leadership made him a pivotal figure in advancing international collaboration both in social development and social work. His life, work, and friendship continue to inspire those of us who strive for greater international understanding and collaboration in our profession.

CONTENTS

6

Social Work in India: Developmental Roles for a Helping Profession

A. B. Bose

71

7

Social Work in Japan: Responding to Demographic Dilemmas

Yasuo Matsubara

85

8

Social Work in Hong Kong, Singapore, South Korea, and Taiwan: Asia's Four Little Dragons

Peter Ching-Yung Lee

99

FOREWORD

Today, even though social workers around the world face the most difficult challenges, they also have new opportunities to improve social and human conditions globally. Events in Asia and Europe, coupled with economic, political, and social issues in the United States, have created a new climate. Isolationism, never a desirable option, is no longer a possibility.

Social workers, as change agents in their own countries and as advocates for the global village, will play an important role in helping policymakers and others understand our interdependence. None of the social problems we face—poverty, homelessness, violence, drugs, racism, and disease—is unique to one country or one region. However, we do not share only the woes of these problems. Citizens of every country also share great strengths and a great capacity for alleviating these social problems. Yet for each country, the political, economic, and social realities may be different. Studying our commonalities and our differences will help all of us learn how we can be more successful in improving the human condition.

At the National Association of Social Workers (NASW), international issues have been a major component of our programming for some time. Recently, we have been engaged in a multiyear technology transfer project, bringing successful intervention techniques and strategies from other countries to the United States. At this time, 21 of our 55 chapters have twinning projects with other countries.

Last year, the Board of Directors adopted the theme of "Global Family Ties" for our annual public service campaign. "Families are the strength of every nation" proclaimed the materials that were distributed to media across the United States and abroad.

NASW's involvement in international activities resulted in a decision to join the International Federation of Social Work (IFSW) in hosting World Assembly '92 in July. Combining NASW's Meeting of the Profession and IFSW's 12 International Symposia, the conference is cosponsored by six organizations from around the world: the International Association of Schools of Social Work, the Council on Social Work Education, the U.S. Committee of the International Council on Social Welfare, the Council of International Programs, the Inter-University Consortium for International Social Development, and Childhope, USA. Social workers from around the world will discuss policies and strategies for improving the human condition by

- strengthening families
- developing human capital
- enhancing empowerment
- dealing with the impact of conflict, violence, war, and disaster
- responding to and managing political, economic, and social change
- meeting the challenges presented by demographic change.

This conference is a most appropriate arena in which to launch *Profiles in International Social Work*.

Knowledge development in issues that affect the global village is an essential part of NASW's programming. We are proud to publish this important new book as a part of that program.

—Mark G. Battle, ACSW
Executive Director

ACKNOWLEDGMENTS

This book is timely because its publication coincides with the gathering of social workers throughout the world in Washington, DC, for a World Assembly co-hosted by the International Federation of Social Workers (IFSW) and the National Association of Social Workers (NASW). The book provides profiles of social work roles and functions in 13 countries. In doing so it offers an overview of the diversity of social work as practiced in those countries and an analysis of social work commonalities across nations. Particular emphasis is given to how the profession is responding to current challenges in different societies.

We welcome this opportunity to bring together a collection of original articles about social work in different countries and express thanks to those who supported the idea for this book and contributed to its completion. Leon Ginsberg, former chair of NASW's Book Committee, was helpful in the initial stages of the project and Judith Davenport, current chair of the committee, was very receptive to our ideas. Linda Beebe, director of publications for NASW, provided constant encouragement and support. Arol Shack, department assistant for the doctoral program at the Mandel School of Applied Social Sciences, Case Western Reserve University, and Sue Imhoff, administrative assistant to the dean at the George Warren Brown School of Social Work, Washington University, had major responsibilities in the preparation of the manuscript. Our thanks also go to Wendy Almeleh for her diligent copy editing and to Steve Pazdan at NASW, who served as production coordinator for this publication.

Most important, we thank the contributors who wrote the case studies of individual countries and collaborated with us in our attempt to provide both a lively and incisive account of social work in the contemporary world. They were always willing to make changes, accept suggestions, and strive to enhance the book's usefulness and relevance.

M.C. HOKENSTAD

S.K. KHINDUKA

JAMES MIDGLEY

1

The World of International Social Work

M. C. Hokenstad, S. K. Khinduka, and James Midgley

Today, international events impinge on everyday life with commonplace frequency. As a result of improvements in travel and communications, enhanced trade, the growth of the global economy, and greater multinational cooperation in science and technology, the world has indeed become a smaller and more intimate place.

Just a generation ago, international travel required lengthy preparation and a major commitment of time. Unlike today, communications were underdeveloped, and knowledge of events in other parts of the globe was limited. Mediating international organizations, such as the League of Nations, were ineffectual, and exchanges between nation-states were marked more often by conflict than by collaboration.

It would be naive to suggest that the contemporary world is characterized by a healthy internationalism that has obliterated conflict; engendered international rather than parochial sentiments; and fostered positive human relations. Regional strife remains endemic; nationalism is still a powerful force in modern politics; and conflict, not cooperation, continues to impede efforts to facilitate global integration. Yet, many would agree that the changes that have taken place in the past few decades have been historically significant and that the countries of the world have become more interdependent.

This interdependence is as evident in the arena of social welfare as it is in the political and economic arenas. In addition to economic development and environmental impact issues, health and welfare problems are becoming progressively international in scope. Acquired immune deficiency syndrome (AIDS) and other infectious diseases require a global response. The resettlement of refugees and similar welfare programs necessitate cooperation and interaction across countries and continents. Both an international perspective and an international response are required for effective problem solving.

In addition to this wider social, political, and economic impact, internationalism has had a profound influence on science, technology, and the professions. Scientific discoveries in one part of the world are now quickly communicated and analyzed, and technological innovations are more readily adapted. In fact, more and more discoveries in medicine and other disciplines are made as a result of international teamwork. With increased travel and other opportunities for sharing ideas, members of many professions are strengthening their links to their colleagues in other nations. This situation offers every profession the opportunity to internationalize both its knowledge base and its practice.

Internationalism and Social Work

Social work has been influenced by these developments and is becoming internationalized. Today, many social workers travel to other countries to attend meetings and conferences; to establish professional contacts; and to study, work, and serve as consultants and advisers. They are now aware of the activities of their colleagues in other nations and have considerable knowledge about the social problems, professional practices, and policies and programs of human services in other parts of the world. Furthermore, international and regional professional social work associations have expanded significantly over the past few decades. Such organizations as the International Federation of Social Workers, the International Association of Schools of Social Work, and the International Council on Social Welfare are stronger than ever. In Africa, Asia, Europe, and Latin America, regional associations have evolved into effective bodies.

However, few would claim that the international dimension in social work is adequate or that there is sufficient information about social work in different societies. In fact, much more needs to be done to foster social work's international activities and to enhance international inquiry in the field. Relatively few social workers have studied social welfare programs or social work practice in other countries during their professional education. Fewer still have had practice experience in another nation or with an international organization. Thus, most social workers have limited, if any, exposure to programs or practice beyond the boundaries of their own countries.

Certainly, social work has not achieved the same level of sophistication in comparative research as have the other social sciences and some of the other professions. In contrast to economics, sociology, and political science, social work's accumulated body of comparative knowledge remains underdeveloped. In addition, there are inadequate opportunities for the dissemination of this knowledge. Few social work journals are devoted specifically to the international field, and most others pay limited attention to international trends and issues. Although international meetings and conferences are now held with greater frequency, relatively few social workers benefit from the ideas and experiences that are shared at these events.

The absence of a comprehensive book about international social work is one indicator of the inadequate knowledge base in this field. It is surprising that despite the growing involvement of social work in international activities, no systematic attempt has been made to examine the profession, its common characteristics and diverse forms, and the challenges it faces from an international perspective. Although there are some accounts of international trends in social work practice (Hokenstad & Kendall, 1988) and in social work education (Brauns & Kramer, 1986; Kendall, 1977, 1986; Rao, 1983; Stickney & Resnick, 1974), no definitive work has been published on the many different facets of international social work. Nor do studies of the "personal" social services (Kahn & Kamerman, 1975, 1980; Munday, 1989) offer adequate insights into the profession in different parts of the world. All these volumes are important contributions to the international literature, but none provides a comprehensive and focused view of the roles and functions of social work across nations.

The lack of a substantive account of international social work is paradoxical in view of the growing interest of social workers throughout the world in gaining more information about their profession in other countries and regions, traveling abroad, and establishing links with colleagues in other societies. Indeed, as Rosenthal (1991) found, many social workers are interested in these issues and many would like to work abroad.

The need for more information about social work in different societies invites the documentation and discussion of the profession—its practice, its limitations, and its achievements—from a broad, global perspective. It is for this purpose that this book has been compiled. The authors—practitioners, academicians, and leaders of the profession from many different countries—have taken the first step toward generating a substantive body of literature about social work cross-nationally. It is hoped that this book will stimulate comparative research and that more studies about the activities, problems, and prospects of social work in many different countries will be published.

The Nature of International Social Work

The term *international social work* is often used to mean different things in different contexts, and its association with the field of international social welfare is not always clear. As is often the case in the social sciences, differences of opinion are particularly marked between those who seek methodological rigor and semantic precision and those who are less concerned about methodology and who use terms loosely. Also, some seek to delineate terms, such as *international* and *comparative,* with a high degree of specificity, whereas others regard them as generally synonymous and signifying the same type of activity.

Although the terms *international social work* and *international social welfare* are sometimes used interchangeably, they should have distinct meanings. International social welfare (sometimes referred to as *comparative social welfare* or *comparative social policy*) has been concerned largely with the social welfare policies and human services of different countries. Numerous authors have addressed issues or provided cross-national comparisons of policies and services in the social welfare field (Elliott, Mayadas, & Watts, 1990: Friedmann, Gilbert, & Sherer, 1987; Heclo, 1974; Hokenstad & Ritvo, 1982; Kahn & Kamerman, 1975, 1980; Kaim-Caudle, 1973; MacPherson, 1982; Rodgers, Doran, & Jones, 1979; Rodgers, Greve, & Morgan, 1968; Thurz & Vigilante, 1975, 1976). Other writers have examined the complex methodological issues attending this research (Higgins, 1981; Jones, 1985; MacPherson & Midgley, 1987; Madison, 1980; Rogers, 1977).

International social work, on the other hand, should focus on the profession and practice in different parts of the world, especially the place of the organized profession in different countries, the different roles that social workers perform, the practice methods they use, the problems they deal with, and the many challenges they face. It may also sometimes refer to the practice of social work in international agencies or programs. In each case, the emphasis is on a cross-national or global examination of what social workers do. It is hoped that this book will contribute to a more precise and well-delineated use of the term international social work. Although the term will continue to cover roles and responsibilities that vary from country to country, there should be sufficient consistency to facilitate communication about and analysis of this arena of practice.

Despite these semantic difficulties, the term international social work has gained currency within the profession. In an early account, Friedlander (1955) noted that the term was first used by George Warren in 1943 to describe professional social work practice in agencies engaged in international activities. These agencies include international governmental organizations, such as the United Nations and its various affiliates; international voluntary agencies, such as the Red Cross; national governmental agencies providing services or international aid to other countries, such as USAID and the Peace Corps; and national voluntary agencies that work in different countries, such as the American Friends Service Committee and Catholic Relief Services. In a subsequent study that focused on international social welfare rather than social work, Friedlander (1975) examined the role of international agencies in social welfare in some detail, but he also drew attention to the development of social work as a profession in different parts of the world.

In this interpretation, international social work is regarded as a distinctive area of practice in which social work knowledge and skills are applied to meet the particular demands of agencies that provide social services to different countries, especially in the developing nations, or Third World.

Although no educational programs have been designed specifically to prepare social workers for practice in these settings, an increasing number of schools of social work now include courses that contain international content (Boehm, 1984). In addition, more literature on social work practice in international agencies is now available. Examples include Myadas's (1983) account of the contributions that social workers can make to the work of international agencies serving refugees and Healy's (1987) review of the opportunities presented for social workers to be employed by international agencies. Also relevant are reports of the increasing involvement of social workers as consultants to agencies that provide social services in different countries (Bogo & Herrington, 1988). The efforts of international professional associations, such as the International Federation of Social Workers and the International Association of Schools of Social Work, to encourage and facilitate the involvement of social workers in these activities further helps to delineate international social work as a field of practice.

Another way in which international social work has been used is to specify the roles that social workers perform in different countries and to examine the similarities and differences in those roles. Although there are fewer such comparisons than for social welfare policy and services, they do provide an approach to the greater appreciation and better understanding of social work as an international discipline. For example, Hokenstad's (1988) examination of the roles of social workers in the provision of services for elderly people in nine countries found that social work is established as a human services discipline throughout the world but that the roles performed by social workers differ significantly from country to country. These roles are influenced not only by governmental policies and organizational prerogatives but by the profession's definition of professional priorities and preferences for practice. The different levels and types of training of social workers are another factor in determining professional status and defining roles. Thus, although there is clearly an identifiable profession of social work internationally, both diversity and commonality must be included in any discussion of international social work.

Midgley (1990) is among those who used the term to connote a wide variety of "exchanges that take place between social workers from different societies and cultures" (p. 295). Doubting that these exchanges actually constitute a distinctive field of practice, he nevertheless used the term broadly enough to include these types of activities. He also used the term to cover the transfer of knowledge and methods of practice between social workers in different societies, so social workers can learn from each other and strengthen the profession.

Another set of terms that need clarification is international and comparative. Several writers have attempted to distinguish between the two. Sanders and Pedersen (1984) argued that the term comparative should be used to designate the methodology of research, whereas the content of such research should properly be referred to as international. As they put it, "It is helpful . . . to view international as the content or the substance of the knowledge that is taught and comparative as a conceptual tool (including models and frameworks) used to organize and analyze knowledge" (p. xv). In her extensive discussion of methodological issues, Rodgers (1977) took a similar position, contending that comparative inquiry is essentially concerned with the ways in which the object of inquiry is defined, research strategies are formulated, and knowledge is collected and analyzed. Mohan (1986, 1987) supported this view and stated that "comparative analysis makes dialectical thought possible; also comparison precedes refutation" (Mohan, 1987, p. 957).

Such distinctions help to avoid the confusion that results from using the terms interchangeably. In social work education, this confusion is evident in the way objectives are defined and in the way content of curricula for international courses is delineated (Hokenstad, 1984). Both teaching and research in the field may contain international content without being comparative and use comparative methodology without including international content. Because both terms have a variety of meanings, it is best to distinguish them clearly.

The purpose of comparative research in the international field also is a matter of some debate. Rodgers (1977), for example, questioned whether comparative social policy should be preoccupied with the production of theoretical generalizations. Comparative research, she argued, should proceed cautiously to generate "constructive descriptions" of welfare systems that will lead to empirical generalizations and perhaps ultimately to more general theoretical propositions. In addition, there is some disagreement about the normative orientation of international inquiry. Although some scholars believe that international investigation should be concerned with the documentation and analysis of global events, rather than with the application of knowledge for meliorative purposes, Mohan (1986) denounced this idea, arguing that comparative inquiry should focus exclusively on social misery and the "critical-evaluative analysis" of those social forces that cause global "illfare" (p. 2). Certainly, international comparisons in social work can both foster understanding and strengthen social work interventions throughout the world.

This book will not settle all the definitional issues involved in the use of these terms. Still, it is important to have a common framework for thinking about and discussing social work as it is practiced around the globe. Although the term international social work will continue to have a number of meanings, there should be a mutual understanding of what it is, so there can be clear communication about it as the international component of the profession grows in importance.

This book also does not seek to resolve the many complex methodological issues attending international inquiry in social work. However, the second chapter is designed to deal specifically with some of these issues and to alert social workers to the need to reflect on the problems of undertaking research in the field, as well as the difficulties of fostering authentic exchanges in international social work.

But ultimately, this book is intended to stimulate greater interest in the subject and to enhance awareness of the need for an international perspective in the profession. It is hoped that its review of social work's common features and diverse applications and the challenges it faces will delineate the field in general terms and provide insights into social work's complex but readily comprehensible world.

Scope of the Book

In attempting to provide a comparative account of social work throughout the world, this book emphasizes three themes that the authors believe characterize the profession in the international context: commonality, diversity, and challenge. As social work reaches the end of its first century of professional growth, these three themes capture its character, commitments, and ideals in many different countries.

Social work in different societies shares many common features. Although the term social work has been translated in different ways in different languages, common elements characterize the profession in most countries. Social work's commitment to respond to all levels of human need; its application of professional skills in individual, group, and community settings; its belief in humanitarian values; its search for professional recognition; and its acceptance of the idea that scientific knowledge should guide professional intervention are just some of these commonalities.

Social workers in all societies are committed to universal human rights and to the development of policies and programs that ensure these rights. They are oriented to social and environmental, as well as individual, change to improve the quality of life. They receive professional training to acquire the knowledge and skills necessary to provide effective social services. Finally, they work primarily within social institutions that each society has set up to serve human needs. These similarities provide them with some common identity cross-nationally.

Despite its common elements, social work is also marked by considerable diversity in its mission, methods, conceptual approaches, organization, and professional roles. The social, political, and economic structures of different countries influence both the structure of the services provided and the emphasis placed on the roles performed. Because social workers are called on to play diverse roles in various societies, it is perhaps not surprising that their commitment to a central core of knowledge, skills, and values should find expression in many different ways. In the international context, it is clear that certain roles and methods are emphasized more in some societies than in others. In many developing countries, social work has stressed macro forms of intervention that address pressing social and economic concerns, whereas in some industrial countries, it has focused on individualistic modes of practice that are based on therapeutic forms of intervention.

Along with the variations in these basic practice orientations, social work's diversity is expressed in its application in different fields of practice and its different approaches to social work education. The level and amount of training that social workers receive varies from society to society. The degree of specialized preparation differs, depending on the level of education and the type of practice roles emphasized in various countries. Because the boundaries of what constitutes social work vary from nation to nation, this diversity is understandable.

Social work today faces challenges throughout the world. In many societies, it does not have the prestige and professional authority that the older, more established professions have secured. This lack of status has implications for the way social workers are able to command resources, exert influence on behalf of their clients, and obtain recognition and reward for their activities. In all countries, social workers deal with an array of complex but urgent problems that place considerable demands on their skills and ability to respond effectively. The pervasive scarcity of resources affects social work everywhere and impedes the profession's ability to respond effectively to pressing human needs. Everywhere social workers struggle for social justice, but in many countries they act in the face of political oppression and seek to promote humanitarian values often at considerable personal risk.

The three themes of commonality, diversity, and challenge are examined in the case studies of countries that are the core of this book and in the concluding chapter. These studies discuss the societal and social policy context in which social work is practiced, including historical, economic, and political trends that have influenced the development and nature of the profession in each country. They go on to examine the roles and functions performed by social workers, the service systems in which social workers work, and the type of training that social workers receive. Finally, they discuss the issues that the profession is facing and future directions it will take in each country. The organization of these chapters and the final chapter will enable the reader to examine similarities and differences cross-nationally.

Each chapter also focuses on a major challenge facing the profession in that country, so the reader may gain insights into how social work is both affected by and has an impact on some of the key social, economic, and political issues of this time in history. For example, E. Maxine Ankrah reports how 20 years of political unrest, tyranny, and civil war influenced the development of social work in Uganda and how the profession is now actively responding to the major challenge of AIDS. Hans Berglind and Ulla Pettersson discuss the reevaluation of social workers's roles in the public social services that is necessitated by the decreasing resources and organizational changes in Sweden. Katalin Talyigas and Gabor Hegyesi analyze the opportunities and challenges for Hungarian social work as that society undergoes basic economic and political changes.

Chris Jones discusses the effects on social work of the ascendancy of the radical New Right ideology in the 1980s in Great Britain, where the welfare state and social work were assailed by Thatcherite approaches that disparaged the profession's historical commitment to serving those in need through public social services. Similarly, A. B. Bose examines the overriding need for social and economic development in a major Third World nation such as India and the challenge this need poses for the profession. In describing social work in South Africa, Fikile Mazibuko, Brian McKendrick, and Leila Patel address how social work has faced the institutionalized racism and oppression of the apartheid system and how the profession is responding to the inexorable forces of political change that are now at work in their society. By focusing on issues of commonality, diversity, and challenge, the book not only raises pertinent issues for the profession but seeks to avoid the descriptive approach that typifies a good deal of comparative research in the social sciences today.

References

Boehm, W. W. (1984). International and comparative social work in the undergraduate and graduate curriculum. In D. Sanders & P. Pedersen (Eds.), *Education for international social welfare* (pp. 3–9). Manoa: University of Hawaii, School of Social Work.

Bogo, M., & Herrington, W. (1988). Consultation in social work education in the international context. *International Social Work, 31,* 305–316.

Brauns, H. J., & Kramer, D. (Eds.). (1986). *Social work education in Europe.* Frankfurt am Main, Germany: Eigen Verlag des Deutschen Vereins fur Offenliche und Private Fursorge.

Elliott, D., Mayadas, N., & Watts, T. (Eds.). (1990). *The world of social welfare: Social welfare and services in an international context.* Springfield, IL: Charles C Thomas.

Friedlander, W. A. (1955). *Introduction to social welfare.* New York: Prentice Hall.

Friedlander, W. A. (1975). *International social work.* Englewood Cliffs, NJ: Prentice Hall.

Friedmann, R., Gilbert, N., & Sherer, M. (Eds.). (1987). *Modern welfare states: A comparative view of trends and prospects.* Brighton, England: Wheatsheaf Books.

Healy, L. (1987). International agencies as social work settings: Opportunity, capability, and commitment. *Social Work, 32,* 405–409.

Heclo, H. (1974). *Modern social policies in Britain and Sweden.* New Haven, CT: Yale University Press.

Higgins, J. (1981). *States of welfare: Comparative analysis in social policy.* Oxford, England: Basil Blackwell.

Hokenstad, M. C. (1984). Teaching social policy and social work practice in an international context. In D. Sanders & P. Pedersen (Eds.), *Education for international social welfare* (pp. 39–55). Manoa: University of Hawaii, School of Social Work.

Hokenstad, M. C. (1988). Cross-national trends and issues in social service provision and social work practice for the elderly. In M. C. Hokenstad & K. Kendall (Eds.), *Gerontological social work: International perspectives* (pp. 1–15). New York: Haworth Press.

Hokenstad, M. C., & Kendall, K. (Eds.). (1988). *Gerontological social work: International perspectives.* New York: Haworth Press.

Hokenstad, M. C., & Ritvo, R. (Eds.). (1982). *Linking health care and social services: International perspectives.* Beverly Hills, CA: Sage Publications.

Jones, C. (1985). *Patterns of social policy: An introduction to comparative analysis.* New York: Tavistock Publications.

Kahn, A., & Kamerman, S. (1975). *Not for the poor alone: European social services.* Philadelphia: Temple University Press.

Kahn, A., & Kamerman, S. (1980). *Social services in international perspective: The emergence of the sixth system.* New Brunswick, NJ: Transaction Books.

Kaim-Caudle, P. (1973). *Comparative social policy and social security: A ten country study.* London: Martin Robertson.

Kendall, K. (1977). Cross-national review of social work education. *Journal of Education for Social Work, 13,* 76–83.

Kendall, K. (1986). Social work education in the 1980s: Accent on change. *International Social Work, 29,* 15–28.

MacPherson, S. (1982). *Social policy in the Third World.* Brighton, England: Wheatsheaf Books.

MacPherson, S., & Midgley, J. (1987). *Comparative social policy and the Third World.* New York: St. Martin's Press.

Madison, B. (1980). *The meaning of social policy: Comparative dimensions in social welfare.* Boulder, CO: Westview Press.

Midgley, J. (1990). International social work: Learning from the Third World. *Social Work, 35,* 295–301.

Mohan, B. (1986). Unraveling comparative social welfare. In B. Mohan (Ed.), *Toward comparative social welfare* (pp. 1–11). Cambridge, MA: Schenkman.

Mohan, B. (1987). International social welfare: Comparative systems. In A. Minahan (Ed.-in-Chief), *Encyclopedia of social work* (18th ed., Vol. 1, pp. 957–969). Silver Spring, MD: National Association of Social Workers.

Munday, B. (Ed.). (1989). *The crisis in welfare: An international perspective on social services and social work.* London: Harvester-Wheatsheaf.

Myadas, N. S. (1983). Psycho-social welfare of refugees: An expanding service area for social work. *International Social Work, 34,* 47–55.

Rao, V. (1983). *World guide to social work education.* Vienna, Austria: International Association of Schools of Social Work.

Rodgers, B. (1977). Comparative studies in social policy and administration. In H. Heisler (Ed.), *Foundations of social administration* (pp. 196–220). London: Macmillan.

Rodgers, B., Doran, A., & Jones, M. (1979). *The study of social policy: A comparative approach.* London: Allen & Unwin.

Rodgers, B., Greve, J., & Morgan, J. (1968). *Comparative social administration.* London: Allen & Unwin.

Rosenthal, B. S. (1991). Social workers' interest in international practice in the developing world: A multivariate analysis. *Social Work, 36,* 248–252.

Sanders, D., & Pedersen, P. (1984). Introduction. In D. Sanders & P. Pedersen (Eds.), *Education for international social welfare* (pp. xi–xxvi). Manoa: University of Hawaii, School of Social Work.

Stickney, P. J., & Resnick, R. P. (1974). *World guide to social work education.* New York: International Association of Schools of Social Work.

Thurz, D., & Vigilante, J. L. (Eds.). (1975). *Meeting human needs: 1. An overview of nine countries.* Beverly Hills, CA: Sage Publications.

Thurz, D., & Vigilante, J. L. (Eds.). (1976). *Meeting human needs: 2. Additional perspectives from thirteen countries.* Beverly Hills, CA: Sage Publications.

2

THE CHALLENGE OF INTERNATIONAL SOCIAL WORK

JAMES MIDGLEY

Although social workers are much more involved in international activities today than in the past, a greater engagement is required if social work is to develop as an internationally recognized profession and a respected applied social science. As an emergent profession, social work requires strong international linkages to consolidate its position. It also needs to test its practice methodologies and knowledge base internationally. As an applied social science, social work must pursue modes of inquiry that enhance the accumulation of empirical data, document trends, and generate universal theoretical propositions that form the basis of all disciplinary endeavors.

Considerable progress has been made in international and comparative research in the other social sciences in recent decades. Methodological procedures have been refined; data collection techniques have improved; and more propositions of universal, rather than domestic, relevance have been generated. Consequently, social scientists know a great deal more about events that are relevant to their disciplinary interests in other countries and regions of the world than they did in the past. Unfortunately, social work has not achieved the same level of sophistication in comparative research. Although social workers now participate more frequently in international activities, the documentation of social work roles and professional commitments in different parts of the globe remains underdeveloped. Although the more frequent publication of articles and books about social work in different countries has enhanced knowledge about social work in the international context, this literature is small.

The international field poses a challenge to the profession. By enhancing international exchanges and by engaging more systematically in comparative research, social work will increase its knowledge base, test and refine its practice methods, share innovations, and develop into an internationally recognized profession. Fortunately, there are many indications that social workers throughout the world are ready to meet the challenge.

THE VALUE OF INTERNATIONAL SOCIAL WORK

In the face of greater global interdependence, it may appear obvious that the need for comparative research is greater than ever. Equally evident is the need for social workers to know about developments in their profession in other societies. But there are other, less obvious reasons for advocating a greater commitment to internationalism: the positive benefits that an international perspective can have on social work's understanding of human problems, its academic knowledge, and professional practice wisdom. Also relevant, although perhaps more self-serving, is the contribution that an international perspective can make to social work's efforts to obtain recognition as a profession.

UNDERSTANDING HUMAN PROBLEMS

By studying social problems in other countries, social workers can learn how these countries identify and define needs, and this knowledge can increase their awareness of social problems in their own societies. For example, as a result of the World Health Organization's widespread dissemination of information about the incidence, nature, and implications of human immunodeficiency virus (HIV) infection, health care professionals who believed that AIDS was foreign to their countries have been educated and prepared to respond as the disease spreads throughout the world. Also, ill-informed but popular beliefs about the etiological association between AIDS and proscribed sexual behavior have been revised as more international information about the true nature of this fatal disease has become available.

Similarly useful lessons have been learned about substance abuse, child neglect, homelessness, and other forms of human need. The preoccupation with substance abuse in the United States has increased the awareness of this problem in other Western countries. Likewise, social workers in Europe have benefited from research on child abuse in the United States, where there has been a greater willingness to discuss this issue than in more traditional European countries, where beliefs about family privacy, honor, and confidentiality have impeded a proper assessment of the incidence of the problem. However, knowledge of this kind has come not only from the United States. American social workers have gained greater insights into their society's social problems by studying similar problems elsewhere. For instance, the problem of homeless teenagers in the United States has been informed by research on street children in Latin America.

ENHANCING THEORETICAL KNOWLEDGE

Social work's attempts to enhance its knowledge base can also benefit from international exchanges. These exchanges permit the rapid accumulation of information and facilitate the adoption of a comparative perspective in social work research that can have significant epistemological benefits.

As an academic subject, social work is seeking to generate its own substantive body of knowledge, but, as is widely recognized, the profession still relies extensively on other disciplines, particularly psychology and sociology, for inspiration. Clearly, the evolution of knowledge in these disciplines is enhanced by international contacts. Through greater international communication among universities, research institutes, and other centers, the accumulation of knowledge accelerates. The active involvement of social work scholars in these international networks increases the production of correct knowledge in the field.

Social work scholars in the United States have undoubtedly taken the lead in the ongoing struggle to identify theoretical conceptions of social work. Although American social work theories and practice approaches have been widely diffused throughout the world, social work in the United States has not been impervious to influences from abroad. The psychoanalytic perspective in social work was a European import that was widely adopted after psychoanalysis took hold in Europe in the early 20th century. Although other European ideas have not had the same impact, existentialism has exerted some influence on social work (Krill, 1978; Sinsheimer, 1969; Stretch, 1967), as have hermeneutics and critical social theory (Clark & Asquith, 1985; Gil, 1985; Scott, 1989). Conceptual approaches emanating from Eastern and other non-European societies have not had the same appeal, but they have, nevertheless, attracted attention and found application in some practice settings (Brandon, 1979; Canda, 1983; Delgado, 1977; Ho, 1987).

Social work can also benefit by adopting the methodology of comparative inquiry in its efforts to generate its own body of substantive knowledge. As has been demonstrated in the other social sciences, comparative research engenders the production of valid and useful propositions. It also facilitates the collection of a larger number of facts than would be possible if research was confined to domestic events. Because facts are relevant in the production of knowledge, the systematic accumulation of factual information on a global scale has obvious implications for the inductive development of propositions and the refutation of generalizations. Comparative research also permits the formulation of propositions of general, rather than specific, validity and permits their testing in many more social situations.

Strengthening Practice

The enhancement of social work practice is perhaps the most obvious benefit of international contacts; indeed, exchanges of this kind have contributed to the refinement of practice methods since the profession's inception. As most American social work students are aware, it was the replication of the English Charity Organization Society and the settlement house movement's respective approaches to poor relief that contributed to the formulation of social casework and group work in the United States at the turn of the century (Leiby, 1978). Similarly, British social work relied extensively on American theories of clinical practice when the first psychiatric social work programs were established in England in the 1920s (Younghusband, 1978). The strengthening of an international perspective in social work can facilitate exchanges of this kind and enhance professional practice in many different settings.

By critically examining, testing, and adapting innovative practices formulated in different societies, social workers can enhance their ability to respond to pressing human needs and hence improve the effectiveness of their practice. Up-to-date knowledge of innovative practices in other countries also provides them with a larger range of options for intervention and permits them to test many more modalities. It also helps them avoid applying practice methods that have caused problems in other societies.

Although it may seem paradoxical, comparative research also increases practitioners' understanding of the usefulness of practice methods within a particular society. As Jones (1985) noted regarding the formulation and implementation of social policy, local approaches to policy are routinely evaluated by systematically comparing them to approaches used by national agencies or local governmental authorities. By extending this technique to encompass international comparisons, social workers can gain more useful insights into local approaches.

A greater awareness of international affairs can also enhance social work's efforts to formulate ethnically sensitive forms of practice. The literature on this subject has grown rapidly in recent years (Devore & Schlesinger, 1981; Green, 1982; Ho, 1987) and has demonstrated the need for practitioners to be aware of the specific needs and cultural differences of clients who come from minority or immigrant populations. Although ethnically sensitive practice does not focus exclusively on the needs of immigrants, an engagement in the international field facilitates a better appreciation of cultural diversity at both the international and domestic levels.

Promoting Professional Development

International exchanges in social work can also contribute to social work's goal of evolving and obtaining recognition as a profession. Although some social workers oppose the idea of professionalism, social work has, since its inception, sought to become established as a profession, and most of those who identify themselves as social workers have acquired formal educational qualifications and aspirations that are commensurate with the demands of professionalism. However, the notion of professionalism in social work is ambiguous in view of the different roles that social workers play, the different forms of educational preparation they receive, the different client groups they serve, and the different ways they perceive and define professional responsibilities. A proper understanding of these issues can help social work formalize its approach and consolidate its position.

The literature on social work as a profession in different countries is surprisingly limited. Although the modes of professional organization, preferred practice methods, employment trends, and similar issues in major industrial countries such as Great Britain and the United States have been well documented, such information about other countries is limited. Consequently, social workers know little about their profession in other countries, and only those who travel to international meetings or who hold leadership positions in international professional associations have a chance to acquire it. This situation occurs even within developed regions, such as Europe, despite the fact that "the European countries have expended much energy in the pursuit of greater cultural, political and economic integration" (Brauns & Kramer, 1986, p. 1). There is clearly an urgent need to document social work practice in different societies so that social workers can have a better understanding of their profession in other parts of the world.

More systematic information is also needed about social work in the Eastern European countries, where it has often been assumed that social work either does not exist or is underdeveloped. However, differences in the degree of professionalization and the deployment of human services personnel should not deter inquiry. It is particularly surprising that there is so little documentation of social work in the former Soviet Union, which is one of the world's largest and most significant countries. Madison's (1968) pioneering research on the Soviet welfare system made limited reference to social work but suggested that human services personnel are not specifically trained and that their activities are widely supplemented by volunteers. In a more recent but brief account, Hegelson (1989) noted that there are indications that the country's *sotsial'nye rabotniki* are being recognized and that professional training programs will be developed. It is hoped that there will be more extensive documentation of social work in the former Soviet Union now that greater opportunities for meaningful exchanges have been created.

A similar observation can be made about the People's Republic of China, where little is known about the human services and the way they are administered and delivered. Dixon's (1981) seminal work needs to be augmented by more specific studies of the role of human services personnel in that country's welfare system and of their similarities to and differences from social workers elsewhere.

On the other hand, a good deal of information has been published about social work in India, which is the world's second most populous country after China. Indian social workers have produced an impressive body of literature about their profession, as well as about the various fields of practice in which they are involved (Chatterjee & Gokhale, 1974; Gore, 1965; Khinduka, 1965; Nagpaul, 1980; Ramchandran & Padmanabha, 1969; Wadia, 1961). In addition, Indian social workers have issued an encyclopedia of social work, and they continue to publish *Indian Social Work,* which is one of the few social work journals from a non-Western country to be read abroad. However, it is a pity that much of the literature on social work in India is not widely available internationally, because, as Midgley (1990) suggested, various innovations in the fields of occupational social work and child welfare that were developed in India are of potential value to social workers in other societies.

Many more accounts of social work in Third World countries are now available. In addition to comprehensive or regional studies of the field (Council on Social Work Education [CSWE], 1967; Hodge, 1980; Midgley, 1981), studies about different aspects of social work have been published in various countries in the developing world (Clifford, 1966; Hebbert, Paras, & Viloria, 1972; Landa Jocano, 1980; McKendrick, 1987; Prigmore, 1976; Weisner, 1972), and they have provided some insights into the profession in these rapidly changing societies. But again, books of this kind are not widely available internationally.

Documentation on social work education around the world is much more extensive and lends support to the idea that social work has now achieved a significant degree of professionalism at the international level. As Stickney and Resnick (1974) reported, the number of schools affiliated with the International Association of Schools of Social Work increased significantly in the post–World War II years. When the association was founded in 1929, it had only a few member schools in Europe and some other industrialized countries. By 1973, its membership had increased to 459 schools in 66 countries. Ten years later, its membership stood at 476 schools (Rao, 1983). Because the extent of professional education is a clear indication of the vigor of a profession, these trends are encouraging. As Kendall (1977) pointed out, social work's achievements in professional education are indeed indicative of its growing professional standing. Despite considerable diversity, she noted, schools of social work throughout the world have many common educational objectives, value commitments, and curricular orientations.

To consolidate and enhance its professional achievements, social work in different countries can obviously benefit from greater collaboration. The growth of professional associations, such as the International Association of Schools of Social Work and the International Federation of Social Workers, has enhanced collaboration and assisted national bodies to obtain greater recognition and better conditions of service for their members. These associations have also helped professional organizations in different countries to respond effectively to problems and challenges. In addition to the work of international professional associations, some national associations, such as the National Association of Social Workers (NASW) in the United States, have made a major commitment to fostering international linkages. NASW's Child and Family Well-being Development Education Project has facilitated the "twinning" of various state chapters with groups of social workers in developing countries. At present, 21 chapters have linked with countries including Costa Rica, Ecuador, Ghana, India, Kenya, Mexico, and the Philippines. These exchanges have greatly enhanced the understanding of how social workers have organized themselves and structured their activities. By learning how colleagues in other countries have formulated proposals and strategies that further professional goals, social work's continued drive for professionalism is significantly enhanced.

Challenges to International Social Work

Although more frequent and substantive international exchanges in social work will be beneficial, there are difficulties to be overcome, some of which are obvious practical problems, whereas others concern the complex methodological issues that attend comparative research. Social workers also need to be mindful of the dangers of ethnocentrism, overstandardization, and the assumption that ideas that emanate from the industrial countries are somehow superior and worthy of emulation. The development of authentic international collaboration in social work requires the emergence of reciprocal exchanges that are based on mutual respect for uniqueness and diversity within the profession.

Practical Problems

An obvious but infrequently recognized difficulty is that international exchanges in social work are not easy to promote. Faced with many demanding responsibilities, social workers are understandably preoccupied with domestic activities. Although interest in international affairs is increasing, international travel remains difficult for social workers in many countries, particularly for those in poor countries with major fiscal and budgetary constraints. Many more social workers attend international meetings and conferences today than in the past, but these events are still disproportionately supported by social workers from the industrialized nations. Also, it is often social workers from the industrialized countries who travel to and serve as consultants in poorer nations. Despite some attempts to assist social workers from these poorer countries to travel more frequently, much more needs to be done.

Similar practical problems impede the accumulation of knowledge based on international inquiry. As was noted in Chapter 1, research and publishing priorities remain focused on local problems, and opportunities for the publication of internationally relevant research are still limited. The problem is particularly acute for social workers from Third World countries, who seldom gain access to mainstream Western social work journals and who have limited opportunities to have their books published in the major Western markets. The role of internationally focused journals in providing opportunities for the dissemination of research from scholars from other parts of the world is commendable.

Greater efforts are now being made to broaden the international perspective in social work education in the industrial countries. In Great Britain, for example, educators in social work and social administration have made a more concerted effort to engender a greater awareness of international issues among their students, and there have been similar developments in the United States. Attempts by CSWE's International Committee to enhance international content in the curricula of American schools of social work are laudatory, but this content area is faced with competition from other content areas that also need to be taught. Nevertheless, it is likely that in the future social work students will, as Boehm (1984) suggested, be more exposed to international content than in the past. And, as more social work educators travel abroad, this content will come not only from courses dealing specifically with international social work but from references to international events in regular courses.

The problem of making contacts with social workers in other countries has been eased by the growth of international professional associations and by the creation of links among schools of social work in different countries. During the immediate post–World War II period, when many schools of social work were established in the colonial territories and the newly independent developing countries, European and North American schools of social work were actively involved in advising on curricular and other matters. Today, these links are usually based on exchanges of students and faculty members, but they are still largely one-sided in that the exchanges are initiated and managed by Western schools.

There are mundane problems as well. Those whose professional commitments require frequent travel to other countries know only too well that the exotic images projected in travel brochures and advertisements are largely fictional, at least for the businessperson or professional. Crowded airports, overbooked reservations, expensive hotels and restaurants, jet lag, inefficient public transportation systems, and dubious taxis are just some of the many challenges that both domestic and international travelers face. Although these and other problems can be overdramatized, they demonstrate the need for adequate preparation.

Adequate preparation is even more vital if the cultural implications of international exchanges in social work are to be properly understood and respected. Even though social workers are trained to be particularly sensitive to cultural issues, it is natural to forget that other societies are culturally different and that behaviors that are commonplace at home are not observed elsewhere. Sometimes, even the best intentions can lead to misunderstandings. For example, the Western proclivity for touching to establish warm interpersonal contacts may be embarrassing and even offensive in other cultures. Similarly, the tradition of showing ceremonial respect for those in authority is not always appreciated by Westerners, who often exude an inappropriate attitude of informality.

Language is an obvious difficulty, but so are the varied customs, beliefs, attitudes, and other subtle cultural nuances that differentiate peoples and societies. Social workers must guard against complacency and be particularly vigilant of the dangers of cultural misunderstanding. The idea that promoting international exchanges in social work requires little more than an adventurous spirit, a willingness to endure discomforts, and a large dose of good intentions is widespread but naive and is likely to result in frequent cultural misunderstandings.

Methodological Problems

The methodological implications of undertaking international and comparative research must also be understood. Although many social scientists do not regard comparative inquiry as a challenging endeavor, others are tantalized by methodological issues, believing that methodological accuracy is a prerequisite for successful international research. For the methodological purists, comparative research is a serious business that requires careful preparation, precise definitions of the research subject, painstaking testing of research methodologies, and the cautious exposition of findings. Purists are particularly irked by those who appear to be indifferent to the methodological rigors of comparative research and who proceed to pepper their work with illustrative examples drawn from other societies.

Social work has not yet grappled to any significant extent with the methodological problems of international and comparative investigation, but as the field evolves, these issues will become more pertinent. In the closely related field of comparative social welfare and social policy, methodological issues have already been vigorously debated (Higgins, 1981; Jones, 1985; MacPherson & Midgley, 1987; Madison, 1980; Rodgers, 1977). But here again, different authorities place different emphases on the need for methodological rigor. Some, such as Titmuss (1971), have made extensive use of international data without expressing any concern about the methodological accuracy of their work. However, methodologically cautious investigators, such as Rodgers (1977), have contended that an appropriate concern with methodological rigor is essential if any plausible knowledge is to be generated. Indeed, Rodgers believed that the methodological obstacles to comparative research are so formidable that she doubts whether much useful knowledge can be gleaned in this way. Her advocacy of a particular methodological approach that relies on "constructive descriptions" of specific countries and their welfare systems is, she argues, a modest attempt to generate at least some knowledge of value.

Although problematic, an understanding of these issues can inform social workers who seek to enhance their knowledge by venturing beyond the confines of their own domestic experiences. By assessing the merits of different methodological orientations, social work researchers can identify approaches that are appropriate to their own needs. Obviously, they can also learn from the achievements and errors of comparative research in other disciplines, and this experience can engender an awareness of the dangers of overgeneralization; the oversimplification of complex phenomena; the imposition of artificial constructs on the real world; and the vexing issues of objectivity, relativism, and ethnocentrism.

An appreciation of methodological issues can alert social workers to the dangers of a glib approach that randomly selects international examples to bolster particular theoretical presumptions or to illustrate certain arguments. It can also warn social work researchers of the risks of reaching conclusions based on inadequate or suspect data. The need to examine data sources carefully is obvious. As scholars who have compared international statistical trends have shown (Estes, 1984; Wilensky, 1975), the data on which these trends are based are often inadequate, and it is difficult to make legitimate comparisons. But comparative investigators are seldom deterred by the inadequacy of the data, and despite caveats about the limitations of their research, their findings are widely accepted as accurate. A good example of this problem is the body of knowledge that has been generated about poverty and inequality in Third World countries. Although this research is based on highly suspect data, trends extrapolated from it have been widely accepted as valid (Midgley, 1988).

Equally problematic is the question of how the object of inquiry in international research should be defined. Although a preoccupation with this issue may result, as Higgins (1981) observed, in the conclusion that nothing can be compared, it is important to be aware that welfare institutions, and indeed social work as a profession, have been defined differently in different countries. Comparative studies of social security by Kaim-Caudle (1973) and Midgley (1984) have shown that the definitions, legal bases, and characteristics of income maintenance programs vary greatly among countries. Systematic comparisons of particular programs are obviously impeded because of these differences. Previous attempts to compare the social work or "personal" social services (Hokenstad, 1988; Kahn & Kamerman, 1980; Munday, 1989; Rodgers, Doron, & Jones, 1979; Rodgers, Greve, & Morgan, 1968) have found that social work is not only defined differently in different societies, but that the tasks social workers perform vary greatly.

However, a concern with methodology should not obscure the fact that comparative research is essentially concerned with asking simple questions to increase knowledge. By asking simple questions about variations in the demography of the family and about family relationships in different societies, sociologists have accumulated an impressive body of knowledge about the family as a social institution. To enhance knowledge, social workers need to ask simple questions about social work as a welfare institution. Although it is not always easy to frame appropriate questions, such efforts provide the impetus for research designs, data collection, theory building, and the other methodological steps on which the discovery of plausible propositions is based.

Problems of Professional Exchanges

Social work's development as a profession is a primary objective of international social work and, as was suggested earlier, international exchanges in social work can promote the attainment of this goal. However, the international promotion of professional goals generates its own set of problems. Social workers in the international field need to be aware of these problems if the profession is to evolve in ways that are mutually beneficial to social workers throughout the world.

One issue that has been widely debated is whether the transfer of ideas and practice methods from one society to another is beneficial to social work's professional development. Obviously, few would quarrel with the idea that social workers can learn from their colleagues in other countries (Midgley, 1990). However, many have been critical of what they regard as the unidirectional diffusion of knowledge and skills from a few global centers where social work is relatively well developed to other countries where social work is still evolving. In this literature, the recipients of diffusional tendencies are usually identified as the developing countries of Asia, Africa, and Central and South America, and the most frequently identified sources of ideas and innovations are Great Britain and the United States. Normatively, such unidirectional exchanges are criticized for fostering the uncritical replication of inappropriate theories and practice methods and for inhibiting the emergence of indigenous forms of intervention that are suited to local needs and realities (Almanzor, 1967; Khinduka, 1971; Midgley, 1981; Nagpaul, 1972; Pathak, 1974; Shawkey, 1972).

Some of these writers have shown that diffusional tendencies have not only resulted in the imposition of inappropriate practice methods but have impeded the development of indigenous forms of intervention that are more appropriate to the local situation. Pathak (1974) argued, for example, that the adoption of American curricular approaches by Indian schools of social work in the 1960s "led to the curtailment of [appropriate] social science content, inadequate emphasis on social action, alienation of social workers from the *Sarvodaya* movement and the neglect of social reform" (p. 178).

Khinduka (1971) reached a similar conclusion in his account of the need for developmentally relevant forms of social work intervention in Third World countries. Such involvement would appear to be self-evident, but it is surprising that textbooks written for students in Third World countries, such as Kenya (Clifford, 1966) and the Philippines (Hebbert et al., 1972), make no reference to activities of this kind; indeed, they are so dependent on American and British clinical approaches that their value in the formulation of appropriate academic and practice knowledge in the developmental context appears to be negligible.

By drawing attention to the problem of unequal exchanges in international social work, scholars have heightened awareness of the need for a critical attitude that subjects professional transfers to careful scrutiny and rigorous testing. There is, as Midgley (1989) argued, evidence that social workers in developing countries are much more aware of the problem than they were in the past and that they are more likely to be selective in the way they adopt approaches from other countries. Such critical attitude should also govern the transfer of social work knowledge and practice methods among the industrialized countries. The assumption that these countries are so similar that innovations from one country can be readily imported requires substantiation.

A related issue is the question of professional standardization in social work. As international linkages have developed, many professions have sought to emphasize commonalities, rather than differences, to foster a unitary, international identity. The trend toward standardization has been marked in many professions, but it is not always socially beneficial. In medicine, for example, where the standardization of procedures, treatments, and technologies would seem to be desirable, variations in morbidity patterns, public health needs, resources, and other factors suggest that different approaches are needed in different societies. However, as Abel-Smith and Leiserson (1978) argued, these realities are often ignored by medical professionals, whose ideals are shaped by international professional standards, rather than by pressing domestic needs.

Social work should be aware of the dangers of overstandardization. Although it is desirable for the profession to have common goals, ethics, knowledge, and practice methods, enormous variations in the nature and degree of social need in different societies; these societies' demographic, economic, social, and cultural conditions; and the opportunities these conditions present for professional practice need to be recognized and respected. The tendency toward standardization can inhibit the profession's ability to respond effectively to local needs and impede the goals of professional development.

On the other hand, social work needs to have a core of common identifying features if it is to claim to be an international profession. Although diversity should be respected, the idea that social work can have a common identity without shared commonalities is difficult to support. Fortunately, there are indications that in many countries the profession does share common features, despite a significant degree of diversity. And it is this apparent paradox—the existence of commonalities together with highly diverse roles, forms of intervention, and challenges—that offers significant opportunities for research in international social work.

References

Abel-Smith, B., & Leiserson, A. (1978). *Poverty, development and health policy.* Geneva: World Health Organization.

Almanzor, A. (1967). The profession of social work in the Philippines. In *An intercultural exploration: Universals and differentials in social work values, functions and practice* (pp. 123–137). New York: Council on Social Work Education.

Boehm, W. W. (1984). International and comparative social work in the undergraduate and graduate curriculum. In D. Sanders & P. Pedersen (Eds.), *Education for international social welfare* (pp. 3–9). Manoa: University of Hawaii, School of Social Work.

Brandon, D. (1979). Zen practice in social work. In D. Brandon & B. Jordan (Eds.), *Creative social work* (pp. 30–35). Oxford, England: Basil Blackwell.

Brauns, H. J., & Kramer, D. (Eds.). (1986). *Social work education in Europe.* Frankfurt am Main, Germany: Eigen Verlag des Deutschen Vereins fur Offenliche und Private Fursorge.

Canda, E. R. (1983). General implications of shamanism for clinical social work. *International Social Work, 26,* 14–22.

Chatterjee, B., & Gokhale, S. D. (Eds.). (1974). *Social welfare: Legend and legacy.* Bobbat, India: Popular Prakashan.

Clark, C. L., & Asquith, S. (1985). *Social work and social philosophy: A guide for practice.* London: Routledge & Kegan Paul.

Clifford, W. (1966). *A primer of social casework in Africa.* Nairobi, Kenya: Oxford University Press.

Council on Social Work Education. (1967). *An intercultural exploration: Universals and differentials in social work values, functions and practice.* New York: Author.

Delgado, M. (1977). Puerto Rican spiritualism and the social work profession. *Social Casework, 58,* 451–458.

Devore, W., & Schlesinger, E. (1981). *Ethnic-sensitive social work practice.* St. Louis, MO: C. V. Mosby.

Dixon, J. (1981). *The Chinese welfare system, 1949–1979.* New York: Praeger.

Estes, R. (1984). *The social progress of nations.* New York: Praeger.

Gil, D. (1985). Individual development and global social welfare. In B. Mohan (Ed.), *New horizons in social welfare and policy* (pp. 15–46). Cambridge, MA: Schenkman.

Gore, M. S. (1965). *Social work and social work education in India.* Bombay, India: Asia Publishing House.

Green, J. W. (1982). *Cultural awareness in the human services.* Englewood Cliffs, NJ: Prentice Hall.

Hebbert, V., Paras, E., & Viloria, E. (1972). *Social work practice: A Philippine casebook.* Quezon City, Philippines: New Day Publishers.

Hegelson, A. (1989). USSR—The implications of glasnost and perestroika. In B. Munday (Ed.), *The crisis in welfare: An international perspective on social services and social work* (pp. 51–80). London: Harvester-Wheatsheaf.

Higgins, J. (1981). *States of welfare: Comparative analysis in social policy.* Oxford, England: Basil Blackwell.

Ho, M. K. (1987). *Family therapy with ethnic minorities.* Newbury Park, CA: Sage Publications.

Hodge, P. (Ed.). (1980). *Community problems and social work in Southeast Asia.* Hong Kong: Hong Kong University Press.

Hokenstad, M. C. (1988). Cross-national trends and issues in social service provision and social work practice for the elderly. In M. C. Hokenstad & K. Kendall (Eds.), *Gerontological social work: International perspectives* (pp. 1–15). New York: Haworth Press.

Jones, C. (1985). *Patterns of social policy: An introduction to comparative analysis.* New York: Tavistock Publications.

Kahn, A., & Kamerman, S. (1980). *Social services in international perspective: The emergence of the sixth system.* New Brunswick, NJ: Transaction Books.

Kaim-Caudle, P. (1973). *Comparative social policy and social security: A ten-country study.* London: Martin Robertson.

Kendall, K. (1977). Cross-national review of social work education. *Journal of Education for Social Work, 13,* 76–83.

Khinduka, S. K. (Ed.). (1965). *Social work in India.* Allahabad, India: Kitab Mahal.

Khinduka, S. K. (1971). Social work in the Third World. *Social Service Review, 45,* 62–73.

Krill, D. F. (1978). *Existential social work.* New York: Free Press.

Landa Jocano, F. (1980). *Social work in the Philippines.* Quezon City, Philippines: New Day Publishers.

Leiby, J. (1978). *A history of social work and social welfare in the United States.* New York: Columbia University Press.

MacPherson, S., & Midgley, J. (1987). *Comparative social policy and the Third World.* New York: St. Martin's Press.

Madison, B. (1968). *Social welfare in the Soviet Union.* Stanford, CA: Stanford University Press.

Madison, B. (1980). *The meaning of social policy: The comparative dimension in social welfare.* London: Croom Helm.

McKendrick, B. (Ed.). (1987). *Introduction to social work in South Africa.* Pinetown, South Africa: Owen Burgess Publishers.

Midgley, J. (1981). *Professional imperialism: Social work in the Third World.* London: Heinemann Educational Books.

Midgley, J. (1984). *Social security, inequality and the Third World.* New York: John Wiley & Sons.

Midgley, J. (1988). Inequality, the Third World and development. *International Journal of Contemporary Sociology, 24,* 93–102.

Midgley, J. (1989). Social work in the Third World: Crisis and response. In P. Carter, T. Jeffs, & M. Smith (Eds.), *Social work and social welfare yearbook* (pp. 33–45). Milton Keynes, England: Open University Press.

Midgley, J. (1990). International social work: Learning from the Third World. *Social Work, 35,* 295–301.

Munday, B. (Ed.). (1989). *The crisis in welfare: An international perspective on social services and social work.* London: Harvester-Wheatsheaf.

Nagpaul, H. (1972). The diffusion of American social work education to India. *International Social Work, 15,* 13–17.

Nagpaul, H. (1980). *Culture, education and social welfare.* New Delhi, India: Chand.

Pathak, S. H. (1974). A quarter century of professional social work in India. In B. Chatterjee & S. D. Gokhale (Eds.), *Social welfare: Legend and legacy* (pp. 170–192). Bobbat, India: Popular Prakashan.

Prigmore, C. (1976). *Social work in Iran since the white revolution.* University: University of Alabama Press.

Ramchandran, P., & Padmanabha, P. (1969). *Professional social workers in India: Their employment, position and functions.* Bombay, India: United Asia Publishers.

Rao, V. (1983). *World guide to social work education.* Vienna: International Association of Schools of Social Work.

Rodgers, B. (1977). Comparative studies in social policy and administration. In H. Heisler (Ed.), *Foundations of social administration* (pp. 196–220). London: Macmillan.

Rodgers, B., Doran, A., & Jones, M. (1979). *The study of social policy: A comparative approach.* London: Allen & Unwin.

Rodgers, B., Greve, J., & Morgan, J. (1968). *Comparative social administration.* London: Allen & Unwin.

Scott, D. (1989). Meaning construction and social work practice. *Social Service Review, 63,* 39–51.

Shawkey, A. (1972). Social work education in Africa. *International Social Work, 15,* 3–16.

Sinsheimer, R. (1969). The existential casework relationship. *Social Casework, 50,* 67–73.

Stickney, P. J., & Resnick, R. P. (1974). *World guide to social work education.* New York: International Association of Schools of Social Work.

Stretch, J. (1967). Existentialism: A proposed philosophical orientation for social work. *Social Work, 12,* 97–102.

Titmuss, R. (1971). *The gift relationship.* New York: Vintage Books.

Wadia, A. R. (Ed.). (1961). *History and philosophy of social work in India.* Bombay, India: Allied Publishers.

Weisner, S. (1972). *Professional social work in Kenya.* Lower Kabete: Kenya Institute of Administration.

Wilensky, H. (1975). *The welfare state and equality.* Berkeley: University of California Press.

Younghusband, E. (1978). *Social work in Britain, 1950–1975.* London: Allen & Unwin.

3

Social Work in Chile: Support for the Struggle for Justice in Latin America

Monica Jimenez and Nidia Aylwin

Social work, as all other human activity, can be understood only within the context of the vast social processes that have forged history and the specific characteristics that those processes have adopted in each society. Thus, to understand social work in Chile, one must first understand the country's history and the most significant characteristics of the social "reality" that its professional social workers face.

Historical and Societal Context

Chile covers an area of 756,626 square kilometers. Of its population of 12,916 million, 84 percent is urban and 16 percent is rural. Youth predominates—67.5 percent of the population is under age 35—and although its demographic growth rate was 1.7 percent from 1985 to 1990, this figure represents a downward trend. Today, life expectancy is 71.8 years, the literacy rate is 95.2 percent, and the infant mortality rate is 18.9 per thousand. Over 80 of each 100 children over age five have had a preelementary school education; for more than 30 years, almost all Chileans have completed elementary school, and 75 out of every 100 adolescents are enrolled in public or private high schools (Ministerio Secretariá General de Gobierno, 1991).

Following a period of harsh structural adjustment, the country is enjoying a period of economic stability. The gross national product grew at an average of 5.8 percent per year over the past five years. Unemployment is currently 6 percent, but "informal" occupations persist among the lowest-income group. Inflation has been controlled at a moderate level, less than 30 percent in the past few years. Despite these indicators, poverty and indigence affect 38.1 percent of all households (Latin American Economic Commission, 1990).

Chile is an integral part of the Latin American community, sharing its cultural roots; language; and historical processes of conquest, domination, and independence. Constituted as a republic independent of Spanish rule in 1810, the country was noted for its institutional stability, democratic advances, and achievements in the political and social fields. Chile's social policies were among the first of their type implemented in Latin America. Advancements in education strengthened the middle class and brought new opportunities to the lower classes, thus contributing to national integration and unity.

Three Decades of Social Change

During the past few decades, Chile has undergone tremendous social change that has had a profound impact on both the way society is structured and on the population's daily life (Arellano, 1986).

The period of radical change began with the Christian Democratic administration of Eduardo Frei, who came to power in 1964 and initiated important changes, including agrarian reform, educational reform, legislation creating neighborhood committees (*juntas de vecinos*), and legislation authorizing the unionization of agricultural workers, among others. This period was characterized by a growth in grassroots organizing and an intensification of the politicization process.

This politicization was further quickened when the socialist administration of President Salvador Allende, who was elected in 1970, sought to construct a socialist society. In addition to radicalizing some of the reforms initiated under the previous administration, Allende introduced new reforms, such as the nationalization of the copper industry and the "stratification" of a number of companies. The government's efforts to introduce structural changes were rejected by its political opponents and eventually led to the institutional breakdown that culminated in the 1973 coup d'etat in which a military government, led by General Augusto Pinochet, came to power.

During the military regime's 17 years in office, a new institutional order was created and the model used for development was altered, giving way to a neoliberal economic system, based on the free market and open international trade. In terms of macroeconomic indicators, this approach was tremendously successful. However, the foreign debt grew substantially, income was concentrated in the hands of the wealthy, and the number of poor people increased explosively. Chile went from being a welfare state to being a subsidiary state in which social spending was reduced and the size of the state was constricted. At the same time, however, social programs focusing on the most needy were instituted. To remain in power, the military government, relying on the national security doctrine, limited public freedoms, and, particularly during its initial period, engaged in grave violations of human rights.

In 1990, Chile began to recover its democratic traditions with the inauguration of President Patricio Aylwin. The new president's transitional government seeks to strengthen the democratic system, foster economic growth, improve the distribution of wealth to benefit the poorest segments of the population, and resolve the human rights violations committed by the previous regime. The neoliberal development model implemented by the military government has been maintained, but social spending has been increased and a priority has been placed on social policy as a mechanism for improving the distribution of income. Thus, new perspectives for social development and for social work have been opened.

Development of Social Work

Chile was the first South American country in which social work emerged, in 1925. The appearance of social work was closely linked to the development of social policies; in fact, that same year Chile passed a set of laws that initiated Chilean social legislation and created a variety of government-run institutions that were charged with implementing the nascent social policies. It was in these institutions that the country's first social workers found employment—a trend that continues to this day, given that the majority of Chile's professional social workers work in governmental agencies. Social workers are also employed by nongovernmental organizations that work in the area of social problems, but there are few private practitioners.

A second important factor in the history of Chilean social work is that the European influence strongly marked the profession during its initial stages of development (Maidagan, 1960). To create the first professional schools, European professors were brought to the country. Thus, the first school of social work in Latin America, named for Alejandro del Rio, founded in 1925, was directed by Belgian instructors Jenny Bernier and Leo Cordemans de Bray. The School of Social Work of the Catholic University was founded in 1929, and its first director was German professor Luisa Joerinsen. It was not until 1945 that the reverberations of American social work began to be felt in Chile.

A third element, related to those just mentioned, is that Chilean casework only occasionally had psychiatric components, and the work was not of a clinical-therapeutic type, except at specialized mental health facilities. From the start, social workers in Chile focused on poor people, with the clear understanding that widespread poverty was not primarily a problem of individual deficiencies but was the result of underdevelopment and inequalities in the distribution of income. Therefore, they understood that poor people did not require therapeutic solutions and never believed that poverty could be overcome through classical casework. Rather, they used individualized attention to educate the population and support the people in confronting and overcoming their hardships.

Chilean social work was profoundly influenced by the reconceptualization of the profession that took place throughout Latin America beginning in 1965. Strongly opposed to practice that sought to explain professional responsibilities without considering the social context and to the predominant individualistic emphasis in other parts of the world, social workers discovered the perspective of social processes, the use of the social sciences for analysis, and the political dimensions of social action. They rejected foreign influences and questioned the critical application of professional models generated in other contexts and cultures. Thus, new forms of professional action, borne of practical experience, were developed, and a new professional identity within the Latin American context of "reality" was sought.

During this period of innovation and search, Chilean social work benefited from the pedagogical knowledge of Freire (1970), an exiled Brazilian educator living in Chile, who proposed a dialogue and "problematizing" orientation to education. Freire's theories strongly influenced a new teaching model that was being created in Chilean schools of social work that would subsequently spread throughout Latin America: The Workshop. The Workshop (Barros & Gissi, 1977) was conceived as an opportunity to combine theoretical and practical knowledge among the student body through collective field exercises among the poorest and most needy groups of society. Freire's strong influence can also be seen in the formulation of the new objectives for social work: participation, organization, and consciousness-raising among the individuals and groups who were receiving attention.

The reconceptualization process was the result not only of the evolution of the profession but of political, economic, and social events in the region that had a strong impact on social work. In Chile, this process emerged in the schools of social work, which fostered and promoted its growth, and created some interest among practitioners. Nonetheless, except for a few groups of social workers, the new practices did not take root among practitioners. Thus, the impact of these new practices was felt more at the academic and theoretical levels than at the practice level. Reconceptualization was strongly stimulated by the University Reform of 1967 and was later influenced by the structural change that the country was undergoing and by the ideological and political currents in vogue in Latin America at that time. These influences contributed to the emergence of reconceptualization's political aspects, which soon came to dominate the field. The shift in priorities had a negative impact on the profession at a time when the country was embroiled in the extreme politicization that eventually led to the 1973 coup.

In 1973, strong limitations were imposed on the exercise of professional social work as a result of both the restrictions on political rights and the characteristics of the new economic model. Moreover, the reduction in public spending and the prohibition against conducting community work further limited professional activity. Social workers who were affiliated with leftist political parties were persecuted, and many went into exile. The power of professional organizations was usurped, and thus the Social Workers Association, the profession's key point of assembly, lost representativeness and importance. Military rectors were appointed and intervened in the administration of the universities; as a result, the schools of social work lost instructors and their curricula were restructured. In some cases, the schools were even closed. A new law on higher education was drafted, authorizing the teaching of social work, as well as other professions, outside the universities. The creation of new schools in nonuniversity academic settings reduced the level of homogeneity in the training of professionals in the field.

Given the historical processes involved, one could say that social work appeared in Chile as the result of the advent of social and political forces that were pushing for change, developed as a profession to the extent that those forces were able to impart cooperative values and consolidate social policies, and entered a crisis—along with the rest of Chilean society—when the reaction against the processes of change shattered the country's democratic institutions. The coup created an authoritarian regime that questioned the value of social consensus, changed the development model, and restricted social spending, resulting in an increase in the severity and extent of societal ills.

Defense of Human Rights

During this period of restrictions on professional practice, social workers, more than any other professionals except attorneys, became active in the field of human rights. The Committee for Peace, the first human rights organization created in Chile, was cofounded by a social worker in 1973. Numerous social workers joined the effort, engaging in important professional work in defense of life and freedom, denouncing violations of human rights, and assisting victims and their families. Given the context in which this work was conducted and the tremendous risks that it involved, their actions can be considered heroic. In fact, several social workers were incarcerated and suffered multiple forms of repression for their efforts.

Social workers also were committed early to the struggle to bring back democracy. This commitment was channeled primarily through educational efforts to enlighten the people about the civil and political rights that they were afraid to exercise after so many years of the authoritarian regime. The Federation of Social Assistants, a member of the nationwide Federation of Professionals, denounced situations of injustice and publicly supported efforts to promote democracy. One social worker created an organization that engaged in the systematic education of the population during the period before the plebiscite of 1988. Subsequently, President Aylwin appointed her to the Commission on Truth and Reconciliation—an eight-member commission that was charged with investigating violations of human rights that resulted in death, identifying victims, and proposing compensatory policies for surviving family members. She worked with the commission's attorneys and a team of six other social workers to design the system used to interview family members and to propose reparation policies.

Today, while Chile is in the first stages of the transition from authoritarianism to democracy, social workers continue to play an important part in the defense and promotion of human rights. This role is carried out as much by providing assistance to the victims of earlier violations or the exiles returning to the country as by promoting more democratic forms of organization and social coexistence.

Social Work Roles and Functions

In accordance with the professional philosophy described earlier, the role of social workers in Chile has been profoundly influenced by the profession's public function and the preeminence of structural origins over individual origins of social difficulties. At present, two basic roles can be defined for the country's social workers: informal social educator and "implementer" of social policy (Aylwin, Briceño, Jimenez, & Lado, 1975).

The educational role is the more important of the two social work roles. Social work professionals have easy access to the poorest members of society, who are most in need of education. Educational services are provided through actions that accompany professional assistance, and it is through these processes that individuals and groups of people acquire the information they require to cope with the problems of daily life. This traditional role of social work acquired a greater emphasis and different content as the result of reconceptualization. In the past, social workers imparted instruction and information through a vertical relationship in which they had most of the power. At present, the teaching methodology favors the establishment of a horizontal relationship, based on the recognition of the existence of "street smarts" that social workers must acknowledge and learn to appreciate.

This new pedagogical relationship is accompanied by an expansion of the focus of educational action. Educational action is understood not only as a way of training the population to cope with their daily problems but as a way of contributing to their formation as citizens by assisting them to take an active and responsible role in the process of social development. Therefore, it is crucial to organize and train natural leaders. This work is conducted by social workers at the community level. In the more recently created nongovernmental organizations, this educational task is frequently effected through a methodology of "popular education" and is conducted in multidisciplinary groups.

Social workers perform the role of policy implementers through the governmental agencies that are charged with providing social services, serving as liaisons between the state and the population at large. It is an extremely difficult task, given the limited resources available and the extent of societal demands. The social workers' role is often that of professional spokespersons for the state. This role requires social workers to be in direct contact with the public, listening to their demands, orienting them to potential solutions to their problems, listening to their complaints, and alleviating the despondency that results from the deficiencies in the services that are provided.

At the planning level, the social worker's role is similar. Here, professionals cooperate in the design of social policies, serving as consultants to teams of policymakers. Nonetheless, it is important to note that in Chile only a minority of social workers participate in this process.

Social workers are active in implementing social policy not only through governmental agencies but through private organizations. In such organizations, they are usually employed in the personnel or welfare section, providing professional services to individuals or groups and helping them make use of the governmental social services.

In practicing their profession, social workers do not separate their role as informal social educators from their role as implementers of social policy. Although some services emphasize one or the other of these two aspects, the vast majority of social workers combine the two. Thus, they teach by implementing policy and implement policy by teaching. In these roles, social workers perform a variety of "functions," including providing assistance, promoting and defending marginalized groups, mobilizing resources, planning projects, and administering services.

The levels of poverty in Chile make the assistance function particularly important. Through this function, social workers provide material assistance and emergency services to individuals or groups whose survival is imperiled. Such dramatic situations may be the result of poverty, which is frequently chronic; other natural disasters, such as earthquakes and floods, that occur regularly in the country; or other emergencies. During the process of reconceptualization, this professional function was strongly questioned. However, it soon became clear that there was a need to focus on real assistance, rather than on "assistencialism."

The promotion of marginalized groups in the society is currently a priority for social workers given that this area is most clearly related to education. Social workers seek to develop individual and group expertise and strengthen organizations so they may take a more active role in voicing their demands within the country's social and political institutions. Training is closely tied to promotion. The "defense function" has traditionally been conducted through support for the demands of individuals or groups who do not have access to the decision makers in a variety of societal institutions. During the past few decades, this function was expanded to include the defense of human rights.

New responsibilities opened up with the incorporation of the defense of human rights into the functions of social workers (Sanchez, 1987). Initially, support was given to the persecuted, to political prisoners and their families, and to the families of the deceased and of those who "disappeared." Also, help was provided in dealing with the problems associated with exile. Later, this function incorporated cooperative organization and action to confront the conditions of poverty in which the most marginalized sectors of the population continue to live. Through this support for the organization and initiatives of the poorest, so-called solidarity workshops, informal grassroots employment "databases," soup kitchens, and community organizations in general were developed.

This "participatory" professional work united the assistance, organizational, and social education functions to facilitate the development of new forms of social involvement at a time when all participation among the marginalized population was prohibited. Such creative forms of participation and social organization later served as the foundation for the reemergence of democratic forms of association. They also provided an opportunity to develop skills and foster a feeling of self-worth within this population.

The mobilization of resources is carried out in two ways. First, in the public and private institutions that provide human services, social workers seek to obtain resources for individuals or groups in their area. Second, at the community level, social workers are active in mobilizing natural and preexisting networks of assistance and make full use of the family and neighborhood networks that are frequently found among indigent individuals.

The project-planning function is increasingly important in the practice of social work because working with social action projects to solve the problems of a given population group has become a fundamental operational aspect in a wide variety of organizations. This reliance on projects is being accentuated by the decentralization of services that is occurring in Chile today. The development of such projects is occasionally done in conjunction with other professionals. The search for participatory forms of planning is an important challenge for social workers who engage in this function.

Last, the function of service administration is conducted by social workers at a variety of levels. A variety of positions require administrative skills, including directorships of social action organizations and high-ranking positions in social welfare departments. Participation in teams charged with implementing a given project also requires a knowledge of administration.

Fields of Professional Activity

According to a study by Lado (1990), the majority of Chilean social workers work in public institutions, whereas the remainder work in traditional private-sector groups and the newer nongovernmental organizations. Most of these professionals attend to the needs of poor people, although a minority does work with middle-income groups. The most important areas of professional activity are the municipalities, youth services, health services, welfare departments in private companies or institutions, and the broad range of human rights activities mentioned earlier.

In the municipalities, social workers are responsible for a variety of activities aimed at promoting local development and providing services to the poorest members of the community. In youth services, social workers develop programs to educate and rehabilitate young people from high-risk groups or those who have come into conflict with the judicial system. In the area of health services, social workers are part of the teams responsible for maternal-infant programs, as well as programs for chronically ill adults and alcoholics. Social workers at health clinics in marginalized areas serve as liaisons between community organizations and other institutions that provide public services.

Another well-developed (and the highest-paid) area for social workers in Chile is the personnel welfare offices in a variety of public and private institutions. In these offices, social workers provide services to employees, organize welfare services, and provide information and training for employees and their families.

Professional Organization

The association that brings together Chilean social workers is the Federation of Social Workers. Created in 1956, it consists of a Superior Council and 18 regional councils throughout the country. Until 1981, affiliation was obligatory. In 1981, a new law modified the functions of professional organizations in general, transforming them into trade associations or eliminating the requirement of affiliation. For this reason, the exact number of social workers in practice is not certain, but the authors believe it is higher than the 7,057 registered members of the Federation of Social Assistants (Lado, 1990).

Training for Social Work

The first school of social work in Latin America was founded in Santiago in 1925 by Dr. Alejandro del Rio. It was dependent on the Benefactors' Council (Junta Beneficencia) and was at the nonuniversity level. Social work was incorporated into Chile's university curricula in the 1940s. At present, of the 17 schools that provide undergraduate education, eight are in universities and nine are in institutes of higher education. Seven of the latter schools are of recent inception (they have yet to graduate their first classes) and are located outside Santiago (Aylwin, 1990; Gonzalez & Rotondo, 1977; Maidagan, 1960).

The fact that less than 50 percent of the training centers for social work are now at the university level is decidedly negative for the profession. It means that there are two clearly different levels of preparation. Still, current legislation is unlikely to produce substantive modification. The new law on universities seeks not to eliminate institutions but to regulate the system by establishing stricter requirements for accreditation.

The 17 schools of social work are training approximately 2,300 students. Nationwide, an average of 300 students graduate annually (Aylwin, 1990; Lado, 1990). This number will increase significantly when the seven aforementioned schools graduate their first students. The students who enter schools of social work are high school graduates and are, on average, 18 years old. They study four to five years to receive their degrees.

The social work curriculum is composed of the following four general areas:

- *Social work:* social problems and poverty, social sciences, institutional resources, and theories and methods of social work. This area includes a practicum (internship) and is the most important part of the curriculum.
- *Methodology:* statistics, social research, planning, administration, and preparation and evaluation of social action projects.
- *Basic social sciences:* sociology, psychology, law, anthropology, economics, philosophy, and political science.
- *Electives.*

Although all the schools follow this basic curriculum, they differ in the emphasis they place on each course within each area, additional material that is incorporated, and teaching methods.

The only graduate social work program in Chile is at the Catholic University of Chile, in conjunction with its counterpart in the United States, the Catholic University of America. This program, which grants a master in education for social work degree, is open to professors and supervisors of the schools of social work and has graduated 42 teachers since its inception in 1982.

Since 1945 the Chilean Association of Schools of Social Work has played an important role in organizing periodic meetings of member schools and has maintained ties at the international level. Since the promulgation of the Law on Higher Education, which authorized the teaching of social work outside universities, the association has played an important role in establishing basic criteria for professional formation that must be met by schools that apply for membership.

Two magazines in Chile are dedicated to disseminating intellectual material in the field of social work: *Revista de Trabajo Social* (Social Work Magazine) of the School of Social Work, Catholic University of Chile, and the magazine *Apuntes* (Notebooks) produced by the Colectivo de Trabajo Social.

Current Challenges and Future Trends

Social work in Chile faces three closely associated challenges. The first is related to the consolidation of democracy, the second deals with social justice and the problems of poverty, and the third has to do with the integration of the national culture.

At this historic moment in Chilean history, when the country is emerging from 17 years of authoritarian rule, all its political actors and social organizations must work together—each from his or her own individual area of specialization—to achieve the common goal of a successful transition. They must dramatically change the nondemocratic forms of conduct and organizational behavior that took root in the country during those years.

Social work has identified as its specific response to this challenge the need to integrate itself into the country's educational and organizational processes, particularly at the grassroots level. This work is inherently democratic, but it can be reinforced with direct training materials on education for democracy.

Not all the country's professional social workers are aware of the role they need to play, and some have failed to assume it as their professional responsibility. Unfortunately, this subject is frequently skirted on the grounds that its political content makes it "untouchable." Efforts to delineate social work's field of action from a narrower perspective could lead to the profession's isolation, making it incapable of contributing to the process of historical change currently under way. Thus, the profession must be involved in the process of social integration.

There will be no authentic democracy as long as the current differences in the distribution of income persist. The problem of poverty—the principal concern for social workers—is also the key obstacle to the establishment of a real democracy. As was indicated earlier, the vast majority of Chile's social workers deal with problems of poverty, but their efforts are almost exclusively at the microsocial level. Therefore, a challenge for the profession is to become active at the policy-planning level to help overcome poverty. The profession must do so, however, without abandoning its position of attending to the needs of the people directly affected by adversity.

The third challenge, as was noted earlier, has to do with cultural integration. In Chile there is a profound schism between the modern culture of the most advanced sectors of the country and the cultural level of poor people. This gap has been widening as a result of technological advances and the concentration of wealth, which is marginalizing increasingly larger sectors of society. One of social work's fundamental challenges, then, is to create a wide awareness of this gap and to promote the development of policies and programs to bring the country's cultural levels closer together.

The future of social work in Chile will be conditioned by the changes that occur in the social context and by the form in which the profession responds to the challenges enumerated here.

The principal trends include the following:

- Research to deepen knowledge of specific areas of specialization
- A greater interest in advanced training and graduate degrees. A variety of graduate programs will be created in Chile, and social workers will have continual access to training courses. Such programs will boost levels of professional preparation
- Growing interest in multidisciplinary work to study social problems and to develop social action projects
- Increasing creativity and innovation, including greater flexibility and a wider breadth in the scope of professional roles, the exploration of new fields, and participation in unique activities that will broaden the profession's employment perspectives
- A focus on the problems of the poor and the environment
- Expansion of the profession into the private sector and a reduction of employment in the public sector among social workers
- Accentuation of the importance of values and ethics in professional practice and an increased presence of these values in the organizations in which social workers are active.

References

Arellano, J. P. (1986). *Políticas sociales y dessarrollo.* Santiago, Chile: Alfabeta Impresores.

Aylwin, N. (1990). *La formación en salud mental del asistente social.* Santiago, Chile: Corporación de Promoción Universitaria.

Aylwin, N., Briceño, L., Jimenez, M., & Lado, W. (1975). El trabajo social como technología. *Revista de Trabajo Social, 13* (School of Social Work, Catholic University of Chile, Santiago).

Barros, N., & Gissi, J. (1977). *El taller: integración de teoría y práctica.* Buenos Aires, Argentina: Editorial Humanitas.

Freire, P. (1970). *Pedagogía del oprimido.* Montevideo, Uruguay: Editorial Tierra Nueva.

Gonzalez, A. L., & Rotondo, M. R. (1977). Visión global del Servicio Social chileno. *Revista de Trabajo Social, 23* (School of Social Work, Catholic University of Chile, Santiago).

Lado, W. (1990). *Informe preliminar sobre diagnóstico del trabajo social chileno.* Cali, Colombia: ALAETS Seminar/Workshop.

Latin American Economic Commission. (1990). *Una estimación de la pobreza en Chile.* Santiago, Chile: División de Estadística y Proyecciones.

Maidagan, V. (1960). *Manual de servicio social.* Santiago: Editorial Jurídica de Chile.

Ministerio Secretaría General de Gobierno. (1991). *Chile 1991.* Santiago, Chile: Morgan y Marinetti.

Sanchez, D. (1987). Trabajo social en derechos humanos: Reencuentro con la profesión. *Revista Trabajo Social, 13* (School of Social Work, Catholic University of Chile, Santiago).

Recommended Reading

Alvarino, P. (1977). *Algunas referencias para la formulacion e proyectos en trabajo social: Apuntes.* Santiago, Chile: Colegio de Asistentes Sociales.

Aylwin, N. (1986). El objeto del trabajo social. *Revista de Trabajo Social, 30* (School of Social Work, Catholic University of Chile, Santiago).

Aylwin, N. (1986). El trabajo social como profesion. *Revista de Trabajo Social, 50* (School of Social Work, Catholic University of Chile, Santiago).

Aylwin, N., Jimenez, M., & Quezada, M. (1982). *Un enfogue operativo de la methodologia de trabajo social.* Buenos Aires, Argentina: Editorial Humanitas.

Barros, N., & Gissi, J. (1977). *El taller, integracio de teoria y practica.* Buenos Aires, Argentina: Editorial Humanitas.

Colectivo de Trabajo Social. (1990). *Concretar la democracia, aportes del trabajo social.* Buenos Aires, Argentina: Editorial Humanitas.

Colectivo de Trabajo Social. (1990). *Trabajo social y derechos humanos.* Buenos Aires, Argentina: Editorial Humanitas.

Garcia, P. (1989). *Servicio social y desarrollo local.* Valparaiso, Chile: Ediciones Universidad de Valparaiso.

Jimenez, M., & Lado, W. (1989). *Desarrollo local: Municipio y organismos nogubernamentales.* Santiago: Catholic University of Chile, School of Social Work.

Matus, T. (1990). *El trabajo social: Una disciplina en tension evolutiva.* Undergraduate thesis, Latin American Institute for Doctrine and Social Studies, Santiago, Chile.

Pizarro, E. (1972). *Que es el trabajo social?* Valparaiso, Chile: Ediciones Universidad de Valparaiso.

4

Social Work in Great Britain: Surviving the Challenge of Conservative Ideology

Chris Jones

British social work is in the midst of its most turbulent period of development since 1945. Faced with an increasingly impoverished client group and strapped for resources, it has been criticized not only for its failures but for its entire approach. Never a popular part of the welfare state, social work now faces hostility and opposition from the state itself. This is a paradoxical situation given that the government employs over 90 percent of all social workers in Great Britain.

This chapter describes the problems facing social work in Great Britain today. It analyzes why the profession remains challenged both by the central government and by substantial elements of the public and suggests what these trends indicate for the future of the profession.

Societal and Historical Context

Although Great Britain ranks among the most affluent nations of the world, the social and economic conditions of its over 55 million people vary widely. In this long-established industrial capitalist society, the majority of the population is urban based, with less than 2 percent of the working people engaged in agriculture, fishing, and forestry (United Kingdom, 1986). Many of the principal dimensions of inequality—social class, gender, and race—have remained remarkably persistent throughout the 20th century, despite the development of an elaborate network of public social services (Reid, 1989). This inequality has been particularly apparent in the major urban and industrial centers, where large populations have been living in long-term poverty and associated distress. This situation gives the country a distinctive regional geography with clear economic and political characteristics.

The country's regional characteristics have popularly been described as the north–south divide, in which the poverty and decline of the old industrial centers (the north of England, Ireland, Wales, and Scotland) are contrasted with the prosperity of London and southern England, with their thriving microeconomies rooted in new high-technology industries and financial services. These regional variations have important implications for social work practice. For example, social workers who practice in the inner cities, where rates of unemployment are as high as 55 percent, housing and environmental facilities are poor, and levels of crime and general harassment are high (especially for black people), face sharply different conditions from those who work in the prosperous and safer suburban areas.

These regional variations are clearly reflected in the voting patterns of the past 50 years (Hudson & Williams, 1989; Reid, 1989). The strength of the Conservative party is largely in the south of England. Except for London, the Labour party won no seats in Parliament during the 1987 general election in this region. However, the Labour party is particularly strong in the old industrial heartlands of northern England, south Wales, and Scotland. What is important for social workers is that the Labour party has been the dominant political force in most of the major cities and has been prepared to support and maintain social services despite fiscal constraints.

Social work emerged as a significant social service after World War II. It expanded rapidly (although unevenly) between 1948 and 1975, the highlight being the 1970 Local Authority Social Services Act that created social work agencies based in local authorities. Over that period, public expenditures for personal social services increased by more than 400 percent (Judge, 1978). With regard to policy, it is important to note that all governments since 1945 have regarded social work as an agency-based service targeted at the poor and marginalized sections of society.

The vast proportion (in excess of 90 percent) of the 25,000 social workers in Great Britain are employed in the public social services departments of local governments (United Kingdom, 1989). The largest percentage of the remainder are employed in the voluntary sector, with private social work being negligible. The social services departments are part of Britain's local governmental system, which is funded jointly by the central government and local taxes to deliver a range of services and goods, including housing, education, leisure and library services, and personal social services. Although there may be important local variations, depending on the political leadership of the local authority, the great majority of the services provided by these departments are governed by central-government legislation. Thus, there is a substantial degree of uniformity in the practice of social work in the public sector.

Public social work in Great Britain is a dynamic activity that has undergone considerable changes and is continuing to change. After the creation of the social services departments in the early 1970s, most social workers were employed as generic professionals in small teams located in particular geographic areas of the local authority. Within these generic teams, they carried mixed caseloads of clients, ranging from older people to children and their families. Recently, many departments have reorganized their social workers into specialist teams that are concerned with specific groups of clients, with services for children, older people, and mentally ill people being the most prevalent. The departments also employ residential workers in such settings as homes for older people and for children. Higher salaries and career opportunities for community-based social workers, coupled with the trend toward community care, have tended to diminish the status of residential social work.

Until the mid-1970s, a range of methods, including group and community work, were used in the social services departments. However, as a result of the subsequent periods of financial constraint and restructuring, most social workers are now engaged in emergency work with individual clients. Today, social work interventions are more likely to be task focused and short term, with little opportunity for counseling or long-term casework. Thus, social work practice tends to be reactive, rather than preventive. However, social workers who are employed in probation, which is part of the criminal justice system, and those in many voluntary organizations, who are under less stress and pressure, have a greater opportunity to use a wide range of social work methods.

The creation of the social services departments brought about a professional career structure for social workers in Great Britain. Professionally qualified social workers tend to be promoted quickly into management and administration, and salary levels, although not high, place social workers among the professional middle class on a level similar to schoolteachers, but well below that of physicians.

For a middle-class occupation, however, social work's professional organization—the British Association of Social Workers (BASW)—is weak. Only a small proportion of social workers are members of BASW, whereas many more have joined white-collar trade unions. Despite its small membership, BASW is widely consulted by the government and the media as being the voice of the profession, and it exercises greater influence than its size would suggest. It publishes one of two weekly social work magazines, *Social Work Today* (the other being *Community Care*), which carries articles on practice issues and national developments. Both magazines are funded largely by revenues generated from advertisements of vacancies in social work positions.

Social Work Education in Great Britain

Since 1970, social work education in Great Britain has been controlled by the publicly funded Central Council for Education and Training in Social Work (CCETSW; Jones, 1979). For 20 years, CCETSW validated two professional qualifications, the certificate of social service (CSS) and the certificate of qualification in social work (CQSW). By the end of the 1980s, more than 85 percent of the social workers who were employed by the social services departments held a professional qualification, and it is now virtually impossible to gain employment as a social worker without a qualification. The two qualifications have reflected the divisions between residential and field social work; the CSS is designed for those in the day care and residential sector, and the CQSW is oriented primarily to community-based practice in the social services departments.

The differences in the status of these qualifications are further reinforced by the fact that CQSW training programs tend to be offered by degree-granting institutions of higher education (universities and polytechnics), whereas the CSS is granted by colleges of further education, which have a lower status and do not offer degrees.

Both the CSS and the CQSW are based on a generic model of social work and are expected to cover all the major social work methods, client groups, and settings. In both programs, approximately half the time has to be spent in supervised practice. However, these parameters have been sufficiently broad to enable colleges to develop a wide range of qualifying courses.

Both these qualifications are now being phased out and will be replaced by 1995 by a single national professional qualification, known as the diploma in social work (Dip SW). Despite vigorous attempts by the CCETSW to persuade the government to introduce three-year training at the undergraduate level, the new diploma has been restricted to two years of study. However, it is innovative in that it acknowledges the move toward specialization and away from genericism. Under the new diploma, students will have the opportunity to focus on what are called areas of particular emphasis. Probably the biggest change is that colleges and universities will no longer be able to determine the curriculum of the training programs but will have to collaborate with agencies to determine educational content. Under CCETSW's new regulations, diploma programs will be offered only as a partnership between social work agencies and colleges.

Despite all the strains of the occupation, social work courses remain buoyant and have many students. This situation is perhaps surprising in view of the serious problems facing social work in Great Britain.

The Conservative Critique of Social Work

Social work in Great Britain was fundamentally challenged by the ascendancy of the New Right and the Thatcher administrations of the 1980s. Much of the attack on social work was part of a wider onslaught on the welfare state. The impact of the restructuring of public health, income maintenance, employment, education, and public housing has been documented elsewhere (Andrews & Jacobs, 1990; Ball, Gray, & McDowell, 1989; Becker &

MacPherson, 1988). This process has been under way since the late 1980s and is still being pursued in the 1990s. It has not been a process of fine-tuning the social services but, rather, a fundamental reordering of the state and its relationship to the increasing number of poor people who have been pushed to the margins of economic and social life (Hudson & Williams, 1989).

This transformation of the welfare state has demanded both structural reforms and an ideological campaign that ridicules and delegitimates the previously dominant social democratic conception of the state (Hall & Jacques, 1983). For about a decade, the government has directed an ideological campaign that has lauded the superiority of market forces and individual initiative over any state-administered enterprise. In terms of social welfare, this has not been an altogether uphill task. The failure of the British welfare state to resolve the problems of poverty and the rising demands and pressures it faced had created, especially for poor people, a monolithic structure that was inadequate, unresponsive, and often impenetrable. The rallying cry of the first Thatcher government, elected in 1979, to get the state "off our backs," hit a responsive chord with many and gave the New Right the upper hand. Yet rather than create an effective and responsive welfare state, the state's provision of services itself has been undermined.

For many New Conservatives, social work provided by the government epitomized all that was wrong with the British welfare state. Social work practice typified the "Nanny State," which Thatcher had ridiculed. With much exaggeration, the New Right held social workers to be left wing and anticapitalist. Because social workers supported demands for an expanding welfare state and opposed the government's plans to cut back services and resources, they were identified as ideological opponents. In terms of practice, social workers were criticized for creating dependence and for being too lenient with those clients whom the Right considered to be "undeserving." It was because of human services professionals, such as social workers, that Conservative critics like Rhodes Boyson (1971)—later a government minister in the early 1980s—claimed that Great Britain had become a society where "no one cares, no one saves, no one bothers—why should they when the state spends all its energies taking money from the energetic, successful and thrifty, to give to the idle, the failures and the feckless" (p. 384).

To sustain their belief in the primacy of individual and familial responsibility, the New Conservatives had to break the link between individual distress and social conditions. In doing so, they confronted the traditions of the social work profession, borne out of social democracy, which contend that the social problems of clients are linked in diverse ways to social, economic, and political factors. Although rarely radical, for social work retained some notions of personal pathology (and, in the case of black clients, racist stereotyping), social work's understanding of disadvantage, reinforced by the significant growth in the feminist and radical social sciences literature, encouraged a form of social work practice in which social workers were prepared to stand by their clients, not as victims of their own inadequacies, but as an oppressed social group. In practice, it entailed social workers acting as advocates for their clients, prepared to confront state agencies to obtain better services and more resources. In many cases, social workers were prepared to accept their clients' manipulation of state agencies, such as the social security office, to maximize their income (Pearson, 1975).

The New Conservatives were vehemently opposed to these theories, and they contended that such thinking had exacerbated the plight of poor and vulnerable people. That is, life was made too easy for poor and vulnerable people, who were protected by social workers from feeling the full consequences of their behavior and indiscipline. What was needed, the New Right argued, was a return to the 19th-century approach that recognized the inextricable link between poverty and labor. As George Gilder noted, "what the poor need most of all in order to succeed is the spur of their poverty" (quoted in Loney, 1987, p. 9).

This New Right attitude has been translated into social policies that have created a reduced and constrained state welfare system. Although the New Conservatives would not permit people to starve or freeze to death, anything beyond that must be justified to those who guard the public purse. These ideas are now being implemented in the context of growing need and poverty in Great Britain. As Becker, MacPherson, and Falkingham (1987) noted, the number of people in poverty in Great Britain increased by 53 percent from 1979 to 1987: "The . . . number of people in poverty exceeds 10 million and the numbers living in or on the margins of poverty are estimated at 19 million people" (pp. 35–36). This combination of minimalist and authoritarian social policies with growing long-term poverty has thrown social work in Great Britain into turmoil.

The New Right critique has found expression in numerous policies and programs that are designed both to weaken state-sponsored social work services and to undermine the profession itself. These policies and programs are discussed next.

Social Work and the Media

One way in which social work has been challenged by the New Right is through the media. Indeed, to make sense of the problems facing social work in Great Britain, one must recognize the extent to which social workers have been the object of the New Conservatives' onslaught. In a profession that relies overwhelmingly on interpersonal relationships rather than on goods and services, the discrediting of social work has meant the discrediting of social workers themselves.

Attacks on social workers in the media over the past 12 years have ranged from the professional to the personal. Social workers have been portrayed as the "sixties generation," which, according to Thatcher, was infatuated with "fashionable theories and progressive clap-trap . . . in which the old virtues of discipline and self-restraint were denigrated" (quoted in Levitas, 1986, p. 7). Rather than being role models of responsible citizenship, social workers were stereotyped as aging hippies, disdainful of legitimate authority, critical of enterprise, and opponents of the family.

Since the mid-1970s, social work has frequently been exposed and humiliated in the media, especially in relation to the issue of child abuse. The media has alternately berated social workers for failing to act appropriately to save a child and for overintervening, particularly in cases of the alleged sexual abuse of children.

The extent of the press's attack on social work has been extraordinary. As Franklin (1989) argued, it indicates the extent to which the British press is largely conservative and rampantly against the public sector. It also reflects the press's particular dislike of social workers, who are taken to epitomize all that is wrong with the welfare state. As Franklin explained, social workers are represented as the "soft" and pandering features of the welfare system, who, in their liberality and naïveté, are easily manipulated by the deviant and the feckless. However, they have also been stereotyped in the press as "bullies." The press's criticisms of social workers who are investigating child sexual abuse often extend beyond the specifics of abused children to the wider role and purpose of social work itself. This bias was demonstrated in the furor over the "Cleveland Affair," when it was disclosed, in summer 1987, that the local social services department had, in the previous six months, taken action to protect over 350 children in the Cleveland area of northern England who were suspected of having been sexually abused. The situation caused an uproar. The popular press, tacitly supported by the government, contended that although sexual abuse might regrettably exist, it had been grossly exaggerated by social workers and some physicians (Campbell, 1988). According to the *Daily Mail* (July 7, 1987), social workers are "abusers of authority, hysterical and malignant, callow youngsters who absorb moral-free marxoid sociological theories" (quoted in Franklin, 1989, p. 2).

As Campbell (1988) revealed in her valuable study of the Cleveland Affair, an important part of the attack on social workers was the accusation that they had approached the issue of the sexual abuse of children from the perspective of feminist theories that point to the abuse of male power within families. As she noted, "Social workers found themselves politically as well as professionally besieged. Child sex abuse was, quite correctly, perceived by people opposed to the diagnosis as no longer belonging to a populist politics of hanging and flogging but to a politics with a critique of patriarchy and power in the family" (p. 139)

This criticism of social work's approach to the sexual abuse of children is also revealed in criminal cases in which defense lawyers sought to demonstrate that social workers were unduly influenced by feminist theories. Some social workers reported that they were interrogated by defense lawyers in court not only about professional activities and opinions but about their personal lives and political beliefs. This questioning of social workers' personal life-styles and politics is indicative of the manner in which Conservative critics have sought to undermine the authority of social work and social workers. Much of social work practice, at least since the 1960s, has been informed and influenced by credible theories drawn from the social sciences. These theories provide perspectives that connect individual problems to wider social and economic factors and that, in recent years, have been more attentive to the corrosive impact of racism and sexism on the lives of many black people and women. However, the attempt to demean the personal characteristics of social workers supports the attempt to present social work as little more than the idiosyncratic behavior of those who are motivated by personal opinion. This attitude makes it easier to dismiss the views of social workers and to avoid more important debates about what is actually happening in British society.

Social Work and the Family

In 1987, Thatcher claimed that "there's no such thing as society, there are only individual men and women" (quoted in Benton, 1987, p. 37). For Thatcher and her supporters, the family was seriously undermined by the encroachment of the welfare state and the activities of social workers who subverted parental authority and weakened family traditions. To restore economic well-being, the traditional family (and, by implication, patriarchy) had to be restored.

The collapse of the authority of fatherhood in the face of feminism was held to be the primary cause of the decline of the family and a resulting increase in social problems, such as lawlessness. The importance of restoring the father to his "natural" place was well stated in 1987 by the New Right journalist Paul Johnson, who argued that Conservatives would put the father back at the "head of the family table." The father, Johnson contended, should be the breadwinner and should be responsible for his children's actions. Years of militant feminism and harmful legislation like the Equal Opportunities Act had, Johnson argued, undermined the "clear biblical concept of the father" (quoted in Loney, 1987, p. 16).

In the domain of child abuse, social workers were not only drawing attention to the problems of contemporary family life but were implicitly focusing on men's abuse of power and authority. In so doing, they posed a challenge to the government's welfare strategy, which advocated transferring responsibilities from the state to the family. The increasing revelation of the sexual and ritual abuse of children has exposed a seam of sickness in British family life and challenged the family's sanctity, harmony, and "normality."

The most widespread reaction within the government and the press has been denial. Rather than trying to make sense of what is happening in families, the press and the government have attacked social workers, complaining that they have overreacted and overstated the extent of the problem.

This response further undermines social work and marks a fundamental disrespect for the expertise and knowledge that social workers have developed in this area. Social workers are once again presented as being driven by self-interest to interpret "every disagreeable condition into a 'problem,' maybe even a deprivation" (Kristol, 1978, p. 248). The implication of these attacks is clear: Social workers can be comfortably ignored.

Regulation, Control, and Agency Imperatives

The Conservative government's persistent attacks on local governments have been particularly disruptive to the human services. In curtailing the powers of local authorities, the government has weakened all services, including social work. Consequently, many social work agencies have been reorganized as each budgetary reduction has been met by organizational change. Many inner-city agencies, which serve some of the most impoverished and marginalized sections of the population, have had to focus on internal reorganizations to the detriment of service delivery. As services are reduced and new rationing procedures are introduced, relationships with clients have become more strained. Thus, social services agencies seem to be moving from being "providers of barely adequate services for the poor, towards becoming underfunded, over-stretched and in, some cases, overwhelmed services for the oppressed" (Balloch & Hume, 1985, p. i).

Social workers' roles are being increasingly governed by agency imperatives, and social workers are finding that they are being compelled to function as regulators and rationers, rather than as providers of services. As the focus of intervention shifts increasingly toward the needs of the agency and away from the needs of the client, helping functions are being replaced by regulatory and rationing functions. This problem has been exacerbated by a new attitude that suggests that because the agency is starved of resources, clients do not have just demands. As agency imperatives become more evident in all areas of social work practice, social workers are being compelled to operate within a supply-led welfare system in which services are determined by budgetary resources, rather than by the needs of clients.

These changes are pushing social workers into more antagonistic relationships with their clients. The combination of the growing distress of clients and the need for agencies to introduce more severe rationing procedures to keep within budgetary limits is having a dramatic impact on social work practice. Becker and Silburn (1990) reported that security issues and the segregation of clients now characterize much social work practice. Describing a typical social services agency, they noted: "Doors can only be opened by tapping in a code number, the separation of client and worker by partitions or glass screens, the increasing use of appointment systems, the air, even the smell, of drab . . . in the waiting rooms, this is now commonly encountered in many places, as though working with the new-poor clients creates a poor working environment" (p. 81).

The growing frustrations of clients are understandable because clients now come to confront social workers who have considerable gatekeeping and rationing powers over the resources that they need. The frustration of clients has led to the rapid increase in the number of assaults against social workers, four of whom have been killed in the past five years. As a Parliamentary panel on social work observed: "The increased pressure upon local authorities to respond to social need whilst coping with a level of funding that fails to meet these needs in real terms, is one factor in the generation of antagonism from sections of the public that sometimes expresses itself in violence against staff" (quoted in National Association of Local Government Officers [NALGO], 1989, p. 14).

The increasing antagonism between social workers and clients has been accompanied by a growing trend toward social workers performing more social-control functions. This trend reflects the clear strategic concern of the government to require social workers to play a more authoritarian and disciplinary role. Informed by a New Right perspective that argues that disadvantaged and marginal individuals are largely to blame for their condition by their indiscipline and lack of morality, governmental policy seeks to make social workers agents of control and discipline, rather than helpers of the needy. Jordan (1988) noted that social workers are showing a greater antagonism toward and are using more coercive measures against their clients. This situation is particularly clear in the field of child care, but other "evidence points also to more punitive ideologies among social workers, more social distance between them and their clientele, and a greater emphasis on decisiveness, which often works against partnership and sharing" (Jordan, 1988, p. 345). It also leads to a process whereby the liberal and humanitarian aspects of social work are systematically stripped away, leaving behind those authoritarian and controlling dimensions that have always been a part of state social work in Great Britain. This harder face of social work is well known to black clients (Bryan, Dadzie, & Scafe, 1985, pp. 1–2), but it is becoming more generalized as social work moves increasingly toward being an agent of a restrictive and punitive welfare state.

Law and Order

The trend toward a coercive tilt in social work is also evident in the recent debates over law and order in Great Britain. Since the passage of the Children and Young Persons Act in 1969, influential groups of police officers and magistrates have been opposed to the significant role allotted by the act to social workers and social services departments in caring for young offenders. In 1976, for example, the deputy chief constable of West Yorkshire complained that social workers and probation officers had become a hindrance, "who made it a work of art getting some young offenders out of the reach of the court. . . . We are fed up with the influence of the so-called specialists . . . the softly-softly, namby-pamby pussy-footing approach to the vicious elements who have never had it so good" (quoted in *Daily Telegraph*, April 19, 1976). These ideas have been echoed by many New Right journalists, such as Peregrine Worsthorne, who believes that "better heads cracked by a policeman's truncheon than souls swamped by society's pity" (quoted in *Sunday Telegraph*, December 2, 1981).

In a reversal of the trend established by the 1969 Children and Young Persons Act, the Criminal Justice Acts of 1982 and 1988 transferred a significant degree of authority from social work agencies to the judiciary and the police. The legislation curtailed social work's autonomy by allowing a court to instruct an agency to place a young person in residential care. This same legislation also introduced new noncustodial measures, such as curfews on young offenders, which were to be supervised by social workers or allied probation officers. Furthermore, the legislation extended opportunities for magistrates to fine parents for the offending behavior of their children. This latter clause may be seen as a further aspect of the Conservatives' strategy of affirming the duties of parenthood. As the government's White Paper, *Young Offenders* (United Kingdom, 1980, paragraph 54) pointed out: "This clarification and extension of the law will encourage the courts to assert the duty of parents to act responsibly towards their children and take all steps within their power to prevent them committing criminal acts."

Ideologically, these measures also challenge and undermine the liberal positions of social work. Consistent with the Thatcherite project of rejuvenating the ethics of free enterprise, the cause of crime is taken to rest within the individual and the family—not in social injustice and inequality. As John Patten, a governmental minister remarked, "I have got more impatient with the analysis of why people commit crime. Five years ago we were told it was the Tories in power and it was unemployment, now the Tories are in power and it's affluence that causes crime. All these things are absurd. In the end people commit crime because they are bad" (cited in May, 1991, p. 109).

Such sentiments were powerfully articulated at the time of the inner-city riots in 1981 and 1985. These explosions of frustration and anger were treated largely by the government and its New Right supporters as symptoms of moral decay and criminality (especially in the black communities). Arguments from within these communities that pointed to the destructiveness of unemployment, poverty, deteriorating housing, racism, and police harassment were systematically rejected by the government (Solomos, 1986). The government's response was to fund and sanction an almost paramilitary role for the police as a means of reasserting control. This reaction was in stark contrast to the softer responses of the 1950s and 1960s, when the government attempted to ease inner-city tensions with a range of urban aid and community programs.

The outright rejection of social deprivation as a cause of these riots has been a recurrent theme of recent Conservative interpretations of social ills. The inadequacy of parental responsibility has been identified as the cause of juvenile crime. Adult crime is attributed to the irresponsibility of individual criminals. The poor health status of the working class and black populations is imputed to their inadequate diets and life-styles. The unemployment of youths is believed to be caused by the welfare state itself; in the words of Thatcher, "It's too easy for some of them, straight out of school, to go straight onto social security at the age of 16. They like it, they have a lot of money, and some of them learn a way of life they should never have a chance to learn" (quoted in Novak, 1988, p. 195).

Responding to the Challenge

Contrary to some expectations, social work has survived under Thatcherism. At the time of writing, more people than ever are employed as social workers (NALGO, 1989), and, to this extent, social work thrives. But, because of all the changes that have been introduced, can it now be defined as an occupation that should be called social work?

Sadly, there are few signs of organized opposition among British social workers today. Social workers seem to be incapable of challenging the authoritarian drift of the welfare state. The profession is not only on the defensive, it is weak and demoralized. Unfortunately, those in practice seem to be overwhelmed with work, which has limited their capacity to resist. As one senior social worker reported, "It's never ending work, you go from one crisis to another, there are so many areas in which you should be doing things that if someone were to check up, they would uncover a whole range of things that simply had not been done. It makes you feel so vulnerable" (quoted in NALGO, 1989, p. 48). The consequence is that social work practitioners are now rarely active politically within their agencies, professional organizations, and trade unions as they were in the 1970s (Jones, 1983; Simpkin, 1983).

However, there have been some attempts to counter the Conservative challenge. Perhaps the most promising site of resistance in recent years has been professional social work education, in part because it escaped some of the new policies but also because during the 1970s, social work education became one of the most active spheres of critical and progressive activity in the profession. Indeed, for some critics, social work courses were one of the major causes of social work radicalism and even of trade union militancy in the profession (Gould, 1977). Although much exaggerated, this critical approach acknowledged the leadership role of social work academics, some of whom like Dame Eileen Younghusband were particularly prominent in the expansion of state social work between 1948 and 1970 (Jones, 1983).

Nevertheless, just as social work agencies have been transformed, so has social work education. It is, as Jones (1989) noted, a prolonged process that began in the early 1980s and is likely to continue through the mid-1990s. The result, apart from the exhaustion of social work teachers, has been the development of a new two-year social work professional qualification, the Dip SW, which supports the government's approach to social work and trains people accordingly.

In introducing this new qualification, the professional validating body, the CCETSW, has legitimated a particularly Conservative definition of social work as being essentially an activity undertaken by those employed as social workers primarily in public agencies. It has also given employers a dominant role in the way the programs are to be designed. Moreover, the new qualification is to be employment led and governed by regulations that are so detailed, directive, and technical that training programs will provide little opportunity for developing the analytical skills that many would argue are essential for effective practice. Above all, the new qualification is essentially antithetical to the development of professionalism. Social workers are thereby denied the possibility of opposing the demands made on them by legislation because they have no professional yardstick with which to assess the tasks being allocated. In addition, the new qualification is disqualified from professional recognition within the European Community, which is "a blow to the standing of British social work and social work education" (Parsloe, 1990, p. 20).

Conservatism has not yet managed to drown all the progressive and radical currents that once characterized British social work. Within agencies and social work education, some people persist in their efforts to liberalize social work and to make it antiracist and antisexist. The assurance that antiracism will permeate the new courses leading to the Dip SW has been an important achievement (CCETSW, 1991). However, initiatives such as these are being attempted within constraining parameters and in a context in which opportunities for addressing the needs of clients are quickly disappearing.

Despite these few hopeful signs, the outlook is gloomy. The plight of those who need and use social work services is now especially dire. For many, social work now contributes to their problems; it does not offer help. It seems that until the political climate changes and there is a popular rejection of the precepts of the New Right, social work will survive as an occupation but may perish as a caring and liberal profession.

References

Andrews, K., & Jacobs, J. (1990). *Punishing the poor.* London: Macmillan.

Ball, M., Gray, F., & McDowell, L. (1989). *The transformation of Britain.* London: Fontana Press.

Balloch, S., & Hume, C. (1985). *Caring for unemployed people.* London: Bedford Square Press.

Becker, S., & MacPherson, S. (Eds.). (1988). *Public issues, private pain.* London: Social Service Insight Books.

Becker, S., MacPherson, S., & Falkingham, F. (1987). Some local authority responses to poverty. *Local Government Studies, 13,* 35–48.

Becker, S., & Silburn, R. (1990). *The new poor clients: Social work, poverty and the social fund.* London: Community Care.

Benton, S. (1987, November 20). Death of the citizen. *New Statesman,* p. 37.

Boyson, R. (1971). *Down with the poor.* London: Churchill Press.

Bryan, B., Dadzie, S., & Scafe, S. (1985). *The heart of the race: Black women's lives in Britain.* London: Virago Press.

Campbell, B. (1988). *Unofficial secrets.* London: Virago Press.

Central Council on Education and Training in Social Work. (1991). *Setting the context for change: Anti-racist social work education.* London: Author.

Franklin, B. (1989). Wimps and bullies: Press reporting of child abuse. In P. Carter, T. Jeffs, & M. Smith (Eds.), *Social work and social welfare yearbook, No. 1* (pp. 1–14). Milton Keynes, England: Open University Press.

Gould, J. (1977). *The attack on higher education: Marxism and radical penetration.* London: Institute for the Study of Conflict.

Hall, S., & Jacques, S. (1983). *The politics of Thatcherism.* London: Lawrence & Wishart.

Hudson, R., & Williams, A. (1989). *Divided Britain.* London: Heinemann.

Jones, C. (1979). Social work education, 1900–1970. In N. Parry, M. Rustin, & C. Satyamurti (Eds.), *Social work, welfare and the State* (pp. 72–88). London: Edward Arnold.

Jones, C. (1983). *State social work and the working class.* London: Macmillan.

Jones, C. (1989). End of the road: Issues in social work education. In P. Carter, T. Jeffs, & M. Smith (Eds.), *Social work and social welfare yearbook, No. 1* (pp. 204–216). Milton Keynes, England: Open University Press.

Jordan, B. (1988). Poverty, social work and the state. In S. Becker & S. MacPherson (Eds.), *Public issues, private pain* (pp. 340–349). London: Social Service Insight Books.

Judge, K. (1978). *Rationing social services.* London: Heinemann.

Kristol, I. (1978). *Two cheers for capitalism.* New York: Basic Books.

Levitas, R. (1986). Tory students and the New Right. *Youth and Policy, 16,* 1–9.

Loney, M. (1987). A war on poverty or on the poor? In A. Walker & C. Walker (Eds.), *The growing divide* (pp. 8–19). London: Poverty Action Group.

May, T. (1991). *Probation: Politics, policy and practice.* Milton Keynes, England: Open University Press.

National Association of Local Government Officers. (1989). *Social work in crisis.* London: Author.

Novak, T. (1988). *Poverty and the state.* Milton Keynes, England: Open University Press.

Parsloe, P. (1990). Future of social work education. In P. Carter, T. Jeffs, & M. Smith (Eds.), *Social work and social welfare yearbook, No. 2* (pp. 197–240). Milton Keynes, England: Open University Press.

Pearson, G. (1975). *The deviant imagination.* London: Macmillan.

Reid, I. (1989). *Social class differences in Britain.* London: Fontana Press.

Simpkin, M. (1983). *Trapped within welfare.* London: Macmillan.

Solomos, J. (1986). Political language and violent protest: Ideological and policy responses to the 1981 and 1985 riots. *Youth and Policy, 18,* 12–24.

United Kingdom, Central Statistical Office. (1986). *Annual abstract of statistics: 1986.* London: Her Majesty's Stationery Office.

United Kingdom, Central Statistical Office. (1989). *Health and personal social service statistics, 1989.* London: Her Majesty's Stationery Office.

United Kingdom, Home Office. (1980). *Young offenders* (White Paper). London: Her Majesty's Stationery Office.

Recommended Reading

Becker, S., & MacPherson, S. (Eds.). (1988). *Public issues, private pain.* London: Social Service Insight Books.

Becker, S., & Silburn, R. (1990). *The new poor clients: Social work, poverty and the social fund.* London: Community Care.

Campbell, B. (1988). *Unofficial secrets.* London: Virago Press.

Carter, P., Jeffs, T., & Smith, M. (Eds.). (1989). *Social work and social welfare yearbook, No. 1.* Milton Keynes, England: Open University Press.

Carter, P., Jeffs, T., & Smith, M. (Eds.). (1990). *Social work and social welfare yearbook, No. 2.* Milton Keynes, England: Open University Press.

Davies, M. (Ed.). (1991). *The sociology of social work.* London: Routledge.

Jones, C. (1983). *State social work and the working class.* London: Macmillan.

Langan, M., & Lee, P. (Eds.). (1989). *Radical social work today.* London: Unwin Hyman.

National Association of Local Government Officers. (1989). *Social work in crisis.* London: Author.

Sullivan, M. (1989). *The social policies of Thatcherism: New Conservatism and the welfare state* (Occasional Paper No. 21). Swansea, England: University College of Swansea.

5

Social Work in Hungary: New Opportunities in a Changing Society

Katalin Talyigas and Gabor Hegyesi

Hungary is one of the Eastern European countries whose political and economic systems, modeled after those of the former Soviet Union, have failed drastically. Therefore, the country faces enormous problems, including the challenge of constituting a democracy.

Historical and Societal Context

The political and economic modernization of Hungary began with the revolution of 1848. By the turn of this century, the last years of the Austro-Hugarian Empire, the development of the bourgeois state had accelerated. Towns had expanded, the railroad network and the educational and health care systems were functioning, the social security system was on a par with those of Western Europe, and the arts flourished. The institutions of a civil society had started to appear, and several organizations were founded. Feudalistic features, however, had not disappeared completely.

As a result of World War I, Hungary lost two-thirds of its territory, and its development was set back by the general political and economic crisis. Modernization gained new momentum from the mid-1920s to the 1930s, after which numerous crises—from the economic depression to World War II and the German occupation of the country—stifled further progress. The parliamentary democracy of 1945–48 provided the framework for the reconstruction of the country and the reorganization of society.

This democratic period was again short-lived. In 1949 the multiparty system was abolished by the Communist party, which took control. From 1950 to 1989, the society was characterized by an immense concentration of power in the state and a centralized economy. The regime claimed to be socialist: It declared liberty, but the country endured Soviet occupation for 40 years; it declared that all people were equal, but new forms of inequality appeared; it declared social safety, which was partially realized, but by 1989 social safety proved to be ineffective.

The year 1989 was a turning point in Hungarian history. The republic was proclaimed on October 23. Following free elections, the multiparty Parliament and a coalition government were formed, a new president of the republic was elected, and local governments were set up. Political change included the establishment of an independent constitutional court. Since then, privatization of the economy has been initiated and modernization has again become a priority.

Despite the favorable changes, Hungary is situated on an area that is experiencing a political crisis. The Stalinist political systems have collapsed irrevocably in Eastern Europe and in the former Soviet Union, but the social-market economies have not yet been established. Today the most important issue in Hungary is how the democratic institutions can be strengthened in the midst of serious economic problems. The country's debt is huge ($2,000 per capita), and its capital assets are small. Although the Parliament has been discussing the issue of privatization, no decision has yet been made as to how state property should be distributed. Should state property be given to the original owners, to those who are working in the industrial or agricultural sector, or to those who have enough money to buy it and run it efficiently? Competition among various interest groups has prevented a national consensus on this issue. The economic crisis, moreover, is mounting. Rising inflation and low wages are leading to mass impoverishment, which is exacerbated by rising unemployment.

The developmental trends of the coming years will obviously be determined by the state of the economy. On the one hand, the new political era may provide a favorable ground for a modern European market economy. On the other hand, there is the danger of the rise of a new dictatorial regime based on nationalism. Democracy as a way of life and new political opportunities can be implemented only if they make an impact on the whole society. At present, however, this political culture is highly undeveloped.

There is some room for optimism given that the prospect of democracy has already released immense human energy. Parties, associations, and societies have been formed, and people are willing to work for clear and well-defined goals. The principle of voluntarism and the development of nonprofit organizations have been gaining ground, and there are opportunities to enter into partnerships with other countries. This openness gives hope that in the future, Hungary will become a successful bourgeois state.

Demographic Profile

Hungary is a small country with 35,912 square miles. Of its 10.5 million inhabitants, 2 million live in Budapest, the country's capital, and the rest live in 3,000 municipalities in 19 counties. The population of the country is aging; 21.9 percent of the people are old-age pensioners (women retire at age 55 and men retire at age 60), and the mortality rate has exceeded the birthrate for a number of years. This situation will produce the following demographic trends:

- The population will decrease in the next 20–30 years. By 2021, it will be below 10 million.
- The number of old-age pensioners will reach 26 percent by 2021.
- The proportion of children aged 14 and under will fall from the present 19.8 percent to 18.8 percent by 2021 (their number will decrease in absolute numbers as well).
- The number of potential active workers will fall from 61.3 percent to 58.8 percent by 2021.
- The proportion of dependents to active workers will not change significantly. At present it is 58.3 percent to 41.7 percent, and it will be 56 percent to 44 percent by 2021.

The composition of families and households also is changing. By 2021 the number of families will decrease by 200,000 (from the present 2.9 million). Similarly, by 2021 the number of adult unmarried people will increase from 782,000 to more than 1 million. This changing family composition reflects the postponement of first marriages, the increase in divorces, and the growing number of single elderly people.

One demographic trend that presents a major challenge to policymakers and service providers is the growing percentage of older people. Hungary is the first country that is experiencing the quick and massive aging of the population without a medium stage of development. At the same time, the infrastructure for this aging population—housing, transportation, telephones, and so forth—is unsatisfactory. Pensions are low, and there are few organizations and services to cater to the special needs of elderly people. In particular, health care for elderly people is inadequate.

Social Policy and Social Services Programs

The sociopolitical system that was in effect from 1949 to 1989 did not pay much attention to social services. Its major concern was to support an economic strategy that was designed to bring about the fastest possible economic growth through the greatest possible accumulation of capital. Wages were kept low to depress the demand for consumer goods, thus reducing the need to produce much for private consumption. Market influences were excluded, and a huge new heavy-industry system was built up.

Private ownership of the instruments and means of production, land, factories, transportation, communications, and the mass media was abolished, and the small holdings of peasants were transformed into socialist cooperatives. A large governmental planning authority was established to regulate directly what was produced, how much was produced, the level of prices and wages, and the allocation of production and resources. The major features of the Hungarian social policy of this period were benefits in-kind, income supports, and social services.

Benefits In-kind and Income Supports

Basic commodities, such as milk, bread, meat, clothing, and services (including transportation, telephones, housing, and electricity), were low priced and subsidized by the state. The value of social benefits in-kind reached 20–30 percent of wages by the 1970s.

Income supports were provided through the price, wage, and social security systems and were linked with the system of mandatory work that abolished unemployment. Everyone had both the right and the duty to work. This social security system was built on low inflation and the promise of a growing population that could provide an ever-increasing reserve of employees, an ever-growing fund for social security through the contribution of employers and the rising number of employees, and the guaranteed maintenance of that fund. One major goal was to establish an indexed pension system with a mandated social insurance contribution. Every Hungarian citizen was to be eligible for an old-age pension.

Today, the big issue is which basic social provisions should be covered by the central government and which should be covered by the local governments. Support should be provided against starvation, homelessness, and impecuniousness by earmarking a fund for local governments through which they could offer free meals, temporary homes, and financial aid. The existence of these institutions is imperative, although the crisis intervention network would not solve social transitions but only address them day by day. Therefore, governmental intervention in the social sector is essential; however, the mobilization of other resources is also needed for the operation of a broad social services sector.

Today, the government and the Parliament seem to prefer selectivity over universality in income-support programs. They claim that the economic problems and the lack of resources allow support only for the neediest. Thus, benefits will be more and more important, especially for large families and unemployed, permanently ill, physically disabled, and mentally retarded people. The maintenance of social and universal provisions, free education, inexpensive nursery and kindergarten programs, and an extensive network of child protection counseling, among others, has become uncertain. Also, the planned privatization of the health care system raises additional questions about universal access.

Social Services

Education and health care services were provided free to all Hungarians under the previous system, although the health care system did not cover the entire population until 1975. Personal social services were not developed at that time. However, the demand for such services grew rapidly owing to a number of changes.

The New Mechanism of Economy, introduced in 1968, abolished the mandatory system of central planning for firms. Its aim was to foster the efficiency and autonomy of firms. The range of systems of subsidizing prices and business was reduced. Unfortunately, this attempt to modernize the economic structure coincided with the oil crisis of 1973, which led the country into debt. The rate of growth fell to a negative percent, while the inflation rate reached 35 percent, in contrast with 2 percent in the 1960s (*Income of People*, 1990).

Inflation had the greatest impact on those who were dependent on pensions because pension income is not fully indexed. Older pensioners have lost the most in recent years. Those who retired more than 10 to 15 years ago find themselves in a difficult position and need different fiscal benefits and relief. There is, however, no fund or other resource to raise their pensions, and the rate of indexing does not match the rate of inflation.

Other factors have contributed to the urgent need for the faster development of a network of human social services. Such factors are closely linked with the process of industrialization; for example, the extensive internal migration from the countryside has caused housing problems in the towns. Similarly because nearly 70 percent of the women have jobs in the towns, they are no longer able to provide care for aged people and for children; consequently, these groups need more organized forms of services.

The shortage of home-help service adds to the stress in the everyday lives of many people, who need efficient caring and preventive networks. The number of problems related to the disorders of social adjustment—suicide, alcoholism, mental disorders, and the abuse of children and youths—have grown rapidly. The following conclusions of a research project completed in 1985 indicate the seriousness of these problems at that time. These problems are even more serious today, since the introduction of the market economy:

> Between 1950 and 1982 the number of suicides has almost doubled and has recently reached 5,000 per annum (out of a population of 10.8 million). Three million people are estimated to be affected by severe alcoholism. . . . The crime rate is relatively low, but recent years have seen some rise, and also a change in its structure; burglary and robbery have become more frequent, child and youth delinquency have increased. Although data concerning the prevalence of mental disorders is scarce, evidence suggests the rapid spread of neuroses which are estimated to affect some 25% of the population. In 1982 the number of young people seeking medical aid for their drug addiction was nearly 3,000 (mainly glue-sniffing) and the number of those who had ex-

> perimented with drugs is estimated at 25,000–30,000. Young people at risk are registered in schools so that they may have access to help; these are numbered at over 120,000. (*Complex Analysis of Disorders*, 1985)

If individuals are detached from the community that shelters them and provides them with norms and values, then they are likely to respond with illness, neurosis, and deviance. Although prevention is important, a pressing task is to expand the scope of certain professions that may help people face and solve their problems. Dealing with these problems is the task not only of the psychological and medical professions but of social work.

In the past 45 years efforts have been made to remedy these problems. The result has been a number of scattered and independently developing welfare networks, including centers for alcoholics, educational and family counseling centers, and centers for mentally ill people. There are also movements for overcoming these problems, such as the mental health care movement.

Expected Changes

It is clear that the social policy that is under development should reflect these societal problems. The expected changes can be summarized as follows: In the "old" system social benefits in-kind were of primary importance, fiscal benefits were of secondary significance, and personal services were of only marginal concern. In the "new" system, personal services will have much more importance, income-support programs also will be important, and social security will be at the center of serious debate. Social benefits in-kind already have a low priority.

If the new policy emphasizes personal social services, the need for social workers who are skilled in various types of social work practice will increase. It is likely that superfluous workers in other fields will find work in this area after having qualified as social workers. Thus, the need for different forms of social work education, both undergraduate and graduate, will increase.

Social Work Roles and Functions

Social workers were employed in Hungary before World War II. However, the profession and training were terminated after the war for ideological and political reasons. According to the ideological explanation, a socialist system is devoid of deprivation, an adequate institutional network can prevent crime and deviance, and illnesses can be reduced. For these reasons, poverty was not to be analyzed and described, and social work as a profession was not to be mentioned. Furthermore, a significant part of the social services activity had been performed by the churches before World War II. However, religion and its institutions were bitterly attacked by the Communist regime, and more than 50 denominations and social organizations were dissolved.

Despite these barriers, certain fields were covered by well-organized professional services without being called social work. Some narrow fields developed counseling systems, such as mothers and infant protection programs, conducted by district nurses. Similarly, educational centers had a developed network of child protection services. These services, begun in 1962, offer psychological counseling and family care to children aged three to 18 and their families. The terms *psychological counseling* and *family care* were first used after World War I, and the services are actually a form of social work.

In 1987 family help centers that provide family therapy were set up. The workers at these centers are usually sociologists or psychologists. Casework and counseling are also conducted by psychologists in psychiatric departments of hospitals and regional neurological outpatient clinics. In addition, the network of services for addicts is provided primarily by physicians and nurses.

Other social services fields are underdeveloped and use professionals other than social workers. For example, probation work is conducted by special teachers, psychologists, sociologists, and lawyers. In the schools, the child protection system usually cannot do more than register cases. The system tries to provide remedies and seeks cooperation with other institutions, such as guardianship authorities and educational counseling centers, only for the most serious and most striking cases. This work is generally performed by teachers.

Employment offices are run by lawyers and economists. There is also a well-functioning career counseling system, staffed by psychologists, for those who are entering careers. On the basis of this foundation, the present government plans to set up a modern system to handle unemployment.

It should be noted here that it has been an accepted practice in Hungary to use the term *social worker* to refer to all persons who perform the functions of "social work" without the appropriate professional training and degrees. This practice is adopted in the following sections because, as is noted in the section on Training for Social Work, students will not graduate from the newly instituted schools of social work until 1994.

In institutional care, Hungary has a specialized type of social worker, called the social organizer. Social organizers are responsible for coordination and administration in institutions. Group work and community work exist only in some institutions, where the staff is willing to learn and use these methods.

The role of representing clients' interests is assumed by social workers in a number of different ways. Some social workers are active representatives in Parliament as members of local governments and various societies. Others have helped to create foundations, such as SZETA (whose aim is to support the poor) and play a major role in organizing political movements, such as the ones that protect ethnic minorities, including Gypsies (PHRALIFE). This is the area in which social workers are most needed: to make society aware of the underprivileged situation of certain groups and communities and to empower them to help themselves.

Need for Social Workers in Various Systems

Personal social services have been largely neglected during the past 40 years. However, there is a universal and free system of mother and infant protection. From the fourth month of pregnancy, every pregnant woman is eligible for medical care; children under age 16 receive free pediatric services, including obligatory inoculations when they are infants; and mothers and children are regularly visited by district nurses.

This system has a long tradition. In the 1950s, the so-called green cross district nurse service was transformed into a district nurse service, provided by social workers and district nurses. The weak point of this highly professional service has been the one-sided mentality of nurses, who focus on health care and lack social and psychological knowledge and methods. The system is valuable as a universal service, but the mentality and methods of its personnel need to be broadened.

Care for elderly people has also been in effect since World War I. Since 1960, several institutions and services have been operating: social homes (nursing homes), clubs for elderly people, home care, and the delivery of meals to homebound elderly people. These provisions are financed primarily by the local governments from the central budget. Today, however, the role of the state in this field is open to question: Should it run the system or appoint private organizations to administer services? The number of church and private organizations with the same function is increasing. Thus, there are opportunities for social workers to work with elderly people. Unfortunately, the demand for services considerably exceeds the available resources.

Unemployment is a new social problem, caused by the economic restructuring in Eastern Europe and the loss of markets in former Council for Mutual Economic Assistance (COMECON) countries. Hungarian products are not yet competitive in the Western European and American markets. As a result, in 1990, 150,000 people were unemployed, and that number reached 300,000 by the end of 1991 (Banfálvy, 1991). Unemployment benefits were initiated two years ago, but the limited period of eligibility and the decreasing amount of benefits present serious problems.

Currently, Hungary lacks a human services component in its employment policy. Retraining, the decrease in the hours of work, the use of part-time workers, and the creation of new jobs require cooperation between the social and economic sectors. Young people, career beginners, unskilled workers, physically or mentally disabled people, and members of ethnic minorities (such as Gypsies) are particularly in danger of losing their jobs. The preparation of employees, retraining, and the handling of social and psychological problems require skilled professionals, and the staff who work in unemployment offices are not prepared for these tasks. Thus, social workers who can mobilize resources in the environment and the individual are needed for this work.

Refugees present yet another new problem. According to official data, 50,000 refugees arrived in Hungary in 1990, but there may be twice as many illegal newcomers (Sik, 1991). The majority of the refugees are Hungarians who fled Romania, and their problems cannot be settled without proper legal arrangements. They also need counseling and the mobilization of resources, which can be provided by social workers.

Prevention and rehabilitation services for substance abuse and addiction need further development, as do mental health services and social services in the criminal justice system. All these service areas will require social workers in the future.

Training for Social Work

Because there was no social work training in Hungary during the Communist period, the tasks of social workers have been performed by other professionals, including psychologists, sociologists, teachers, and lawyers. Now social work education has been initiated and is growing rapidly. The newly organized training is offered at several levels: in secondary and higher education, in postgraduate courses, and in further training.

Social assistance training has been launched in five high schools and in on-the-job courses in six cities. These courses offer high-level, though not professional, training, and students have the opportunity to continue their studies in higher education. There has been much debate whether this level of training is needed. However, because admission to colleges and universities is still limited, it does not provide an opportunity for an initial form of training.

Colleges and universities offer four-year programs in social work education that lead to a general social worker diploma. This four-year program may be followed by a two-year program for specialized education, for which graduates receive a specialized social worker diploma. Graduates of the two-year program are eligible to continue their studies for higher academic degrees. The subject areas include social work, social organizing, social policy, social administration, mental health care, and communication theory. There are now 10 programs available at seven colleges and universities in three cities.

In 1989 the 10 programs that were then planning to offer social work training formed the Association of Schools and worked out a standard curriculum. The members of the association agreed that the curriculum should follow the Hungarian educational plan and the recommendations of the International Association of Schools of Social Work. The following subjects are taught in all 10 schools: social policy, theory of social work, sociology, psychology, law, health care, and a field practicum. A minimum of 900 hours are required for field practice. Each student also attends a 200-hour program on personality development.

Full programs of social work education at the university level did not start until 1990. Thus, the first group of students will not graduate until 1994. It is expected that after all 10 programs are fully under way, there will be 200–250 graduates each year.

Social work training is closely linked with research programs in universities and the Academy of Sciences. Research on minorities and on current social problems and programs is conducted by faculty members and is included in some student projects. The social work departments of the two schools in Budapest—Eotvos Lorand University and "Gusztav Barczy" Training College for Special Teachers—also publish a journal.

Challenges for Hungarian Social Work

Social work must be seen as a new and developing profession in Hungary. Thus, it must define and develop itself within a difficult and changing economic and political situation. Whereas the former economic and political system was outdated and unable to handle social or economic problems, the major changes of the past several years have produced new problems, such as unemployment, and accentuated other problems, such as poverty. At the same time, state subsidies have been withdrawn and social expenditures have been cut. Thus, Hungarian social work faces many challenges.

This situation requires new institutional forms, including nonprofit service organizations and state- and church-owned agencies. New services, such as employment counseling, will require training for new and developing social work roles, including voluntary social work and community social work. It will be some time before social work in Hungary matures, but promising workshops and experiments that have been recently initiated mark the birth of a new social services network and thus opportunities to develop clearly defined roles and functions for social workers.

In 1992, the greatest challenge for the profession is the limited resources of the social sector because of the radical cuts in the state budget. The government no longer offers subsidies but has introduced the so-called application system, in which a limited amount of money is allocated for the numerous applicants who will not automatically receive financial aid the next year. This system has created strong competition in the social sector but inadequate resources to meet human needs. On the recommendation of the Association of Hungarian Social Workers, the Association of Social Professionals and Organizations is being set up to protect social welfare interests.

The mobilization of nonstate resources, such as support by foundations, companies, and private individuals, is yet another task. Research has been hindered by the lack of public recognition of social work. Now that social work training has been launched at colleges and universities, there will be an opportunity to highlight social work's contribution to society.

Future Directions

The authors are full of both hope and anxiety about the future of Hungarian social work. They believe that social work will be accepted as a new profession. However, its success will depend on the social-political situation in the coming years. If the economic crisis prevails and human and social services do not receive proper political, economic, and social support, social work will be restricted to crisis intervention. Nevertheless, it is likely that the profession will effect changes in the micro- and macrostructure of society. To achieve such objectives, both highly qualified social workers and a fully developed service system are essential.

The founding of the social work profession in Hungary is taking place at a time of democratic changes, when social work can serve as an example of ethical values, tolerance, solidarity, and caring for others. Although the next 10 years will be difficult, social workers will have the opportunity to participate in the democratization of the society. They will be able to conceptualize their experiences and thus create a practical and theoretical body of knowledge for the profession.

References

Banfálvy, C. (1991). *Unemployment and its societal consequences.* Budapest.

Complex analysis of disorders: A report of the Ministry of Welfare. (1985). Budapest: Ministry of Welfare.

Income of people. (1990). Budapest: Bureau of Statistics.

Sik, E. (Ed.). (1991). *Refugees.* Budapest: Hungarian Institute of Political Sciences.

Recommended Reading

An analysis of social pathologies: Report of the Ministry of Social Affairs. (1985). Budapest: Ministry of Social Affairs, Hungary.

Bang, R. (1973). *The targeted conversation.* Budapest: Tankonyvkiado.

Bang, R. (1980). *The helping relationship.* Budapest: Tankonyvkiado.

Bjornson, B. (1982). *Therapy.* Budapest: Europa.

Buda, B. (1978). *Empathy.* Budapest: Magveto.

Csizmadia, A. (1977). *Changes in social care in Hungary.* Budapest: Allames Jogtudomanyi Intezet.

Ferge, Z. (1980). *Studies in social policy.* Budapest: Gondolat.

Ferge, Z. (1989). *The fourth road.* Budapest: Kozgazdasagi Konyvkiado.

Ferge, Z., & Varnai, G. (1987). *Social policy today and tomorrow.* Budapest: Kossuth.

Gayer, G. (1980). The Conference on Family Care in Pecs, 1979. *Csaladgondozo Fuzetek, 1.*

Gayer, G. (1981). Family care as a form of social policy. *Munkaugyi Szemle*, pp. 4–5.

Gayer, G. (Ed.). (1986). The social work profession: A code of ethics. *Szocialpolitikai Ertesito, 2.*

Gondos, A., & Hegyesi, G. (1984). Preventive family care. *Kultura es Kozosseg, 2.*

Hankiss, E. (1977). *Values and society.* Budapest: Magveto.

Hegyesi, G. (1987). *Major issues of integrating theory and practice for the establishment of social work education in Hungary.* Unpublished master's thesis, Monash University, Melbourne, Australia.

Hoffman, G. (Ed.). (1976). *The tasks of the family carer.* Budapest: Pedagogiai Intezet.

Horanyi, G. (1979). Family care in the educational counseling centers of Budapest. *Munkaugyi Szemle, 4.*

The income distribution of the population. (1990). Budapest: Central Statistical Office.

Jeney, S., & Zombori, G. (Eds). (1991). *Social security in transition.* Budapest: Fraternite.

Losonczi, A. (1978). *Values in objects, lifestyles, and time.* Budapest: Gondolat.

Molnar, E., & Sebes, A. (1981). Reflections on the article of Mrs. Gayer. *Munkaugyi Szemle, 9.*

Talyigas, K., & Hegyesi, G. (1984). Proposal for the training of social workers in Hungary. *Kultura es Kozosseg, 2.*

Talyigas, K., & Hegyesi, G. (1990). An outline of social worker training. *Felsooktatasi Pedagogiai Szemle.*

Telkes, J. (1986). *The basics of family care.* Budapest: Orzsagos Pedagogiai Intezet.

Woods, R. (1991). *Voluntary social work in Hungary.* Paper presented at the Conference on Voluntarism, Barcelona.

6

Social Work in India: Developmental Roles for a Helping Profession

A. B. Bose

India is the world's largest democracy. With a population of 844 million in 1991 (Registrar General and Census Commissioner, 1991), of whom almost 30 percent are categorized as poor, the challenges facing the country are indeed phenomenal. Social work is uniquely placed to contribute to the country's social development efforts.

The Challenge of Social Development

India has a federal structure. It also has laid down certain principles of state policy that are primarily in the area of social development and are of special significance for the social and economic well-being of the people, particularly those who are disadvantaged. In addition, the central government has framed specific national policy statements on social development related to education, health, housing, children, child labor, and youths. Social development concerns are also reflected in the legislation enacted after independence in 1947 to protect and promote the interests of women, children, and other disadvantaged groups.

India guides its development efforts through five-year plans that lay down developmental goals and strategies, identify policy instruments and programs (including those related to social development), and indicate budgetary outlays. The formulation and implementation of the five-year plans are the joint responsibility of the central and state governments.

The current status of the Indian population on indicators of social development suggests the colossal tasks ahead, even though there have been significant improvements in welfare since the time of independence. India's large population and the high rate of growth of the population (23.5 percent from 1981 to 1991; Registrar General and Census Commissioner, 1991) tend to offset the gains from development and put severe pressures on resources for providing community and social services. Attempts to contain the growth of the population through family planning have been of limited success, because the birthrate has declined only 6.4 percent in the past 19 years—from 36.9 in 1971 to 30.5 in 1989 (Registrar General of India, 1990).

Estimates of the population (derived from national sample survey data on household expenditure) with incomes below the poverty level in India in 1987–88 suggest that as many as 238 million people (29.9 percent of the population) are poor. Although India is self-sufficient in the production of food grains, a large number of people do not have the purchasing power to maintain a nutritionally adequate diet or a reasonable level of shelter and clothing. Poverty is one of the major contributors to the unsatisfactory health and nutritional status of mothers and children.

Only 52 percent of the population aged seven and above is literate. Among women, the literacy rate is 39.4 percent. Although there is nearly universal primary school enrollment, retention rates are low (Department of Education, India, 1991). The main causes of dropping out of school are poverty; a sociocultural environment that places a lower priority on education than on work; and an unattractive school environment with inadequate physical facilities, low motivation of teachers, and poor instructional methods.

Although India has a large health care system that provides both curative and preventive services, the health status of the population is still unsatisfactory. Despite significant improvements in health standards, the infant mortality rate is high and there is a large incidence of malnutrition among poor women and children. In 1988, the deaths of infants accounted for 27 percent of all deaths, and the deaths of children below age five accounted for 40 percent of the total deaths. Furthermore, only one-third of poor preschool children have adequate nutrition.

The backlog of housing in India is estimated to be 23.3 million units. Sanitation in rural areas and urban slums is unsatisfactory. Even though India is one of the lesser urbanized countries, the size of the cities is phenomenal. The urban population was 217 million in 1991, with more than 23 million urban agglomerations, two of which have populations of more than 10 million each. A related problem is the increase in slums because of the country's inability to meet the housing needs of urban poor people. In the large cities, the proportion of the population living in slums varies from 25 to 33 percent (Planning Commission, India, 1983).

Gender differences are evident on most social development indicators, despite constitutional and legislative guarantees of equality and the improvement in the status of women since independence. Despite the significant increase in the enrollment of women at all levels of the educational system and women's higher rate of participation in the modern sectors of the labor market, disparities still exist. For example, the illiteracy rate among women is far higher than that among men, and the school dropout rate for girls is much higher than that for boys, because families give a much lower priority to the education of girls and girls drop out much earlier than do boys (Department of Education, India, 1991). Early childhood mortality is higher among girls than among boys, indicating that families neglect nutrition and access to health care for girls. Other constraints facing women are early marriage, high fertility, and social customs that assign a subordinate role to women and restrain their participation in nontraditional activities.

There are wide disparities between rural and urban areas on almost all economic and social development indicators. In addition, rural areas, where three-fourths of the population live, have lagged behind urban areas in the development of social services, a physical infrastructure, and economic development.

Changes in social and economic structures and institutions have resulted in the emergence of new social problems. Destitution and deprivation among children, women, and elderly people; family breakdown; and an increase in delinquency, crime, drug addiction, and other manifestations of social deviance require urgent attention. Marginalization of those who are disadvantaged and increased economic inequalities are creating social and political tensions and new alignments of forces owing to demands for alterations in the social and economic structures for a more equitable share of power and of the benefits of development. Women, particularly those who are urban educated, are seeking a redefinition of their traditional roles and responsibilities and are demanding a readjustment of relationships and new social services so that they will be able to participate more effectively in all spheres of life and cope with the demands of a modernizing society. They are also demanding the equality that has been guaranteed to them by the Constitution and by specific legislative enactments.

There has been massive investment by the state in economic and social development, with direct policy and program shifts for the benefit of poor and disadvantaged people. Much more, however, needs to be done. This situation presents a challenge to social workers to engage more actively in development and to focus their attention more effectively on the poorest and most disadvantaged groups in society.

Social Work Education

The foundations of professional social work education in India were laid with the establishment in Bombay in 1936 of the Sir Dorabji Tata Graduate School of Social Work (renamed the Tata Institute of Social Sciences in 1944) and the offering of a two-year graduate diploma in social services administration (Desai, 1985). Three more graduate programs were established toward the end of the 1940s, but enrollments were small. In fact, the four programs only had about 160 students in all at the end of the decade. Given the estimated population of about 356 million at this time, this number was a veritable drop in the ocean.

The 1950s saw the expansion of professional social work education. As more university departments of social work, including affiliating colleges that offered social work, were established within the university system of higher education, the trend toward establishing programs in social work by autonomous bodies that were independent of the university system was reversed. The institutions that had begun as autonomous schools gradually affiliated with the universities to overcome their financial problems by gaining greater access to university and governmental funds, to acquire the status of being a part of the university system, to afford university pay scales for their teachers, and to award degrees that would enable students to compete more effectively in the employment market.

By the end of the 1950s, there were 14 graduate- and three undergraduate-level programs in social work. The total annual number of students was about 500. In addition, three institutions offered nondegree certificates or diplomas in social work. During this period, Lucknow University established the first doctoral program in social work in the country. This program marked the beginning of the trend toward establishing higher academic programs in social work education and conforming to the pattern followed by other social sciences disciplines in the higher education system.

During the 1960s and in subsequent decades, social work education developed rapidly, and the number of students increased to about 2,000 per year by the end of the 1980s. However, this is still a small number compared to India's population of about 830 million.

The distribution of institutions offering social work education is uneven both among states and within states. The location of these institutions has not been based on an assessment of the need for trained personnel or been a part of an overall plan for the development of social work education facilities in the states. Numerous courses were started without adequate preparation of faculty or infrastructure or attention to the design of curricula (including field practice) that could respond to the needs of different areas. Thus, there is considerable variation in the standards of social work education throughout the country.

India began professional social work education at the graduate level, and graduate education has predominated ever since. At the end of the 1980s, 14 institutions were offering bachelor's degree programs, 42 were offering master's degree programs, 15 were offering Master of Philosophy (M.Phil.)–level programs, and 24 were offering doctoral programs. Thus, most institutions offer programs that lead to master's or higher degrees. In fact, several institutions that started at the bachelor's level sought to upgrade their programs to the master's degree level at the earliest opportunity because of pressures from the students to better their prospects for employment and from the faculty to increase their status and prospects for promotion.

The increase in higher level programs even though there is only a small market for professionally trained personnel at this level (usually required for teaching and research positions) indicates the growing tendency toward the academization of social work education, especially because the M.Phil. and Ph.D. programs are usually not practice based and except for choice of subjects, there is little difference between these programs and the other social sciences.

Commenting on this trend, the Second Review Committee on Social Work Education in India (University Grants Commission, 1980) observed: "The Committee finds the growth of social work education lopsided—there is a push for growth at higher levels, but very little development of the front line worker at the bachelor's and lower levels where the bulk of workers are required." The paradox is that in the absence of a definite recruitment policy by the state and the projection of demand for trained social welfare personnel, even the small number of graduates of bachelor's degree programs do not find it easy to get employment. If anything, they are more disadvantaged in getting jobs than are those with master's degrees because the organized sector of employment in urban settings does not recognize the bachelor's degree as the essential qualification for social welfare positions and, therefore, the students either have to opt for poorly paid positions in nongovernmental agencies or seek admission to master's degree programs.

The curricula of postgraduate social work programs range from the generic to those that offer specializations, usually in the second year and, more often, some special interest papers. A truly generic postgraduate program is offered only by a few institutions. The most common specialization offered is in the field of labor welfare, personnel management, and industrial relations, in which since its inception the largest number of graduates have found employment, good salaries, and an assured career ladder facilitated by legislation that requires the appointment of welfare officers in the larger industrial establishments. Other specializations that are available to students in different schools are correctional services, psychiatric and medical social work, family and child welfare, rural development, and social welfare administration.

In the prevailing employment market for professionally trained social welfare personnel, the relevance of specialization has been attenuated because the students seek and usually acquire positions in fields of social welfare that are different from their specializations. Even for positions like medical social workers or welfare officers in prisons, recruitment is not confined to those who specialized in these fields; other social work graduates are also recruited (Ramachandran, 1977).

The early curricula of the schools of social work in India did not emerge from India's socioeconomic realities (characterized by social and economic inequalities and deprivation among large segments of the population) and the role that the profession could play in response to them. It was strongly influenced by the pattern of social work education in the United States, where disadvantaged people were a minority in a system that, by and large, demonstrated its ability to meet the basic needs of society. The influence was reflected in the way the curriculum for the first school of social work in the country was designed, the level at which the courses were started (postgraduate level), and the types of client groups (unadjusted, destitute, and maladjusted people and those who were vulnerable in urban industrialized settings) that students were equipped to handle upon graduation.

The methods courses in India drew heavily on American texts, particularly until the 1960s, and focused more strongly on casework and group work (with their emphasis on therapy to help unadjusted and maladjusted individuals) and, to some extent, on community organization. These methods were to be applied within the overall framework of current systems and structures for helping client groups, in which the role of social work was perceived as an enabling process and its focus on the functioning of the individual. Concepts, methods, techniques, and principles that were developed in an entirely different sociocultural setting were being used here. They were of limited relevance in the context of Indian society, which necessitated major reforms in social, economic, and administrative structures; bold strategies in social and economic policy; and strong political will to improve the conditions of the masses and to prepare the people for change and development. The American model of social work education, developed in response to the needs of the American society, could perform only a perfunctory role when adopted for use on Indian soil (Nagpaul, 1972).

A major challenge to social work education in India was posed when the need for developmental and preventive functions were forcefully advocated at the International Conference of Ministers Responsible for Social Welfare in 1968 (United Nations, 1969). This advocacy, which had great relevance for developing countries in which large segments of the population are disadvantaged and marginalized, was echoed in subsequent regional and national forums of social work educators. It was clearly evident that the remedial approach that had been so widely adopted by social workers in developing countries was of limited value in the context of such massive social and economic problems as poverty, unmet needs, and the widespread inequalities and limited provision of social services.

The implications of this approach for social work education were far reaching. If the need for developmental and preventive functions was accepted, social workers could no longer be educated only to help enhance the functioning of the individual but should be prepared to contribute to the attainment of wider social development goals. Such an approach also would imply that social workers could not continue to seek solutions to social problems by working within the prevailing system but needed to focus on the economic and social conditions of disadvantaged people and, when necessary, to question inequalities and injustices and advocate their restructuring in the direction of social justice.

For some time, Indian social work educators had also been uneasy about trying to integrate professional goals and academic content with the realities in the field. The inadequacies of conventional social work models and the need to deepen the search for solutions were becoming apparent. Social work educators recognized the value of the new developmental thrust in the context of India's development needs and realized that social work education should widen its concerns and focus on the mass of the disadvantaged population, so they could participate in the mainstream of national development. The Second Review Committee on Social Work Education (University Grants Commission, 1980) made a strong case for redesigning the social work curriculum in response to India's social needs, as did Desai (1985). The report of the Curriculum Development Center in Social Work Education (University Grants Commission, 1990) endorsed this approach when it observed:

> The major task would be to promote social change and development, while recognizing that groups or individuals already affected by the problems emanating from the structural factors in society will need help in meeting their immediate problems or needs. Hence, while the overall thrust of the task of social work should be developmental and promotive, tasks which are remedial and rehabilitative cannot be overlooked.

Social Work Practice

Before the 1950s, most professional social workers found employment in nongovernmental organizations or in industrial enterprises as labor welfare officers. The vast majority found employment in urban settings, usually in junior positions in organizations that catered to destitute, maladjusted, and handicapped clients. Because the number of graduates of professional schools was small, the supply more or less met the demand. The agencies that employed professional social workers did so through informal networks established with social work educators. The vision of social work's role in society was modest. Hardly any social workers set up in independent practice. Societal recognition of the value of professional training in social work and of its contribution toward the significant improvement of the quality of services to meet clients' needs was hazy.

In the 1950s, the public sector became the main generator of employment, with the state or state-funded agencies the primary employers. Thousands of jobs, which were of the nature of welfare functionaries, were created at the field level. These jobs were in community development, family planning, work with backward classes, and social welfare programs, mostly in the rural areas. A number of supervisory positions in these sectors were created at the district level and in urban areas for the implementation of programs and the training of functionaries.

The 1970s and 1980s witnessed the rapid growth of social development programs. Poverty-alleviation schemes and minimum-needs programs became focal concerns of the rural development strategy. Health, family planning, nutrition, education, environmental sanitation and hygiene, and other programs in the social services sectors expanded phenomenally. The social welfare sector, too, received a tremendous boost with the launching in 1975–76 of the national program of Integrated Child Development Services.

In all these services and programs, the following types of positions were created:

- Field-level functionaries, for which a postmatriculation two-year social work education program would be adequate. Thousands of jobs were created
- Supervisors of the field-level functionaries (about 4 percent of the field-level functionaries), for which a three-year bachelor's degree in social work would be adequate
- Planning, programming, monitoring, and administration at the middle level, for which a two-year master's degree would be adequate. Several hundred jobs were created
- Research and evaluation, for which a Ph.D. in social work would be a desirable academic qualification. About 200 jobs were created
- Training and education, for which a Ph.D. in social work would be a desirable academic qualification. About 200 jobs were created.

The irony is that for the first type of employment, which could be called paraprofessional social work, the schools of social work had no programs of study. The training of these functionaries was assigned to institutions that were set up or supported by the government. For the second type of functionaries, only a few schools were offering bachelor's degree programs. Thus, the existing schools of social work would have been in no position to meet the massive requirements had there been a demand for these levels of social workers by the employing agencies. Furthermore, almost the entire student community (almost half of whom were girls) was drawn from the urban middle class and was disinclined to take supervisory jobs in rural settings. Yet another problem was the weak preparation of students for the types of jobs that were being created in the field.

Although estimates of the number of trained personnel who were needed tends to create an impression of a frightening shortage of trained social workers who had the unenviable privilege of several job offers, the reality in the field was the opposite: Those with social work degrees did not readily find jobs suited to their qualifications. This paradox arose because there was no clear governmental policy regarding the recruitment of trained personnel.

The current employment pattern of social work graduates indicates the market that exists for professionally trained social workers. The largest number of graduates have gone into industry as labor welfare and personnel officers. Some have found employment in the field of correctional services or as medical or psychiatric social workers, community workers, superintendents in welfare institutions, or social welfare officers in administration—almost entirely in urban settings and in salaried employment in the state or state-assisted sector. Unlike other professionals, few professionally trained social workers have set up independent practice because there is hardly any demand for such services from the client groups who are poor and disadvantaged and could not be expected to pay for the services they need. One exception may be family counselors or psychiatric social workers, but their numbers, too, are small. The demand for their services by clients who can pay for them is limited because the value of such services to clients is not recognized. Social workers, therefore, have to look primarily, if not totally, to salaried employment.

An important characteristic of professional training is a society's clear recognition of its need, manifest by the acceptance of the qualitatively superior service that such training makes possible. This recognition is expressed in the employment of trained personnel and societal pressure to ensure that people without professional training are not assigned positions that require professional education. In India, however, the society does not—even after more than five decades since the first school of social work was set up—recognize that social work training is essential for proper standards of services and therefore does not object to the employment of untrained people in welfare positions.

The administration structure in India gives a preeminent status to the generalist administrator—a situation that shows no signs of changing. Today, there is virtually no possibility of professionally trained social workers being employed in decision-making positions that require social work expertise. It was a distinct possibility in the 1950s and early 1960s when the professional associations were strong, and by the 1980s it had become a fond hope. The Association of Schools of Social Work and the Indian Association of Trained Social Workers, which could have played a strong advocacy role and mobilized political and public support to ensure the employment of professionally trained personnel, were ineffective.

Currently, government departments that implement social welfare programs have not identified positions that require professional training in social work. Even when some positions are designated as technical posts for the purpose of recruitment, the educational qualifications that are prescribed usually place social work on par with the other social sciences—a clear indication that the necessity and value of professional education for social welfare positions are neither understood nor recognized, even though the job description relates almost entirely to the field of social welfare and the duties require knowledge, understanding, and skills that are unique to social work.

The administration has extensively promoted an alternative system to meet the requirements of trained personnel. Under this policy, a short period of training and orientation for supervisory staff is all that is considered necessary to enable a generalist to perform social work tasks "satisfactorily," thus considerably diluting the need and value of professional education. Social work educators have occasionally been involved in designing curricula and sometimes running the training courses on grants from the government. Thus, unwittingly, they have supported a process and a structure that systematically devalued the two-year professional program. The first Review Committee on Social Work Education (University Grants Commission, 1965) cautioned against this trend. The Second Review Committee (University Grants Commission, 1980) reiterated that short-term training is no substitute for professional training. In practice, short-duration social work orientation became accepted as a substitute for a full professional education program.

Toward a Developmental Perspective

The current scenario for Indian social work education may be summed up as a paradox in which even the small annual output of around 2,000 trained bachelor's and master's degree holders are not sure of their employment prospects in social work or a career ladder in a country of 844 million people with massive social development needs.

Social work in India urgently needs to redirect its focus so that it can contribute more effectively to the country's social development efforts. However, if it is to make a significant contribution by performing appropriate development roles, it will first have to address the problems it currently faces.

Social work in India must redefine its role and mission and work harder to convince political leaders, government administrators, members of other professions, and the public at large of its value. The profession was in search of recognition and status in the 1950s, and the situation has not changed significantly since then. It is still knocking at the door for acceptance as a profession and seeking an identity that is separate from that of the other social sciences.

Social work's narrow role, which had initially focused on helping the destitute and maladjusted in urban areas, rather than being at the forefront of efforts to address the country's massive problems of poverty and deprivation, also has prevented it from making a wider contribution to social development. Because of its concern with remedial social welfare, social work has often been regarded as marginal to the nation's development efforts. Therefore, it can make a positive contribution only if it changes this focus and seeks to respond to the problems of social deprivation, works to secure social justice, and prepares to motivate the masses for change and development.

The failure of social workers in India to create effective professional associations has undoubtedly exacerbated the problem. The national professional association of social workers is inactive, and the Association of Schools of Social Work does not play an active advocacy role. Both associations have made little effort to function as pressure groups to get qualified social workers appointed to positions in the human services and social development fields.

The relatively small number of professionally trained social workers in the country limits their visibility. The public has little understanding of the role of professional social workers. Large segments of society, including opinion leaders and those in senior decision-making positions, are generally ignorant about social work. The common perception is that any person who is engaged in public welfare is a social worker, and there is little understanding of the need for professional education in the field.

Social work education in India has developed in a lopsided manner, ignoring the huge need for personnel at the paraprofessional level and thus preventing the development of a sizable base from which it could have generated upward mobility in education and training and pressure for recruitment to supervisory positions to establish a career ladder. It has also failed to develop a ladder approach in social work education that would match the requirements for personnel at different levels.

Social work education programs must be redesigned to contribute to development. The curriculum needs to be changed to expose students to the country's most pressing social problems and to provide training in appropriate interventions. The excessive academization of social work education and its efforts to emulate the other social sciences should be reviewed, so that social work education programs can establish a distinct identity with a strong practice orientation that is suited to social development. It is also necessary for social work education to be in harmony with personnel requirements at different levels. It is unfortunate that the expansion of social work education and the expansion of social development programs took place independently of each other, even though both have been largely dependent on government funding. It is time that social work educators and government planners begin to collaborate more closely so that social work and development efforts can be linked more closely.

The neglect of paraprofessional training is another problem that should be addressed. Schools of social work cannot continue to ignore the pressing needs for personnel who can work at the field level in rural areas. In this regard, changes in the curriculum are needed to prepare graduate-level personnel for supervisory and similar positions in social development agencies.

There can be no doubt that social work has much to offer the field of social development. Its primary client group is disadvantaged people. Its social philosophy and values champion human dignity, social justice, human rights, equal opportunities, and people's participation. The fact that social work education has played a limited role in India's social development effort does not imply that the profession has little to contribute. On the contrary, social development programs in India are suffering because of the absence of appropriately trained professional personnel. Social work can make a positive contribution not only to the delivery of direct services but in administration and planning and in the preparation of client groups for change and development and effecting changes in the system. It thus has to train personnel to function at both the micro- and the macrolevels.

A restructuring of the curriculum is necessary to equip social workers to perform preventive and developmental roles to help disadvantaged people, while retaining their traditional remedial and rehabilitative functions. Thus, a curriculum, teaching methods, and learning tools must be developed that focus on problems and issues and involve the use of one or more methods of social work. Fieldwork settings that are consistent with these goals have to be identified and developed. Social work education has to be indigenized. In the 1960s, this need was strongly emphasized by several social work educators (Nagpaul, 1967).

As the century comes to a close, it is crucial that social work in India make a concerted effort to gain recognition and acceptance as a profession and that it restructure its current approach. If the profession is to be relevant to India's needs, it must make a major contribution to social development. Social work has chosen the right goals, tasks, and paths of development. Organized action by the profession is now necessary.

References

Department of Education, India. (1991). *Annual report, 1990–91.* New Delhi: Government of India.

Desai, A. (1985). The foundations of social work education in India and some issues. *Indian Journal of Social Work, 46,* 41–51.

Nagpaul, H. (1967). Dilemmas of social work education in India. *Indian Journal of Social Work, 28,* 269–284.

Nagpaul, H. (1972). The diffusion of American social work education in India. *International Social Work, 15,* 3–17.

Planning Commission, India. (1983). *Report of the Task Force on Shelter for the Urban Poor and Slum Improvement.* New Delhi: Government of India.

Ramachandran, P. (1977). *Social welfare manpower in greater Bombay.* Bombay: Somaiya Publications.

Registrar General and Census Commissioner. (1991). *Census of India, 1991, India* (Paper 1 of 1991, Provisional population totals). New Delhi: Government of India.

Registrar General of India. (1990). *Sample Registration Bulletin, 24*(2), 3.

United Nations. (1969). *Proceedings of the International Conference of Ministers Responsible for Social Welfare.* New York: Author.

University Grants Commission, India. (1965). *Social work education in Indian universities.* New Delhi: Government of India.

University Grants Commission, India. (1980). *Review of social work education in India.* New Delhi: Government of India.

University Grants Commission, India. (1990). *Report of the Curriculum Development Center in Social Work Education.* New Delhi: Government of India.

7

Social Work in Japan: Responding to Demographic Dilemmas

Yasuo Matsubara

Two interrelated issues complicate the future of social work in Japan: an aging society and the need to reform the post–World War II system of social welfare services. Perhaps more so than any other industrial nation, Japan is experiencing a "graying" of its people. With the advent of a new age of technology in medicine, coupled with the economic boom, Japanese people are living longer, the infant mortality rate has been reduced, and the needs of handicapped people are being met in better ways in a better system. But as the average person lives longer than did his or her parents, the ability of the system to provide adequate services is being taxed. The 1990s offer Japan the opportunity to rethink and reshape the purpose and structure of its social welfare services so that it can not only continue to meet the needs of the conventional recipients of such services but can began to accommodate the emerging classes and incipient trends of a society in transition.

Historical and Social Context

After World War II, Japan instituted its new Constitution in which the basic rights of its people were recognized, the government ensuring its people of their "right to maintain minimum standards of wholesome and cultured living." By the 1960s, the Diet had legislated a system of social welfare services to uphold and secure this tenet. Indeed, the provision of social services in Japan has been, in principle, the responsibility of the government. The government also has shaped the role that private, nonprofit organizations play in delivering social services. The private sector does its work primarily under contract to both the national and the local governments.

The initial stages of the social welfare system were established during the Allied occupation of Japan. As a consequence, Japan virtually imported and applied the U.S. model of social work to meet the needs of its society. The ease of introducing a ready-made system significantly eclipsed the need to integrate Japan's culture into the model, at least in the beginning. For example, tradition, especially as it relates to the role that the family plays in the life of the individual, affects how social services are best delivered in Japan. Since the Allied occupation, efforts have been made to establish an indigenous system based on Japan's own social practices; however, the U.S. model of social work, particularly that of social casework, has continued to have a strong influence on the development of social work in Japan (Nakamura, 1980).

Yet, Japan has its own identity, its own history, and thus its own social problems. The high pace of economic growth that began in the 1960s, the result of Japan's increasing role in the international marketplace, also had an effect on domestic issues, for with prosperity came the responsibility to address emerging social conditions, and the need for a social welfare system finally was recognized in the early 1970s. However, as an industrial nation, Japan's economy is vulnerable to the supply of oil, a fact of modern commerce that the oil crisis of 1973 proved. Thus, the social welfare systems must meet the effects of the recent economic stagnation that will test the fabric of society. Social welfare will secure Japan's future, ensuring the "minimum standards" laid down by the Constitution. Japan must acknowledge how a shifting market affects the quality of its society. It must acknowledge, too, how changing demographics—whether an aging population that is sustained by welfare services or infants who are born healthy because of advances in medicine and prenatal care programs—are signs of its economic health. In short, a mutable society constantly poses challenges for the delivery of social welfare services.

Demographic Profile

Japan's demographics have undergone significant changes since World War II. As of 1990, the average life expectancy for men was 75.91 years and for women, 81.77 years, compared to 56.2 years for men and 59.8 years for women in 1949. Japan's rate of longevity is one of the highest in the world, because of the low rate of infant mortality (5 per 1,000 live births) and the increase in life expectancy of persons over age 65.

The percentage of people over age 65, which was 4.7 percent of the population in 1940, rose to 11.2 percent in 1988 and 12 percent in 1990. Indeed, it is estimated that the percentage of the population over age 65 will continue to increase until 2021, when it will peak at 23.6 percent (Ministry of Health and Welfare, 1990b). The mounting challenge of Japanese society is to support generations who will live longer.

When aging people retire from the labor market, they usually need economic assistance in addition to their pensions and individual savings. But aging brings about more than social changes. It is marked by numerous physiological changes. As a result, many elderly people require physical as well as financial assistance in some form to maintain their personal well-being and independence. The increase in the elderly population has created an acute need for a system of income assurance and an improvement in the delivery of social services and health care. Although the percentage of people over age 65 who live with their adult children is gradually decreasing, the number still remains close to 70 percent (Ministry of Health and Welfare, 1990b). Because these elderly people receive care and assistance from their extended families, an important goal in reforming the social welfare system is to reinforce traditional efforts to provide care.

The decreasing birthrate is another social concern. The birthrate in Japan has continued to decline since the second phase of the baby boom of the 1970s for a number of reasons: (1) the decrease of women of childbearing age; (2) the tendency to marry at later ages, which further decreases the number of married women of childbearing age; and (3) the decrease in the number of children born to married women (Ministry of Health and Welfare, 1990b). The average number of children per married couple was 1.53 in 1990. In view of the increasing number of elderly people, the disparity between the higher proportion of elderly people, who will need both government and familial support, and the lower proportion of young people, who will help provide such support through taxes and direct care, will continue to grow.

The acceleration of economic growth also has contributed to the changing profile of the Japanese family, which, in turn, has placed new burdens on the social welfare system. Since the economic boom, social services in child care have expanded, particularly in major urban areas, as more and more women enter the workplace. Also, with 70 percent of the children living in nuclear families, it has become more difficult to pass on traditional values from generation to generation, especially those related to child rearing (Shoji, 1990). The breakup and perhaps passing of the traditional family in Japan—in other words, the movement in recent decades toward the nuclear family as society's paradigm—is related to Japan's economic success, as more families become transient in the pursuit of employment. Such transience changes the character of communities, a component that has long been important to the success of the social welfare system. In a mobile society, an individual may have fewer roots in his or her new community. Consequently, the system of mutual aid, which has traditionally existed in historically stable communities, is a potential casualty of Japan's new economic prosperity.

Reform of the Social Welfare System

The 1980s was a period of economic stagnation in Japan. During this period, austere fiscal measures and the more efficient administration of the government were necessary. Adjustments were required in the social welfare system as well. Since the enactment of the Old Age Persons Health Law in 1982, elderly people have had to pay for part of their medical care, which was free from 1973 to 1982. The review of the pension system in 1986 established basic levels of payment. In addition, in 1985, subsidies from the state to local organizations were reduced and the rights and authority of local bodies were strengthened. During this period, the government restricted the rendering of welfare services by private commercial organizations to elderly individuals. In 1987, the Certified Social Worker and Certified Care Worker Law established a system of national qualifications for social workers (Ministry of Health and Welfare, 1990a).

In the prevailing spirit of reform, new laws revised the social welfare system that was established after World War II. The main areas of reform were (1) home welfare services, which had been established by individual local organizations, are now regulated by law; (2) home welfare and other institutional welfare services became the responsibility of local governments; and (3) provisions were made to obtain the personnel who are needed to deliver these services (Ministry of Health and Welfare, 1990a).

Social Work Roles and Functions

Direct Service

The social work technique used most extensively in Japan is social casework. In social casework, civil service personnel in charge of public benefits seek solutions to problems together with the recipients of such benefits. Public facilities, such as welfare offices, child guidance centers, and hospitals, have instituted social casework. For example, as Japan's population ages, more elderly people will use hospitals. Health insurance covers the basic portion of medical expenses, but both patients and their families are insecure about the costs of hospitalization, the kinds of services that are available, and the quality of life that patients will have and the support they will receive after their release from hospitals. Moreover, as caseworkers, social workers at hospitals are expected to render services to all patients, not just to elderly patients.

The public relief system in Japan consists of monetary benefits and counseling to help clients achieve independence and self-support. Essentially, social workers in this system are responsible for visiting public relief recipients regularly to offer consultation and guidance. The combining of monetary benefits and casework has elicited some criticism (Kato, 1979), but it has enabled the social welfare system to deal with overlapping problems.

Group work is being encouraged as a method of meeting the needs of elderly people, handicapped people, and children who require day care and residential services. However, elderly people are not as accustomed as are others to acting in groups; elderly patients tend to be reserved or shy, especially in the initial stages, or refuse to participate in group activities. However, by encouraging them to join groups and by supporting group activities, social workers have helped elderly people to take collective action to formulate various programs.

Case Management

Case management has become a focus of attention in Japan, particularly in the field of welfare for elderly people. An aging society requires more welfare services to meet its needs. Therefore, welfare policies and measures for the aged population are constantly being initiated and refined. Although welfare services in Japan are diverse, many people do not use them either because they do not know how to gain access to them or because they find them to be inefficient. In Japan, rivalry over jurisdictions hinders cooperation among the various institutions that deliver welfare services. This lack of cooperation results in overlapping services, separate case files with different information, and the failure of institutions to share information.

Case management should help overcome the lack of continuity in services and make services available in an effective manner to those who are unable to make use of them. In Japan, case management centers mainly on the coordination of services and is not involved in the purchase or financial administration of services. Profit-making organizations in the private sector are increasing but still play a minor role in delivering services. Services primarily are furnished through public channels and care provided by family members.

In 1991, the report of the National Council on Social Welfare (a nongovernmental professional organization) recommended the extensive use of case management (Research Group on Case Management, 1991). Henceforth, it will be necessary to build a network of services not only for elderly people but for various groups, including handicapped people and children. As the social welfare system expands to meet the needs of its diverse constituency, agencies should avoid the pitfalls of bureaucracy. The public will see case management as a way to ease the seemingly innate difficulties of delivering services and learn to trust the social welfare system.

Community Work

The formation of service networks is premised on the existence of social resources in each local community, which are developed by community work. The advantages of furnishing social welfare services through a publicly operated system are that these services are guaranteed as a right and are provided according to identical standards throughout the nation. The disadvantages include the difficulty for social welfare activities to take root. Even in districts where such activities have begun, community work tends to be secondary to services rendered by other sources.

Community work in Japan has three roles to play: (1) to identify the need for social services in line with the special conditions of a district and if these services are to be handled by public resources, to revise the existing systems; (2) to promote the establishment of private service organizations within the cultural context of Japan, despite the difficulty that private organizations have had in flourishing; and (3) to restore the capability of local communities, which have been weakened by transience since the onset of rapid economic growth, to offer mutual support and assistance.

It is particularly important for Japan to identify and predict current and future needs, so that it can plan to provide more comprehensive social welfare services. To date, the reform of the social welfare system has involved the delegation of authority from the prefectural governments to city, town, and village governments. The prefectural governments formulate social welfare plans and programs and consult with local municipalities. These plans are not limited to the administration of programs but include the work of private organizations and the activities of community residents. Thus, the prefectural governments' formulation of plans to administer welfare is but one portion of the entire social welfare plan. For the formulation of local plans, the participation of the Council on Social Welfare is essential (Makisato, 1991).

Importance and Usefulness of Social Work

Health Care System

In the 1990s, the reform of the social welfare system will involve the coordination of the fields of social welfare and health and hygiene. The unification of social welfare offices with health care centers is currently being studied. Local municipalities have already initiated experimental projects. The aim is to improve the delivery of services.

The nation's 848 health care centers are the frontline public institutions in the health and hygiene field. Social workers are playing an active role at health care centers and mental hospitals. The health care centers are receiving a greater number of telephone calls for help from, for example, young mothers who feel insecure about changes in the Japanese family structure and the decline of mutual support and assistance in their communities. Health care centers treat maternal and child health problems, as well as problems related to environmental hygiene. In addition, they cooperate with mental hospitals in caring for patients. The recent trend in mental health is to care for patients in their communities, whenever possible, through such alternatives to hospitalization as day care and night hospital services.

Family Court

The family court consists of the Household Affairs Department and the Juvenile Department, the former mediating and arbitrating household matters and the latter dealing with cases related to juveniles and criminal cases of adults who violate the welfare of juveniles. Besides judges, the court is staffed by research specialists in social welfare, pedagogy, sociology, and psychology and well-known volunteers, who play an active role in local affairs and who are appointed to the mediation committee.

The family court seeks to save young children from abuse and delinquency and works closely with child guidance centers. Although it works in as effective a judicial manner as possible, follow-up to the judicial intervention is needed. By offering continued support and assistance, social workers help individuals and families do what the court decrees.

Personnel and Training for Social Work

Of the some 800,000 people who are engaged in social welfare, about 590,000 work in social welfare institutions (Health and Welfare Statistics Association, 1990). The staff at these institutions may be generally categorized as administrators, providers of direct care, and counselors of patients and family members. Yet, in Japan, workers have not been clearly classified according to areas of specialization. This lack of definition is reflected in the placement of university graduates who have studied social welfare as direct care workers in residential institutions. It is not surprising, then, that cases of abuse or mistreatment involving personnel who are charged with care are rare in comparison with the United States. Nonetheless, this relative upgrading of the quality of care is achieved at the expense of social workers who are trained to do more.

Because there has been a severe shortage of social workers in social welfare, much effort has been devoted to finding ways to fill this void. The shortage seems as much a problem now as it will be in the future. However, the increase in elderly people who will require care and the reform of the social welfare system will necessitate an additional 200,000 social workers in the next 10 years.

The shortage of social workers is attributable to the low wages of social welfare positions, which have prompted social welfare students to seek positions in businesses during the recent years of economic prosperity, and to the fact that in Japan the majority of personnel remain with their first place of employment until they retire. Workers need to be trained for both public agencies and the private sector. Moreover, they need to feel that as they age and develop skills, they will have opportunities for promotion.

Yet, in one form or another, training continues. Welfare study classes and departments at universities and colleges are preparing new generations of social workers. However, because there is no formal degree in social work, students tend to receive a bachelor's degree in sociology or literature. Specialist schools for training nursery school teachers and colleges specializing in nursing and health care provide the personnel needed for social welfare services. Graduates of four-year university courses may qualify to take the state examinations for certified social worker if their curricula meet the requirements prescribed by the Certified Social Worker and Certified Care Worker Law. State examinations have been conducted three times thus far, with some 1,500 to 2,500 persons taking them and over 1,000 passing them. Certified care workers with three or more years of on-the-job experience can, on passing the state examinations, also become qualified. About 30,000 of these workers have taken the three state examinations conducted thus far, and about 9,000 have passed them.

Also, graduates of training institutions that are designated by the Ministry of Health and Welfare become qualified as certified care workers by registration. Every year some 5,000 persons graduate from such training schools and close to 70 percent find positions in social welfare–related work.

The training of social workers at the graduate level is still in an early stage, so that few social welfare workers have been prepared to fill leadership positions. But the system of practical training has vastly improved. For instance, the National Council on Social Welfare conducts practical training sessions for staff members of various facilities and institutions throughout Japan. Some prefectures have established social welfare training centers that are also conducting practical training. Because of the lack of specialization, people with no education and training frequently have been appointed to social welfare positions.

To summarize, the professionalization of social work in Japan is only in the beginning stage. Social workers, therefore, lack professional autonomy. They are often hired in nursing homes and other institutions simply as caregivers—just to provide hands-on services, such as handling pots and pans—rather than as true professionals.

Challenges and Issues for Social Work

Challenges

In many communities, those who need social welfare services cannot or do not make use of them. The nonusers include those who do not know about services, those who have a deep-seated mistrust of social institutions, those who hesitate to use social services because of traditional values, and those who have no access to services because of old age, infirmity, or physical handicaps. Of course, poverty and illiteracy also contribute to nonuse, and such conditions may underlie any of the reasons just listed.

Elderly people tend to regard the use of social welfare services not as their right but as an occasion to suffer embarrassment. The value that caring for old people is to be handled by family members contributes to their hesitancy to use services. Yet, because the traditional support system of the Japanese family has been affected, if not undermined, by the increased mobility of the population, social welfare services are essential to meet the needs of elderly people. Although social welfare services can identify the needs of elderly people or other groups at an early stage, the provision of services that are required at the appropriate time cannot be achieved merely by a reform of the system of supplying such services. Social work will need to undertake new functions; that is, it must devote its efforts to reaching those who do not intend to use services or who have reservations about using them.

Among elderly people, handicapped people, and children are those who at some time will need services that can be furnished only by an institution. Entering institutions once meant isolation from the community; it meant the lack of privacy—a life controlled by the institution's staff. But the recent reform of social welfare has brought about changes in some institutions. By consulting with community residents and maintaining a dialogue between institutions and communities, social workers are helping to create an atmosphere of openness and cooperation so that patients can still see themselves as part of their communities.

The weakening of ties in the community and the increase in nuclear families have led social welfare services to try to meet the needs that traditionally have been met by the family or the community. These changes have affected both the young and the old. For example, a new mother may lack the simple but essential information to rear her child properly. Or an elderly person may not be able to secure his household against fire or theft. Granted, the needs of each individual are diverse. And if it were possible to deploy a specialist for the multitude of problems each person might face, there would still be a limit to what a single social worker could do.

In short, social workers are being asked to reorganize and revitalize society. Surely, it is a difficult task. But a spirit of mutual assistance can be reawakened in Japan. The Council on Social Welfare and other welfare organizations in local communities are trying to establish a system that furnishes services that are designed especially for community residents. If the moral imperative of communities is rebuilt, individual residents will also gain.

The Japanese tend, however, to resist any form of counseling. Meeting with a counselor or a psychiatrist has strong negative connotations: It lowers one's self-esteem as well as one's prestige in the community. Therefore, providers of direct services in Japan should not seek in-depth involvement with individuals. Rather, they should adopt the role of spokespersons for those who need services. They should attempt, for instance, to coordinate services and reduce anxiety and hardship. Thus, it is paramount that social workers understand people who need treatment but resist it.

Issues

In the 21st century, Japan is likely to experience social changes of all kinds, including those that will affect the social welfare system and social work. For example, there will be significant changes in the way social welfare services are delivered, an increase in the number of women in the labor force, and a greater dependence on foreign labor to fill the shortage of personnel, as well as changes in education and in the way related specialist fields interact.

In Japan, the majority of services have been furnished through a system that was established by law. Thus, the spontaneous development of a system of services provided by nonprofit, private organizations has been retarded, and services by private enterprise have been all but nonexistent. But with the increase in the number of elderly people, which will tax the present system, there undoubtedly will be an increase in private, mainly profit-making enterprises. The government is prepared to permit the private sector to expand into this area, but it will need to consider some form of sliding fee scale, because if rates are set irrespective of income or the ability to pay, some groups would be excluded from using these services. The government could also subsidize services for low-income users.

To ensure an adequate family income, it is common for both husbands and wives to work. The more women participate in the labor market, the more need there will be for society to provide for the care of children and elderly people.

The shortage of social workers has been anticipated since the 1980s. The Ministry of Health and Welfare (1990b), which identified the problem, has suggested solutions, including the use of foreign laborers, mainly Asian, to staff basic positions in the social welfare system. However, care should be taken not to impose inferior working conditions on foreign laborers or to allow the quality of care to suffer.

Japan's schools no longer can meet all the country's needs. Indeed, the educational system has its own emerging problems. Middle school is the compulsory level of education in Japan, yet about 95 percent of middle school graduates go on to high school and specialized training schools. The average level of education in Japan is among the highest in the world. Japan truly enjoys the benefits of an educated populace. But the tendency of parents and children to seek advancement in education as life's sole objective has affected society adversely. Studying to pass entrance examinations in which they compete for a limited number of spaces causes unbearable stress for children. It is difficult to give sufficient attention in the classroom to children who will not or cannot compete in this stressful race to pass entrance examinations. In turn, schools, and the children, must suffer the consequences of the stress of studying for these examinations—high school dropouts, an increasing number of children who are unwilling to attend classes, and bullying and other misconduct. This clearly is a social problem, but in Japan the tie between education and social welfare is insufficient, and no social workers are employed in schools.

But specialist fields, like the problems they face, are interrelated. In the future, the connection between social work and medical care will become stronger, but not without complications. For instance, physicians are at the top of the hierarchy in the field of medical care, and it is not acknowledged that social work in hospitals is a specialty that is equal to that of medicine. Furthermore, because diagnosis is conducted under the health insurance system, hospitals will not be compensated for social workers' activities unless the profession is accepted as a specialty that falls within the scope of health insurance.

Future Directions

U.S. social work has strongly influenced social work theory in Japan since its introduction after World War II. However, traditional values and ways of thinking in Japan remain deeply rooted, and what is characteristic of Japan will continue in spite of the social conditions in the country. Cultural values—for example, the way the Japanese perceive embarrassment or differentiate between individual and social matters and between public and private concerns—are not likely to change in the next 10 to 20 years. Therefore, social work in Japan must acknowledge and accommodate the elements of Japan's culture.

Up to now, volunteers in social work have mainly been housewives and students who are seeking extra income. This narrow pool of workers is the result not only of the cultural environment that fails to encourage and promote volunteerism, but of the complexities of daily life, such as the long hours spent commuting between the workplace and home. Social work in Japan should expand its programs to accommodate the lives of potential volunteers because with the aging of the society, public social services alone will not be able to meet Japan's needs. Therefore, one of the most crucial tasks facing social work in Japan is to clarify the respective roles of public sector services, private sector services, and community residents and to strengthen volunteer activities. Such measures would supplement the efforts of professional social workers.

The fit between society and social work is becoming better defined to all. Certified social workers and certified care workers, who are now bound by law, are beginning to be viewed by the public as specialists in their respective fields. Article 45 of the Certified Social Worker and Certified Care Worker Law prohibits acts that cause welfare workers to lose credibility; Article 46 safeguards confidential information. The recognition of professional standards of conduct should lead to the acceptance of social welfare workers as qualified specialists. However, the further development of theory and public discussion of the role of social work are still necessary to secure the future of Japanese social work. The U.S. model should not be rejected, but Japan must acknowledge, both in theory and in practice, what works best for social work in Japan.

References

Health and Welfare Statistics Association. (1990). *General trends in the peoples' welfare.* Tokyo: Author.

Kato, S. (1979). The Nakamura–Kishi controversy. In N. Sanada (Ed.), *Social welfare issues of controversy during post–World War II in Japan* (pp. 39–78). Tokyo: Horitsu Bunkasha.

Makisato, T. (1991). Community work and comprehensive networks. *Social Welfare Studies, 50,* 81–85.

Ministry of Health and Welfare. (1990a). *Major implications of amendments of 8 laws pertaining to social welfare.* Tokyo: Dai Ichi.

Ministry of Health and Welfare. (1990b). *White paper on health and welfare.* Tokyo: Gyosei.

Nakamura, Y. (1980). *Casework classroom.* Tokyo: Yuhikaku.

Research Group on Case Management. (1991). *Case management.* Tokyo: National Council on Social Welfare.

Shoji, Y. (1990). The present situation of child care in terms of family changes—Conflicts between socialization of child care and baby-sitting business. *Social Welfare Studies, 48,* 25–32.

Recommended Reading

Arakawa, Y. (1991). *Supervision in health settings.* Tokyo: Kawashima Shoten.

Kawai, K. (1990). *Home welfare service of the future.* Tokyo: Akebi Shobo.

Maeda, T. (1988). *Issues faced in the practice of modern-day social work.* Kyoto, Japan: Minerva Shobo.

Matsubara, Y. (1991). Working with the multiproblem family at a child welfare office. *The Meiji Gakuin Sociology and Social Welfare Review, 86,* 145–167.

Nakamura, Y., & Akiyama, T. (Eds.). (1988). *Manpower requirements for welfare.* Tokyo: Chuo Hoki Shuppan.

Nakamura, Y., Miura, F., & Abe, S. (Eds.). (1989). *Social welfare classroom.* Tokyo: Yuhikaku.

Ooi, T. (1991). Techniques of interviewing those suffering from alcoholism. *Social Work Research, 16*(4), 30–35.

Sakata, S., Liang, J., & Maeda, D. (1990). Effects of negative and positive aspects of social support on depressive symptoms among Japanese older adults. *Social Gerontology, 31,* 80–90.

Taniguchi, M. (1989). Toward innovation of staffing in municipal authorities. *Social Welfare Studies, 46,* 46–52.

8

Social Work in Hong Kong, Singapore, South Korea, and Taiwan: Asia's Four Little Dragons

Peter Ching-Yung Lee

The economic growth of the newly industrializing countries (NICs) of Asia—Hong Kong, Singapore, South Korea, and Taiwan—has been virtually without historical precedent and, as a result, these countries have become known as Asia's "Four Little Dragons" ("Asia;" 1990; Midgley, 1986; Tai, 1989; Weiss, 1989). In their outward appearance, these NICs have embraced Western capitalism and are Westernized, yet the people of these countries pursue a way of life that remains essentially Oriental. This blend of Western capitalism with Oriental culture has had a significant impact on the socioeconomic conditions of these societies. To place the NICs' achievements in a social work perspective, this chapter explores the socioeconomic development trends in these countries; how the Four Little Dragons are dealing with their recurrent social, political, and economic dilemmas; and social work's contribution to the future economic and personal well-being of the people in these countries.

Societal and Historical Context

Hong Kong, Singapore, South Korea, and Taiwan are economically prosperous and more industrialized than are most other countries in the Asian-Pacific region. In the past four decades, the Four Little Dragons have experienced remarkable growth in their gross national products (GNPs), together with a more equitable distribution of income and full employment; their annual rate of growth (6.6 percent) is more than double that of the Asian-Pacific region as a whole (Chai & Clark, 1991; James, Naya, & Meier, 1989). The social progress of these NICs has been equally impressive, according to Estes's (1990) Index of Social Progress, which ranks them in the second quartile of the world's most socially advanced nations. Without question, the Four Little Dragons are among the so-called high human development nations of the world, as measured by scores on the United Nations'

Human Development Index (United Nations, 1990). However, it should be noted that, overall, the four countries' commitment to social welfare is relatively limited, despite their governments' obligation to make policy concerning social welfare (see Table 1).

The governments of Hong Kong and South Korea may be considered democratic, whereas those of Singapore and Taiwan may be classified as "dominant party" states in which opposition parties are rarely permitted to come to power. Except for Hong Kong, defense spending, as a percentage of the government's expenditures for 1987, exceeded 15 percent (Estes, 1990; United Nations, 1990). This level of defense spending clearly reflects the high level of political instability that stems from long-standing intraregional tension (Singapore), internal political unrest (North and South Korea), or uncertain territorial futures (Taiwan).

To explain these remarkable economic and social achievements, observers often point to the many similarities among these countries—their common physical attributes, historical circumstances, strategies of develop-

Table 1.

Demographic and Socioeconomic Profile of the Newly Industrializing Countries

MEASURE	HONG KONG	SOUTH KOREA	SINGAPORE	TAIWAN
Population (in millions)	5.7	45.9	2.7	20.4
Area (1,000 km²)	1	99	1	36
Life expectancy (in years)	76	70	73	73.5
Per capita GNP (in U.S. dollars, 1987)	8,070	2,690	7,940	3,095
Per capita GDP (in U.S. dollars, 1990)	13,910	4,830	12,790	4,969
Social welfare expenditure as a percentage of the GDP (1986)	2.4	0.3	6.21	4.1
Adult literacy rate (1985)	88	95	86	90
Ratio of highest 20 percent to lowest 20 percent of income (1986)	8.7	6.8	—	4.9

SOURCES: International Monetary Fund (1987), *Kaleidoscope* (1990), Malik (1991), *OECD Economic Surveys* (1988), *Taiwan Statistical Data Book* (1991), United Nations Development Programme (1990).

NOTE: GNP = gross national product; GDP = gross domestic product. Dash indicates data not available.

ment, shared traditions, and cultural heritage. What is less scrutinized is the societal context of their development—the different trends in the four NICs.

South Korea

South Korea is a nation of private companies with strong industrial groups, including Samsung, Hyundai, and Daewoo (Weiss, 1989). As in Singapore and Taiwan, economic planning is an integral function of the government. South Korea is split by religious and regional conflicts—more so than Japan or Taiwan. Since 1945, when the country gained independence from Japan, Christians have been politically active. Their activities have led to the evolution of mass media that are more independent and directly critical of the government than are the mass media in the other three NICs. Regional splits between the northeast and southwest and conflict with North Korea also plague South Korea and contribute to the political polarization and rigid policymaking of recent decades, something not seen in Taiwan and Singapore. Although Korea's economic development has been significant, it has yet to fulfill major social needs in such areas as the provision of social services, adequate medical care, care for elderly people, and a good quality of life for all its citizens (Chai & Clark, 1991; D. B. Lee, 1989; Roh, 1989).

Singapore

Situated midway between China and India, Singapore enjoys one of the highest per capita GNPs in Asia (Chai & Clark, 1991). Within the NICs, Singapore is the most diverse society, with three officially recognized racial groups—Indian (7 percent), Chinese (74 percent), and Malays (15 percent). Soon after it achieved independence from British rule in June 1959, Singapore's leaders decided to build a strong society in which the expansion of trade and industrial growth could take place. The priorities were to industrialize the nation, to lower unemployment and raise income levels, to provide decent housing for all, and to build a national identity and a national consciousness. In its pervasive moralism, Singapore's public policy is thoroughly Confucian. Singapore, a well-run authoritarian government, governs this city-state with a paternalistic hand and dictates on such aspects of life as morality, cleanliness, and even the prohibition of gum chewing. The creation of a relatively stable political climate has been the prerequisite for multinational corporate investment in Singapore. A dedicated labor force that respects work efficiency and law and order has strongly supported the government's economic policy.

Alone among the ruling regimes of the NICs, Singapore's People's Action Party is of socialist origin and has long been a member of the Socialist International. Ideologically and politically, the government believes that it is in its best interest to offset the negative effects of the multinational corporations on the country's distribution of income with positive social welfare programs of its own (Hofheinz & Calder, 1982; Weiss, 1989). An example of Singapore's commitment to social welfare is its housing policy. Almost 90 percent of the Singaporeans who live in public housing units hold title to those units, compared with one in 10 in Hong Kong. Since 1975, the Singapore government has also invested considerable resources to establish about 300 residents' organizations (called Residents' Committees) for dealing with neighborhood needs and for residents' participation in community development (Vasoo, 1990).

Hong Kong

Hong Kong is not an independent sovereign state like the other NICs. Rather, it has been a crown colony of Great Britain since the British took it from China in the so-called Opium War of 1842. A market economy, a dedicated labor force consisting largely of immigrants from China, an ideal geographic location with a deep-water harbor, and relative political stability have all contributed to its prosperity. Today Hong Kong is the world's third largest container port, the third largest gold-dealing center, and the third largest banking and financial center. Hong Kong differs from its NIC neighbors in two important ways: It is the only city-state still ruled by foreigners, and it lives completely in the shadow of its enormous neighbor, China. Will its dynamic character change when Hong Kong is formally ceded back to China in 1997? Initially, the Chinese government promised to maintain the economic system and the free press; however, its shifting policy has created uncertainty about Hong Kong's future.

Although social welfare in Hong Kong made much progress in the 1980s, the gap between the supply of and demand for most human services is still great (Kwan, 1988; Kwan & Chan, 1986; Social Welfare Department, 1985). The biggest problems in the human services are and will continue to be housing and inadequate resources. The care of elderly people is becoming a progressively more serious problem given that Hong Kong still does not have a pension system. Other problems that demand the attention of social workers include juvenile delinquency, the disintegration of the family, and the rehabilitation of mentally ill people.

Taiwan

Defeated by the Chinese Communists, the Chinese Nationalist government (known as the Kuomintang) of Chiang Kai-shek took over Taiwan in 1949, calling itself the Republic of China. Learning from past experience, the government started a major land-reform program in Taiwan. This program, along with a series of long-range economic plans, started in 1953, helped Taiwan's economy to grow rapidly. In the wake of urbanization and expanded international trade, national income levels rose, as did the GNP, and unemployment virtually disappeared. Since then, Taiwan's standard of living has increased, while its social structure has undergone dramatic changes. The result has been the creation of the new middle class, who are the beneficiaries of tremendous upward mobility since the 1950s. Currently, more than 85 percent of Taiwan's population is employed in business- and service-oriented industries. The industrial products' share of the gross domestic product (GDP) rose from 18 percent in 1952 to 44 percent in 1987, whereas the per capita GDP during the same period increased from U.S.$151 to U.S.$4,969 (Lin, 1991).

Of the Four Little Dragons, Taiwan's social welfare effort was higher than that of Korea's and Hong Kong's and below that of Singapore's in 1986 (see Table 1). Despite the Taiwanese government's opposition to the welfare state, its program of land reform, nationalization, and the provision of human services has produced one of the most equitable patterns of income distribution in the world (Lin, 1991; Midgley, 1986; Tai, 1989; Weiss, 1989). However, as Lin (1991) indicated, Taiwan's social welfare efforts have lagged behind those of advanced industrial countries at similar levels of economic development.

Social Work Roles and Functions

Among the Asian NICs, social welfare is considered, in part, the state's responsibility, and social work is officially recognized as a profession. Each nation wants to provide the social services desired by every modern society: relief for impoverished people, adequate health care, education, and social security. Yet *social work* and *social welfare* are misleading as umbrella terms, for the relative quality and quantity of social welfare programs vary substantially from country to country. To understand social welfare and social work in the Four Little Dragons, one must first understand what each state does and does not contribute to social welfare and the collective influence of the family, the culture, and the state.

Types of Social Work Roles

In the NICs, the roles of social workers and their abilities to address societal issues vary with the level of intervention required. Social workers may be employed at the grassroots level, working door to door, or they may directly make policy. Their education is based on different conceptions of professional identity, and in most of the NICs they are in short supply. The three most basic roles of social workers in these countries are in social policy, social administration, and direct services.

At the social policy level, social intervention is often political or ideological and is inevitably tied to economic development. All four governments have established policy directives for social welfare programs, using a system of selective social benefits. In determining who has a priority to be helped, the NICs deploy their resources to meet the most obvious threats to their present and future welfare. Decisive factors, such as welfare ideology, the labor movement, and the particular state structure, have most likely played significant roles in shaping the development of modern social welfare in all four NICs (Lin, 1991; Midgley, 1986; Roh, 1989). As a result, the principal policy features are clear. First, levels of benefits are based primarily on the principle of basic minimum provision, and the volume of services is proportional to the nation's economic standing. Second, in South Korea and Taiwan, social policy targets children, elderly people, handicapped people, and poor people, whereas in Hong Kong and Singapore, with their urban orientation, social policies place more emphasis on public housing, medical care, labor welfare, and care of elderly people. In all the NICs, social policies are rudimentary, restricted, and lack the institutional framework that is necessary for the effective delivery of human services.

Two patterns of administrative decentralization are common in the NICs. One pattern is decentralization according to locality, as in Hong Kong; the other is decentralization according to organizational subunits within the framework of control by the central government, as in Singapore, Taiwan, and South Korea. In the NICs, the administrative role of social workers focuses on the planning and management of social welfare services in relation to the political and economic institutions and on the distribution of national resources to meet social needs. In this context, social administration is directly linked to the social work profession, but from the broader vantage point of other political and economic influences on the national development of social welfare.

All four NICs have statutory educational, housing, social security, child welfare, health, and mental health services, but their social services departments are cast mostly in the role of "enablers," which subsidize and coordinate the efforts of private social services organizations, rather than of providers of direct services. Social workers in the NICs are employed in a variety of human services systems, such as community services, public assistance, mental health services, corrections and probation, family welfare services, services for elderly people, and rehabilitation. In Taiwan, for example, most social workers are assigned to the local social services departments, where they are responsible for a population in a geographic area, not for a caseload that is screened according to regulations that are barriers to eligibility. As another example, in Hong Kong, voluntary agencies are unique in that although they are subsidized by the state welfare department, they provide most of the direct social work services, including family services, child care services, rehabilitation services, services to elderly people, and community development projects.

Social workers in the NICs are well aware of the importance of the family and the community and have developed techniques of group work and community work to ensure that clients gain access to available welfare resources. Nevertheless, social workers who are actively trying to change existing social policies have been limited by their relationship to their employers. In most cases, they work under public-sector auspices and are expected to implement the policies of the government, not to engage in political activities against those policies. Furthermore, there are too many tasks for them to perform with clients given that families and communities are becoming less and less capable of keeping a benevolent eye on their members (Jones, 1990) because of changes in family structure and family life.

One significant change is the aging of the population (7 percent of the population of Singapore and 11 percent of the population of Hong Kong are over age 60) and changes in attitudes toward the aging (United Nations, 1990). Despite the traditional view that caring for aged individuals is an honorable duty, an increasing number of elderly people are living alone and are left to care for themselves.

Other changes in the family are also noteworthy. There has been an alarming rise in the divorce rate (Kim & Kang, 1984; Kwan & Chan, 1986; D. B. Lee, 1989; P. Lee, 1988). In addition, more and more women are working outside the home (in 1988, they constituted one-third of the labor force in the NICs; Leung, 1989; *Taiwan Statistical Data Book*, 1991; United Nations, 1990). These two changes have created additional problems for the families involved, as well as for social welfare institutions that are concerned with child care and placement and care of elderly people given that women have been the traditional caretakers of the young and the old.

Importance of Social Work

In the past four decades, the governments of the NICs have focused on economic growth and political development to the detriment of social development, which has been treated as a "residual" element in the pursuit of national development. Also, most of the social welfare laws in these countries were not instituted until the 1970s. The result has been a proliferation of an almost confusing variety of social programs, ranging from massive emergency relief to individual care. For the NICs' societies, where the family still assumes the major responsibility for meeting the needs of its members, it is important to strengthen the function of supportive systems, including the extended family, friends, and neighbors. A review of the social policies of all these societies indicates, however, that none has yet developed comprehensive family policies and programs for the provision of services (Chow, 1986a, 1986b; Kwan & Chan, 1986; D. B. Lee, 1989; Lin, 1991).

Social workers in these countries continue to focus on individual functioning and on services that ameliorate, stabilize, or modify problems. Still, they have developed unique services, including the guaranteed housing program in Singapore and the government–voluntary sector partnership in Hong Kong.

Although there is growing recognition of social work as a profession, the role of social workers in the broad arena of social development remains limited. There are several reasons for this situation. One is the fear that the traditionally oriented support systems (the family and the local community) will be eroded. As the public sector has become increasingly overloaded with social demands and responsibilities in recent years, the NICs have become more apprehensive of their social commitments. Also, economists in the NICs (Chai & Clark, 1991; Lau, 1990) have warned that the expansion of entitlements and the spread of generous social programs may weaken—if not destroy—the efficient operation and continuous growth of their economies. In their view, too much public support for social services diminishes traditional support, erodes savings, and inhibits the motivation to work.

Despite an increasing public awareness of the importance of social spending, there has been counterpressure from the growing middle classes of the NICs because the social welfare clientele includes narrowly targeted problem groups, rather than the entire population. The trend in the NICs is toward a dual welfare system, with publicly provided assistance for poor people and other disadvantaged groups, such as mentally ill people and elderly people, and other services, including high-quality medical care, for the middle class and the rich populations (Kwan, 1988; D. B. Lee, 1989; P. Lee, 1988; Leung, 1989; Lin, 1991). Financial support for services for poor people remains limited, the amount and quality of professional services is eroding, and the vicious circle of the stigmatization of targeted groups, such as mentally ill people and recipients of public assistance, continues. The situation is similar in many ways to that of the United States.

Social Work Education and Training

Social work programs in the Four Little Dragons offer diplomas and bachelor's, master's, and doctoral degrees. Furthermore, these countries have a network of good schools of social work. For example, nearly all faculty members of the Department of Social Work and Psychology in the National University of Singapore have doctoral degrees.

Most schools of social work in the NICs are members of the Asia and Pacific Association of Social Work Education (APASWE), a strong association of schools of social work and educators, with about 130 members (Cox, 1991). The Asia and Pacific Regional Seminar on Social Work, held biennially, has provided an avenue for both scholarly and practical exchanges among educators and professionals in this region.

At present, South Korea has more social work education programs than do all the other NICs combined (see Table 2). It began supporting social work as a profession when it established a social work program at Ewha

Table 2.

Social Work Training Programs in the Newly Industrializing Countries

MEASURE	HONG KONG	SOUTH KOREA	SINGAPORE	TAIWAN
Total social work programs	12	30	1[a]	13
Master's-level programs	2	9	1	6
Doctoral-level programs	0	6	1	0
Number of graduates (year)	927 (1987)	1,286 (1990)	65[b] (1990)	731 (1989)

SOURCES: *Educational Statistics of the Republic of China* (1991), Ichibangase, Ogawa, & Ohashi (1990), Kwan (1987), Tiong, Liang, Black, Vasoo, & Bentelspacher (1991).
[a]Combined master's- and doctoral-level program. [b]Estimated.

Women's University in the 1940s. Except for two independent graduate schools of social work, the majority of Taiwan's social work programs are affiliated with sociology departments at universities and colleges. Only one university in Singapore has a social work program, and that program offers bachelor's, master's, and doctoral degrees. Started in 1950, the University of Hong Kong first introduced a two-year social work diploma. With the establishment of the Social Work Training Fund in 1961, Hong Kong has developed many high-quality professional degree programs in social work (Kwan, 1987).

Issues and Curricula

There is no uniform philosophy or curriculum in these countries, owing to the different historical contexts of social work education and of political and socioeconomic circumstances. National priorities undoubtedly reflect this diversity as well. For instance, both Hong Kong and Taiwan face an acute shortage of labor in social work and are funding programs to produce more graduates in the next few years (George, 1991; P. Lee, 1990; Lin, 1991). A curriculum study conducted by the APASWE (Cox & Britto, 1986) highlighted this diversity of education and practice.

As a result of colonial ties, the British model has influenced the social work curricula in Hong Kong and Singapore. There is also a strong tendency in the NICs to favor the North American model of social work given that a significant number of social work educators hold postgraduate degrees from universities in North America (George, 1991). In Taiwan, for example, nearly all the social work educators are American trained (P. Lee, 1988).

The core curricula in the NICs do not always emphasize equal training in casework, group work, community work, fieldwork, and research (Cox, 1988). In most schools, students take courses in casework and community work but are not offered courses in social policy. In many schools, students may choose to pursue one of several degrees. In the Polytechnic in Hong Kong, for example, students may enroll in a graduate program that qualifies them as "professional" social workers according to governmental salary criteria, whereas other students may enroll in a diploma program that qualifies them to be employed as social work "assistants."

Social work educators have a common inclination to design social work training so it reflects a social development perspective, rather than the remedial, traditional social work practices already in place (Cox & Britto, 1986). Even though social development combines policy analysis, social planning, community organization, administration, program evaluation, and social advocacy, much conceptual work awaits serious students of social development given that the concept has not been developed in depth.

Social work education also reflects the urbanization that is common to all NICs. More than three-fifths of the South Korean population live in cities, and Hong Kong and Singapore are overwhelmingly urban. The agricultural sector is more important in South Korea and Taiwan than in Hong Kong and Singapore, but the share of the agricultural sector in the GDP of both countries has declined sharply. Naturally, in much of the social work curricula in the NICs, social work practice that is geared toward the urban environment seems to have been widely accepted (Cox, 1991; Kwan & Chan, 1986).

"Indigenization" of the Curricula

The concept of "indigenization" is applied by Western and Western-minded professionals to denote strategies of adapting Western models to the indigenous conditions of the developing nations (Ragab, 1990). Since the 1970s, indigenization of the curriculum has been a marked trend in many of the NICs' social work programs. Many schools, particularly in Singapore and South Korea, have developed socioculturally relevant teaching materials and curricular designs to adapt Western social work concepts to their local contexts (Ichibangase, Ogawa, & Ohashi, 1990; Tiong, Liang, Blake, Vasoo, & Bentelspacher, 1991). The newly published *Asian Pacific Journal of Social Work* seeks to encourage the study and dissemination of culturally relevant models of practice and education in the region.

However, two important issues related to indigenization remain unanswered (George, 1991). The first is whether social workers should seek local solutions to local problems; that is, whether intervention should be based on a socioculturally relevant frame of reference or on Western approaches. The second has to do with the apparent incompatibility of locally oriented

indigenization and comparative internationalism. How can both localism and cross-culturalism be encouraged at the same time?

At the heart of this debate seems to be the continuing doubts about the effectiveness of the European or North American models of social work education and practice in Oriental cultures. Midgley (1981) even argued that the practice of individual casework is inappropriate for social workers in developing countries and is a form of cultural imperialism. The resolution of this debate must take place within the profession itself, through its people and institutions. Until political and educational decisions (or compromises) can be reached, the question of the indigenization of social work education will remain unanswered.

Challenges for Social Work

Although economic growth has greatly contributed to the disposable revenue for social spending in the four NICs, these countries are faced with economic challenges that have serious social implications. Since the 1970s, most of the NICs' social programs have evolved as a result of the continuous ad hoc interplay or conflict between policymakers in the economic and social sectors. The economic institutions and basic economic decisions have remained strong and dominant. Decisions about social goals and policies have played a relatively secondary role (Estes, 1990; Lin, 1991; Roh, 1989). Thus, the balancing of economic growth and equity remains a fundamental challenge.

Although less wide than in some other countries, the gap between the rich and the poor classes, especially in Taiwan and South Korea, seems to have grown wider since the early 1980s and will probably have serious sociopolitical consequences (James et al., 1989; Lin, 1991; Roh, 1989). Obviously, an extensive social agenda is awaiting South Korea: Although housing and other living standards have improved in the past two decades, infant mortality is still high and health care is costly and often limited (United Nations, 1990).

The extent to which new social programs can develop is contingent on how well the fruits of economic growth are distributed. However, entrenched values and cultural mores—often revolving around Confucianism—have played a major role in shaping social policy. For example, in these societies, the family is the basic social group that unites individuals. Family ties are permanent, and all individuals are supposed to uphold the interests of the group—from the family to the nation—above their own. This ideal of the common good, intertwined with national priorities, has allowed these NICs to put social needs on the back burner as they have striven to achieve their national economic goals.

However, the NICs' governments are now feeling pressure from those who complain of overcrowding and of the tremendous ecological price that has been paid for industrialization. The Four Little Dragons are among the world's most densely populated countries, and although environmental policies and protection are starting to take effect, the side effects of industrialization continue to take their toll on public health and on the quality of life. For example, by the early 1970s, the major causes of death in these NICs—neoplasms and diseases of the circulatory system—had assumed a pattern similar to those in the developed countries (*Korean Statistical Year Book,* 1990; Kwan & Chan, 1986; *Singapore Annual Report,* 1990; *Taiwan Statistical Data Book,* 1991; United Nations, 1989). Similarly, the problem of industrial pollution is becoming acute. Except for Singapore, the rapid industrial growth in the other NICs since the 1970s has resulted in the deterioration of the environment, including ruined fishing beds, contaminated drinking water, uncontrolled use of pesticides and fertilizers, and worsening photochemical smog in urban areas (Hofheinz & Calder, 1982; James et al., 1989; Lau, 1990).

The changes in family structure and family life mentioned earlier also present a challenge. For example, the aging of the population and the declining birthrate mean that, in the future, there will be fewer wage earners to support the increased number of retirees. In addition, the growing number of working women and the rising divorce rate will necessitate more child care services and services for elderly people. Despite their profamily rhetoric, none of the NICs' family welfare programs provides benefits specifically for dependents or supplements for needy families. The scale of human problems generated in the Four Little Dragons is such that relatives and friends can no longer be expected to cope without professional advice and support. However, a review of existing social policies in the NICs (Ichibangase et al., 1990; D. B. Lee, 1989; P. Lee, 1988; Leung, 1989; Lin, 1991; Roh, 1989) indicates that none of these societies has yet developed a social welfare program that specifically addresses the effect that changing social mores are having on the individual family.

Professional Issues

Given the rapidly changing political, economic, and social conditions in the NICs, it would seem appropriate for social work to lay claim to professional status. Clearly, social work is beyond the status of an occupation and is a stable, although changing and developing, social institution in all four countries. The growth of social work in the NICs has been phenomenal in the past three decades, and there is no reason to think that its development will decrease in the future.

The number of trained professional social workers is still limited, but the demand for their services will grow rapidly with the expected focus

on social development. To be consistent with this direction, the profession may have to reconceptualize the role of social workers not solely as caregivers but as change agents. In this regard, the use that these societies want to make of social work must be considered, and the effect that social workers would like to have on these societies must be distinguished from the influence that social workers can and do exert. It should be noted that there will be special problems in redefining social work in the NICs given that the basic goals and objectives of the profession, which have never been well defined, seem to be in substantial transition. At the same time, it is clear that the changeover period in the next decade will offer a special opportunity to redefine social workers' roles.

Future Directions

The Four Little Dragons no longer have low labor costs; strikes have become commonplace; and exchange rates have appreciated significantly, affecting the countries' international competitiveness. They must transform and upgrade their industrial structures to remain competitive in the world market, and they all have to face increasing protests against certain aspects of their social and environmental policies (Lau, 1990). As Estes (1990) indicated, the tenacity of the NICs' developmental dilemmas—despite their considerable new wealth—suggests that gains in per capita income alone will not sufficiently enhance social development. Thus, a fundamental issue facing these NICs is not whether they are spending too much for social welfare but whether what they are spending will contribute significantly to the development of a better society. It is clear that if they are to achieve significant gains in social development, effective strategies will require close cooperation and technical assistance between the economic and social sectors.

The funding of social welfare programs will remain the greatest challenge to social work in the future. Despite the continued importance of economic development in the next decade, an emphasis on growth must not be allowed to obscure the need to establish social policy objectives. The NICs, with limited natural resources, will have to develop their wealth in human resources, including an increasing emphasis on education to complement their shift toward technologically advanced industries that demand highly skilled workers. Thus, if the problem of poverty is to be addressed seriously, it is essential that these countries provide more educational opportunities for poor people.

Furthermore, the social problems of the Four Little Dragons can no longer be addressed solely through beneficent private organizations; the governments must become more involved in creating and funding social policies that emphasize the entire family and the importance of family support systems. Not only must social policies offer families both economic opportunity and social protection, but these governments must move away from the incremental, fragmented form of policymaking that characterized reform efforts of the past.

With regard to a social development perspective for formulating family policies, two interrelated dimensions should be noted. The first is the need to foster the capacity of families to work continuously for their own welfare; the second is the alteration or development of the societies' institutions so that the needs of families are met quantitatively and qualitatively at all levels.

The major question facing social work in these countries is how to address local needs effectively. It is conceivable that social work in the four NICs may become an instrument of social change, but it is not now such an instrument. As social work educators and practitioners challenge traditional methods of practice and experiment with new approaches, definitions of intervention will change. More than simply modifying the social work nomenclature, educators and practitioners—if given the chance to develop new techniques—will change the very nature of intervention. When circumstances permit, social work students in the NICs should be prepared to study and work with changing family structures in their political-economic contexts.

Social work educators and practitioners must reconceptualize and experiment with new practice methods, while reevaluating the broad missions of social work in general. The new *Asian Pacific Journal of Social Work* is committed to just such a reevaluation and deserves strong support from the region. In calling for a greater degree of collaboration between schools and scholars in the Asian-Pacific region, Cox (1991) also proposed some important strategies that clearly emphasize institutional development. These strategies include the cooperative development of an advanced social work education program that reflects regional more than national realities.

The final factor that will inevitably influence the future of social work in most of the NICs will be the nature of the transition from old to new political leaderships. The governments of Hong Kong and Taiwan, for example, are particularly consumed by their changing relationship with China. Ultimately, the future of the NICs' development will depend greatly on narrowing the gap between the changing sociopolitical realities and good social policies. But if this gap is to be narrowed, the political leaders will have to pay more attention to social development and improved social welfare programs.

References

Asia: Mega-market of the 1990s. (1990, Fall). *Fortune*, Special Issue.

Chai, W., & Clark, C. (Eds.). (1991). *Political stability and economic growth: Case studies of Taiwan, South Korea, Hong Kong and Singapore*. Chicago: Third World Institute for Policy Research.

Chow, N. (1986a). A review of social policies in Hong Kong. In A. Kwan & D. Chan (Eds.), *Hong Kong society: A reader* (pp. 137–153). Hong Kong: Writers' & Publishers' Cooperative.

Chow, N. (1986b, Fall–Spring). Social security provision in Singapore, Hong Kong, Taiwan and South Korea: A comparative analysis. *Journal of International and Comparative Social Welfare,* pp. 1–10.

Cox, D. (1988). *Social work education trends in the Asian-Pacific region.* Paper presented at the Seminar on Social Work Education in the Asian and Pacific Region, Beijing, China.

Cox, D. (1991). Social work education in the Asia-Pacific region. *Asian Pacific Journal of Social Work, 1,* 6–14.

Cox, D., & Britto, G. (1986). *Social work curriculum development in Asia and the Pacific: A research report.* Melbourne: Asian and Pacific Association of Social Work Education.

Educational statistics of the Republic of China. (1991). Taipei: Ministry of Education, Republic of China.

Estes, R. (1990). *Development trends in Asia and the Western Pacific: Assessing adequacy of social provision, 1970–87.* Paper presented at the 1990 Sino–American–British Conference on Social Policy, Taipei, Taiwan.

George, J. (1991). Rhetoric, reality and strategy: Issues in regional social work education. *Asian Pacific Journal of Social Work, 1,* 15–25.

Hofheinz, R., Jr., & Calder, K. E. (1982). *The East Asia edge.* New York: Basic Books.

Ichibangase, I., Ogawa, T., & Ohashi, K. (Eds.). (1990). *Professional education in the social welfare field* [in Japanese]. Tokyo: Koseikan.

International Monetary Fund. (1987). *International financial statistics.* Washington, DC: Author.

James, W., Naya, S., & Meier, G. (1989). *Asian development: Economic success and policy lessons.* Madison: University of Wisconsin Press.

Jones, H. (1990). *Social welfare in third world development.* London: Macmillian.

Kaleidoscope: Current world data. (1990). Santa Barbara, CA: ABC-CLIO.

Kim, Y., & Kang, S. (1984). A study on the social structure of Korean families. *Korean Journal of Social Policy, 5,* 3–35.

Korean statistical year book. (1990). Seoul: Economic Planning Board.

Kwan, A. (1987). *Social welfare services in Hong Kong* [in Chinese]. Hong Kong: Ji-Suan.

Kwan, A. (1988). Suicide among the elderly: Hong Kong. *Journal of Applied Gerontology, 2,* 248–259.

Kwan, A., & Chan, D. (Eds.). (1986). *Hong Kong society: A reader.* Hong Kong: Writer's & Publishers' Cooperative.

Lau, L. (Ed.). (1990). *Models of development: A comparative study of economic growth in South Korea and Taiwan.* San Francisco: Institute for Contemporary Studies.

Lee, D. B. (1989). Family disintegration in changing societies: Social welfare implications. *Social Development Issues, 2,* 35–50.

Lee, P. (1988). *Dimensions of social welfare transition: Sino–British perspectives.* Taipei: Chu Liu Book Co.

Lee, P. (1990). *Social work professional system: A reader* [in Chinese]. Taipei: Ministry of the Interior, Republic of China.

Leung, B. (1989). *Social issues in Hong Kong.* Hong Kong: Oxford University Press.

Lin, W. (1991). The structural determinants of welfare effort in post-war Taiwan. *International Social Work, 2,* 171–190.

Malik, M. (Ed.). (1991). *Asia 1990 yearbook.* Hong Kong: Far Eastern Economic Review.

Midgley, J. (1981). *Professional imperialism: Social work in the third world.* London: Heinemann.

Midgley, J. (1986). Industrialization and welfare: The case of the four little tigers. *Social Policy & Administration, 3,* 225–238.

OECD economic surveys. (1988). Paris: Organization for Economic Cooperation and Development.

Ragab, I. A. (1990). How social work can take root in developing countries. *Social Development Issues, 3,* 38–51.

Roh, C. (1989). Disparities between economic development and social development: The case of Korea. *Social Development Issues, 2,* 23–34.

Singapore annual report. (1990). Singapore: Government of Singapore.

Social Welfare Department. (1985). *The five year plan for social welfare development in Hong Kong—Review 1985.* Hong Kong: Government Printer.

Tai, H. (Ed.). (1989). *Confucianism and economic development: An Oriental alternative?* Washington, DC: Washington Institute for Values in Public Policy.

Taiwan statistical data book. (1991). Taipei: Council for Economic Planning and Development, Republic of China.

Tiong, T. N., Liang, N., Black, M., Vasoo, S., & Bentelspacher, C. (1991). Report on curriculum review of the social work program at National University of Singapore. *Asian Pacific Journal of Social Work, 1,* 101–113.

United Nations Development Programme. (1990). *Human development report 1990.* New York: Oxford University Press.

United Nations, Statistical Office. (1989). *Demographic yearbook.* New York: Author.

Vasoo, S. (1990). Studying neighborhood leaders' participation in resident's organizations in Hong Kong and Singapore: Some theoretical perspectives. *International Social Work, 33,* 107–120.

Weiss, J. (1989). *The Asian century: The economic ascent of the Pacific Rim and what it means for the West.* New York: Facts On File.

Recommended Reading

Copper, J. (1989). Taiwan: A nation in transition. *Current History, 537,* 173–176.

Hamilton, C. (1987). Can the rest of Asia emulate the NICs? *Third World Quarterly, 4,* 1225–1256.

Harris, R. (1990). Beyond rhetoric: A challenge for international social work. *International Social Work, 33,* 203–212.

Lee, P. (1990). *Social work professional system: A reader* [in Chinese]. Taipei: Ministry of the Interior, Republic of China.

Midgley, J. (1988). Inequality, the Third World and development. *International Journal of Contemporary Sociology, 25,* 983–1003.

Rose, R., & Shiratori, R. (Eds.). (1986). *The welfare state: East and west.* New York: Oxford University Press.

Sanders, D., & Fischer, J. (Eds.). (1988). *Visions for the future: Social work and Pacific-Asian perspectives.* Honolulu: University of Hawaii, School of Social Work.

Shorrock, T. (1988). South Korea: Chun, the Kims and the constitutional struggle. *Third World Quarterly, 1,* 95–110.

9

Social Work in South Africa: Coping with Apartheid and Change

Fikile Mazibuko, Brian McKendrick, and Leila Patel

The Republic of South Africa extends over 1,220,000 square kilometers of the southernmost part of Africa, an area greater than that of France and Germany combined. It contains some of the most fertile agricultural land in Africa, and beneath the land is one of the world's richest concentrations of mineral wealth.

Societal and Historical Context

Three-quarters of the population of 37 million people are Africans, the indigenous people of the continent. A further 13 percent are white, descendants of Europeans who settled in the country from 1652, and the remainder are people of Asian extraction (2.6 percent) or of mixed origin, termed "colored" in South Africa (8.6 percent). The various ethnic and cultural heritages of the population have not been melded into the single identity of "South African." On the contrary, up to 1990 the policy of the country was to emphasize racial differences and to separate people on this basis (South African Institute of Race Relations, 1990).

Dutch, English, and other European settlers, who were advantaged by superior technology, established themselves as the ruling elite, separated and distanced from the indigenous peoples and subsequent immigrant groups by their shared Christian religion, "civilization," ethnocentrism, and self-interest. Despite divisive incidents, such as the Anglo-Boer War, these commonalities enabled whites to bond into a ruling caste. The distinctive hallmark of their rule has been the promotion of white hegemony—political, economic, and social—together with the oppression of "nonwhite" aspirations.

When the National Party came to power in 1948 and established its policy of apartheid, racial segregation and injustice were not new notions to South Africans. Apartheid only legally institutionalized and more deeply entrenched racial advantage and disadvantage. Although the right to vote (for separate houses of Parliament) was extended to Asian and colored South

Africans through the Republic of South Africa Constitution Act of 1983, whites retained economic and political power (South African Institute of Race Relations, 1990).

Apartheid has been maintained at a high price, over and above its heavy toll in human degradation and indignity. Some of these costs include slow economic growth in the country given that the majority of people have been relatively excluded from education and opportunity; the permeation of society by political violence; and the gross waste of money through the duplication of state structures on racial and ethnic criteria. For example, 18 different state departments handle "social welfare" policies and programs (South African Institute of Race Relations, 1990).

The consequences of apartheid are felt in all aspects of everyday life and are mirrored in demographic data. Despite South Africa's potential wealth, its overall profile is that of a poor country. The per capita gross domestic product is only U.S. $2,978, the life expectancy is only 52 years for men and 55 for women, the mortality rate is 104 per 1,000, and the literacy rate is 46 to 100 (South African Institute of Race Relations, 1990). However, when broken down into apartheid's racial divisions, the data reveal a sophisticated, urbanized group of whites; less advantaged Asian and colored groups who are also largely urbanized; and a highly disadvantaged African population, the majority of whom live in poverty, both in the rural areas and in urban townships and squatter settlements. The median family income of whites is double that of Asians, three times greater than that of coloreds, and eight times that of Africans. Conversely, the infant mortality rate of Africans, which is 80 per 1,000, is almost twice that of coloreds, more than four times that of Asians, and more than seven times that of whites (South African Institute of Race Relations, 1990). In terms of the Gini coefficient, a measure of the disparity between the rich and the poor in a society, South Africa has the world's highest measure of inequality (Wilson & Ramphele, 1989).

In February 1990, the white South African government indicated a desire to abandon its apartheid policies and to share power with the disenfranchised African majority. Since then, some legislative pillars of apartheid have fallen, and others have been marked for demolition. Nevertheless, concurrent with these reformist actions have been instances of governmental reluctance to abandon white privilege. So, for example, in February 1991, a governmental minister was still assuring whites that they would be able to retain their "own" schools ("Race Not Issue," 1991), and state welfare officials were still advocating "revisions" of the welfare system that would leave racist structures intact and encourage the state's divestment of welfare responsibility (South African Welfare Council, 1990).

Contrary to popular belief in some countries, the process of bargaining and negotiation that, it is hoped, will lead to a nonracial democracy in South Africa is only in its early stages, and when it is achieved, the effects of centuries of racial injustice and decades of apartheid will linger for many years. Hence, South African social workers are faced with tasks of construction and reconstruction. They are challenged to develop new localized programs and services that will support South Africans in a changing, industrializing society and to reconstruct existing services that deliberately or inadvertently promote the goals of apartheid. Above all, they are challenged to redefine the roles and priorities of their profession so that social work will make a meaningful contribution to human development and well-being in a future democratic South Africa.

Roles and Functions of Social Work

Social work practice in South Africa takes place in two principal contexts: the formal welfare system, within state-organized parameters and with state subsidization, and "alternative" structures, usually associated with an antiapartheid, prodemocracy ideology and without financial aid from the state. These parallel structures are both contradictory and complementary, and the auspices of each determine the opportunities for and limitations of social work practice. These two approaches are revealed in most fields of social work practice in South Africa and can be clearly demonstrated in social work with families and children.

Social Work with Families and Children: The Formal System

The formal welfare system is divided into seven fields of practice, of which "married life, family and child care" is one (South African Welfare Council, 1990). This system, comprising state and voluntary agencies, is guided by four principles: (1) racial division in the provision of services, which results in whites having the widest range and greatest depth of social work services; (2) a rejection of "socialism," so that the state does not routinely accept responsibility for the welfare of its citizens; (3) a move from residual, therapeutic services to community-based and preventive services (not yet realized); and (4) a "partnership" between the state and the community, whereby the state accepts responsibility for the planning of services and the delivery of some statutory social work to adults and other children and provides limited subsidies to private welfare organizations that conduct approved activities (McKendrick, 1987b). To these has been added another principle that is, in some respects, an extension of the second, namely, privatization. This principle implies the increased responsibility of individuals, families, and communities for the provision of services and a reduction in the already limited involvement of the state (South African Institute of Race Relations, 1990).

Within the field of social work with families and children, the most prominent group is that of the child and family welfare societies that are affiliated with the South African National Council for Child and Family Welfare (Hoffman, 1991). The council has 173 affiliated societies, many of which employ social workers. McKendrick and Dudas (1987) reported that the bulk of the social work undertaken by these societies was casework in the areas of foster care, "reconstruction" services with families, day care services, child neglect, marital problems, unmarried mothers, and adoption. More recent data suggest that this pattern remains constant, except for the increased response to child abuse, again through casework but with the occasional use of family therapy and group work ("Statistics," 1989).

The overwhelming emphasis of social work is on individual therapeutic work at the rehabilitative level. Indeed, a survey of social work in South Africa's largest metropolis, Johannesburg, in which child and family welfare services were the largest type of service provided, found that 90 percent of social work services consisted of casework counseling (McKendrick, 1990b). This focus may be due to the high demand for therapeutic services (individual caseloads often exceeded 100 families with serious problems), but it may also be a result of the state's method of subsidizing services, which lays heavy stress on traditional casework. The survey also indicated the limited use of group work for therapeutic, educational, and developmental purposes and a small amount of community work, largely concerned with either the development of localities or social planning to develop new services. Advocacy was also evidenced but, with the one exception discussed later, it focused on traditional "welfare" issues, such as sexually and physically abused children, battered wives, and changes in child welfare legislation. The survey also noted that most recipients of services were whites and that the management boards of most agencies were dominated by whites.

A few voluntary social work organizations in the formal sector have broken the mold and have courageously attempted to provide services in response to people's real and immediate pain. One such organization is the Johannesburg Child Welfare Society (JCWS), a nonracial body, which was the only formal agency in South Africa's province of Transvaal to respond to the state's incarceration without trial of children who were suspected of political involvement in the 1980s. Other child welfare societies did not react because they regarded attempts to protest the government's action as "belonging in the political domain" and outside their range of activities (Thomas, 1990).

JCWS's social workers were denied access to children in detention, but by networking with other concerned groups, they retained attorneys to bring pressure on the authorities to have the children released. Direct intervention was initiated with released children, their families, and the families of children who were still detained. Short-term crisis intervention was introduced with the children, reinforced by the sharing and mutual support of group activities and family counseling. Ongoing networking with alternative groups enabled the children and their families to be linked to medical and legal facilities and to be given material aid. Throughout, the JCWS played a prominent role in publicizing the conditions under which children were detained, as well as the consequences of detention for children and their families.

Of late, many social work organizations that are affiliated with the South African National Council for Child and Family Welfare have expressed concern that services should be expanded and altered to meet current human needs. At a brainstorming session of a number of societies in 1990, there was agreement that services, especially those to alleviate poverty, unemployment, and inadequate education and to foster community development, should be extended to meet the needs of urban and rural families of all races and should be provided on a nonracial basis ("Welfare for a New Decade," 1990). However, being locked into a dependence on governmental financing may inhibit these developments.

Social Work with Families and Children: The Alternative Structure

Borne out of popular resistance to apartheid, an alternative or progressive welfare structure, comprising two main groupings—services associated with nonsectarian antiapartheid organizations and services under church auspices—has evolved. Social workers are employed in both, although in much smaller numbers than in the formal system.

At the grassroots level, nonsectarian antiapartheid organizations have given life to their democratic and humanitarian ideals through local developmental initiatives in response to inadequate social, political, and economic resources and the formal sector's neglect of developmental work. Many of these organizations are affiliated or are aligned with the United Democratic Front or the Congress of South African Trade Unions. In a recent survey, Patel and Taback (1991) located 175 such grassroots organizations that provide direct services to children and families, and in her ongoing research on social services programs of resistance movements to apartheid, Patel has shown that social workers who are employed in these organizations are part of community-based social development programs that are concerned with preventive, promotive, developmental, and curative services.

Church-sponsored services are offered by the prophetic Christian churches, which hold that the world and the church cannot be divided and that churches have a role to play in the daily lives of their members, particularly in opposition to apartheid; in advocacy for social justice and human rights; in instances of state oppression and other forms of violence; and in response to basic human needs. The major church groups include, among others, the South African Council of Churches, the Southern African Catholic Bishops Conference, the Institute for Contextual Theology, and Diakonia. Church-sponsored services to families and children cover a wide spectrum, from community-advice offices to educational programs and from the support of persons on Death Row and their families to reintegration programs for political exiles and those who were detained without trial. Social workers are part of many of these programs, often in senior positions.

Five striking features of the activities of social workers in both antiapartheid and church-sponsored organizations clearly distinguish social work in these settings from most social work in the formal welfare system. First, social workers in alternative structures are not usually employed under the occupational title "social worker." They enter organizations as citizens who wish to fight apartheid and to promote social justice. Once they are in these organizations, their social work knowledge and skills are appreciated and used. Many social workers occupy managerial, facilitative, enabling, and coordinating positions, under such titles as "program developer," "project manager," and "project coordinator."

Second, in alternative organizations, social workers are usually part of a team of social services workers, comprised of grassroots people and professionals from the fields of law, religion, health, education, and agricultural development. Social workers become valued team members because of their expertise in group work, community development, and effective communication; their specialist knowledge of child and family care, crisis intervention, problem solving, and networking, as well as program design, implementation, and evaluation; and their understanding of the impact of social, economic, and political forces on people's lives. Within programs, social workers' knowledge and skills are directed toward the development and empowerment of the grassroots participants in efforts to bring about change.

Third, a constant characteristic of the management and delivery of alternative programs is the large-scale involvement of local people. Patel (1989), for example, found that up to 250 community volunteers were involved in a single program. Social workers play an important part in the preparation and training of these indigenous workers.

Fourth, given the tradition of resistance and the linkage of grassroots programs with the movement for democracy and social justice, there is an emphasis on advocacy and community action. Friere's (1972) concepts of "conscientization," reflection, action, and empowerment of oppressed people have been highly influential in determining the social-development intervention of popular movements and in shaping the part that social workers play in them.

Fifth, social work activity in the alternative sector, even in such ostensibly "therapeutic" programs as those aimed at helping the victims of political violence, is developmentally oriented. Hence, social workers perform roles, such as nonformal educators, community development catalysts, networkers, and coalition builders, in popular social movements to shape the direction of social development policies and programs. Developmental social work also implies the development of a practice suited to the local political, economic, and sociocultural context and to mass issues, such as oppression and poverty.

Training for Social Work

Training for social work in South Africa was begun in the 1920s as a response to the problems of "poor whites" at that time. The theory on which it was based was taken directly from North America and Europe, with little adaptation to specific local conditions, and the majority of people trained for the profession were whites (McKendrick, 1987a). Although an increasingly large number of African, Asian, and colored people have been drawn into the profession over the past two decades, whites still predominate. Of South Africa's 6,767 registered social workers, 66 percent are whites, 16 percent are Africans, 12 percent are colored persons, and 6 percent are Asians.

All South Africa's 20 universities offer recognized professional-preparation programs for social work through four-year bachelor's degrees. In addition, two nonuniversity institutions, Huguenot College and Minnie Hofmeyr College, offer nondegree training programs in social work that are also recognized as professional qualifications. Graduates of the universities and these programs are eligible to register as social workers with the South African Council for Social Work, a statutory body that is charged with the regulation of social work profession and the training of social workers. To practice social work for gain without registration is a punishable offense (McKendrick, 1987a).

In theory, undergraduate education for social work is open to people of all racial groups at all universities, but the residues of apartheid have ensured that, with the exception of English-language urban universities, many universities have virtually uniracial faculties and student bodies.

The aim of all basic social work education programs is to produce "generic" social workers, who have beginning competence for responsible entry to social work practice. By generic, two dimensions are implied: beginning competence in the practice of all methods of social work in an "integrated" approach and beginning competence in all social work fields. In reality, however, the training emphasizes preparation for individual practice that is therapeutic or restorative, directed largely at urban, not rural, people (McKendrick, 1990a).

For a developing, industrializing country, South Africa is unusual in that the only entry to social work is through a four-year qualification obtained at an institution of higher education, usually a university and usually in the form of a degree. There are no intermediate-level social workers, although the South African Council for Social Workers is currently exploring the introduction of lower-level training for "social auxiliary workers."

In addition to basic undergraduate preparation, all South African universities offer master's and doctoral degrees in social work through independent research. Recently, some universities have introduced, or are in the process of introducing, "specialist" course work for master's degrees in medical social work, industrial social work, clinical social work, statutory social work, and supervision.

Challenges for Social Work

The process of bargaining and negotiating to achieve a nonracial democracy is just beginning. The national liberation movements, political parties, the Nationalist government, and popular social movements are developing policy positions on a wide range of social, political, and economic issues. In this climate of free political activity and debate, both the formal welfare sector and the alternative sector are engaged in shaping the debate about a future welfare policy (Lund, 1990; Patel, 1989; Snyman, 1989; South African Welfare Council, 1990). The opportunity also exists for grassroots participants to influence the development of social policy. A major challenge facing the social work profession is to conduct appropriate research and thereby to contribute to the formulation of policies and the content and direction of social policies in a future South Africa. It is critical for the profession to do so: Not only will social work make a valuable contribution, but its actions will go a long way toward changing the negative public image of social work and social welfare in the country. However, a change in the profile of social work will necessitate redefining the profession and its focus in line with national reconstruction and social development.

Traditional versus Developmental Social Work

Because of its origins and development in South Africa, the social work profession has been widely perceived as an instrument of domination and control over the majority of the population and as a means of furthering the aims of apartheid. In addition, the profession, as practiced in the formal sector, has been associated with residual interventions that are designed to maintain an unjust social system, rather than action to change the system.

The progressive or alternative welfare sector, on the other hand, emphasizes the need for social services professions, including social work, to reexamine their values, principles, and methods of intervention to contribute to the building of a new national identity that will stress the nonracial character, languages, cultures, religions, and geographic diversity of the future society. There is also a need for national reconciliation, based on an acknowledgment of the negative impact of apartheid on the lives of people and the removal of spurious social divisions that have been created among different population groups.

Supporters of the alternative sector believe in the social and economic development of the society, through innovative social policies, strategies, and methods of service delivery that will have an impact on the massive poverty and inequality. A focus on developmental roles for social welfare will undoubtedly receive the highest priority. Closely linked to this focus is the need to develop appropriate forms of practice in the social services that will locate social programs within the political, economic, and sociocultural context and contribute to the development of authentic social services methods in response to local needs.

All these ideals are dependent on the institution of a democratic system that will guarantee participation as a principle and as a means to empower those who are disadvantaged to influence the flow of resources in their direction. Building a democratic culture is crucial in a society in which the majority of people have been denied this basic human right. Thus, the traditional "developmental" role for the profession will, by itself, be insufficient. Social workers will also have to be advocates for social and distributive justice. Moreover, their methods will have to be aimed at empowering people to advocate on their own behalf.

Earlier in this chapter, social work roles and functions were discussed with reference to the formal and alternative sectors. It is apparent from this discussion that two forms of social services delivery coexist in a complementary and contradictory way in present-day South Africa. The development of these two forms is interrelated given that the alternative sector emerged in direct response to the inappropriateness and inequity of the formal sector. A major challenge facing the welfare sector as a whole is to evolve a framework for a social welfare policy that is based on the realities of what a postapartheid society will inherit and on the positive elements in the social policy and social services programs of the two sectors. In this way, the possibilities and limitations of integrating these two forms of service delivery can be assessed, and strategies can be devised to facilitate such an integration.

However, these two forms of service delivery will probably continue to coexist for some time. The two are rooted in different paradigms of social and economic development, each emphasizing different roles and functions for social work. The process of integrating these disparate forms will not be smooth or consensual but will involve conflict among political groups and between economic and social forces that are contending for power.

The unequal resources that are due to the constraining effects of apartheid on economic development and the economic isolation of South Africa from the international community will be major obstacles to meeting people's needs. A postapartheid government will be faced with the challenge of instituting socioeconomic upliftment policies and programs to satisfy rising expectations and demands on the state to meet needs at the grassroots level. Because of the distorted nature of apartheid, shortages of skills will be a further obstacle to reconstruction, particularly in the area of developmental social welfare.

The social welfare bureaucracy is staffed largely by whites, who monopolize key positions in planning social services, formulating policies, allocating financial resources, and managing the human services. Resistance to change from people occupying such powerful positions may be anticipated. In the process of transition, the structures and institutions of service delivery are likely to reflect the ideology of the old system, despite legislative changes.

The changing political, economic, and social context demands a change in the values, principles, methods, and focus of the social work profession from a First-World model of service delivery aimed at a predominantly urban, middle-class white minority, to the majority of the population, which is battling to survive under conditions of massive urban and rural poverty. These changes will define the developmental role of social welfare.

There is a consensus among experts on developmental social welfare about the obligation of social welfare programs to respond to the needs of the most disadvantaged people, to promote self-reliance in decision making, and to organize integrated services that are family oriented and community based. Developmental social welfare programs also give high priority to social development and preventive functions, redressing gender inequalities and the reduction of regional, rural–urban, sectoral, and social disparities. Although intersectoral initiatives have been high on the agenda of the alternative social development programs, territorial, elitist, hierarchical, and other barriers still exist among professionals in different fields. Social workers in alternative welfare programs have facilitated a better understanding of social work roles and functions among other professionals.

One major feature of the South African context is that as a result of the harmful consequences of apartheid, there is a great demand for curative and rehabilitative services. Finding the balance between developmental and therapeutic roles will not be easy. Presently, social workers are most skilled in social casework, and the incorporation of developmental roles within their repertoire will require retraining, changes in policy, and greater financial resources. In addition, the vacuum between highly skilled professional social workers and community volunteers will have to be filled by recruiting and training grassroots developmental workers. Grassroots organizations, church groups, and some formal welfare organizations are currently experimenting with community-based rehabilitation programs. These programs give priority to community development principles, integrate curative services with preventive interventions, and involve community participants in the delivery of services. This approach has been used successfully by a home program that was developed to assist mentally handicapped children (Solarsh, Katz, & Goodman, 1990). It has also been implemented in counseling and supportive services to individuals, families, and communities who have been traumatized by repression and the escalation of political violence (Thomas, 1990).

Future Roles for Social Workers

Different roles are indicated for social workers if they are to have an effect on a society in transition. These roles are related to mediation skills, networking, conflict management, popular education involving work with small groups, and public education. The integration of new values and principles into social policies and programs will be a further major challenge for the profession. Social workers will also need to link small localized interventions with macrosystems and broad developmental strategies. South African social workers have always been good at individual intervention, but the new situation demands additional skills in research and social planning; in the formulation, implementation, and evaluation of social policies; and in the management and planning of human services.

There is no doubt that one of the most effective strategies to change the nature of social work practice is to change the nature of social work education. Social work education is almost totally concerned with preparing highly skilled therapists to deal with First-World types of social problems. To respond to the developmental needs of the future South Africa, social work education will have to be adapted to reflect the priorities just identified. Moreover, there is a strong need to recruit African people into social work education, so the profession becomes more representative of the wider South African population.

In conclusion, the transition from apartheid to social justice within a nonracial democracy will require a total rearrangement of the existing social order. The process of dismantling apartheid and making up the socioeconomic backlog suffered by the black majority will not take place smoothly but will involve conflict among a wide range of social, political, and economic forces about the direction of change. A clear assessment of the obstacles to change, as well as the proactive forces that are facilitating change in the society at large and in the social welfare sector, will be necessary. Social work faces the challenge of redefining its role in relation to all these forces, while remaining true to its professional commitment to promote peace, social justice, equity, and democracy.

References

Friere, P. (1972). *Pedagogy of the oppressed.* Harmondsworth, England: Penguin Books.

Hoffman, W. C. (1991). South African social work practice in family and children's services. In B. W. McKendrick (Ed.), *Social work in action* (pp. 47–83). Pretoria, South Africa: HAUM.

Lund, F. (1990). Moving beyond slogans: Transforming welfare in South Africa. *Critical Health, 31–32,* 12–15.

McKendrick, B. W. (1987a). Social work education. In B. W. McKendrick (Ed.), *Introduction to social work in South Africa* (pp. 178–205). Pretoria, South Africa: HAUM.

McKendrick, B. W. (1987b). The South African social welfare system. In B. W. McKendrick (Ed.), *Introduction to social work in South Africa* (pp. 20–44). Pretoria, South Africa: HAUM.

McKendrick, B. W. (1990a). Beyond apartheid: An alphabet of challenges for social work education. *Social Work/Maatskaplike Werk, 26,* 241–250.

McKendrick, B. W. (1990b). The future of social work in South Africa. *Social Work/Maatskaplike Werk, 26,* 10–18.

McKendrick, B. W., & Dudas, E. (1987). South Africa. In J. Dixon (Ed.), *Social welfare in Africa* (pp. 184–217). London: Croom Helm.

Patel, L. (1989, May). Towards a democratic welfare system—Options and strategies. In *Proceedings of the National Social Welfare Policy Conference* (pp. 21–25). Johannesburg, South Africa: Concerned Social Workers.

Patel, L., & Taback, R. (1991). *Feasibility study to assess the social development initiatives pertaining to children in South Africa.* Unpublished report, Concerned Social Workers, Johannesburg, South Africa.

Race not issue for state schools. (1991, February 5). *The Star,* p. 3.

Snyman, I. (1989). *Some perceptions of the public on privatization and community participation.* Pretoria, South Africa: Human Sciences Research Council.

Solarsh, B., Katz, B., & Goodman, M. (1990). *START integrated programme.* Johannesburg, South Africa: Sunshine Centre.

South African Institute of Race Relations. (1990). *Race relations survey, 1989/90.* Johannesburg, South Africa: Author.

South African Welfare Council and the Interdepartmental Consultative Committee on Social Welfare Matters. (1990). *Voluntary welfare initiative and the financing of the welfare system. Report of the Working Committee of the South African Welfare Council and the Interdepartmental Consultative Committee on Social Welfare Matters.* Pretoria, South Africa: Department of National Health & Population Development.

Statistics: Doing more with less (News Item). (1989, November–December). *Child Welfare, 14,* 11.

Thomas, A. (1990). Violence and child detainees. In B. W. McKendrick & W. Hoffmann (Eds.), *People and violence in South Africa* (pp. 436–464). Cape Town, South Africa: Oxford University Press.

Welfare for a new decade (News Item). (1990, April). *Child Welfare, 16,* 1–2.

Wilson, F., & Ramphele, M. (1989). *Uprooting poverty. The South African challenge.* Cape Town, South Africa: David Philip.

Recommended Reading

Letsebe, M. A. (1989). The South African social welfare policy: Responses and critiques. In *SABSWA papers* (pp. 4–5). Johannesburg: South African Black Social Workers Association.

Mazibuko, F. (1989). Privatization of welfare services: Implications. In *SABSWA papers* (pp. 18–21). Johannesburg: South African Black Social Workers Association.

McKendrick, B. W. (Ed.). (1987). *The contribution of social work in a changing South Africa.* Johannesburg, South Africa: University of the Witwatersrand, School of Social Work

McKendrick, B. W. (Ed.). (1987). *Introduction to social work in South Africa.* Pretoria, South Africa: HAUM.

McKendrick, B. W. (1990). Beyond apartheid: An alphabet of challenges for social work education. *Social Work/Maatskaplike Werk, 26,* 241–250.

McKendrick, B. W. (1990). The future of social work in South Africa. *Social Work/Maatskaplike Werk, 26,* 10–18.

McKendrick, B. W., & Hoffman, W. (Eds.). (1990). *People and violence in South Africa.* Cape Town, South Africa: Oxford University Press.

Patel, L. (1987). Towards a critical theory and practice in social work with special reference to South Africa. *International Social Work, 30,* 221–236.

Patel, L. (1989, May). Towards a democratic welfare system—Options and strategies. In *Proceedings of the National Social Welfare Policy Conference* (pp. 21–25). Johannesburg, South Africa: Concerned Social Workers.

South African Institute of Race Relations. (1990). *Race relations survey, 1989/90.* Johannesburg, South Africa: Author.

Wilson, F., & Ramphele, M. (1989). *Uprooting poverty. The South African challenge.* Cape Town, South Africa: David Philip.

10

Social Work in Sweden: Professional Identity in the Welfare State

Hans Berglind and Ulla Pettersson

To understand the meaning of social work in a society, one has to know something about that society—its historical background, its basic structure, and its main concerns. One also has to separate social work from other activities—activities that may be referred to as "social work" in one society but not in another.

Some characteristics of Sweden have to be emphasized in this context. First, Sweden is a small country, with a population of only about 8.6 million people. In area, it is the third largest country in Western Europe—almost twice as large as Great Britain and somewhat larger than the state of California.

Even if its population is not as highly concentrated in cities as is true of many other European countries, there are still vast areas, especially in northern Sweden, that are sparsely populated. This fact is important to remember because the economic and social problems that face social work may not be the same in all parts of the country. For example, with regard to unemployment, although the national rate has been low compared with many other countries—only about 1.5 percent of the labor force—the rate for some areas may be double that figure or more. And when unemployment increases during an economic decline, as it did in 1991, it increases particularly in small communities with one dominating industry that has to close down.

In this context, social work can be seen as either the front line of the welfare state or as the last resort for those who fall through the safety net of social policy. Sweden spends 35 percent of its gross domestic product on welfare expenditures, an internationally high figure (*The Cost and Financing of the Social Services,* 1990).

The majority of trained social workers are employed by the municipal social services, working in the areas of individual and family care. Of the total expenditures on social welfare in 1989 (429 billion krone, or approximately U.S. $70 billion) only about 2 percent was spent on individual and family care, including social assistance expenditures and social workers' salaries. The means-tested programs, operated by the social services, are limited in scope, and the general welfare programs are supposed to take care of the needs of the majority of the population (Berglind & Hokenstad, 1981; Korpi, 1990). Less emphasis on means-tested assistance, of course, makes social work different from what it would be in a society with a less-developed general welfare system. At the same time, such a welfare system is costly, and among the main concerns today are the economic constraints that increasingly face a welfare state with a stagnating economy and an internationally high level of taxation.

Historical Highlights

In fewer than 100 years, Sweden was transformed from a poor agrarian country to a rich industrial society. As late as 1870, about 70 percent of its population obtained their subsistence from agriculture and subsidiary activities like fishing. In 1970 only 8 percent worked in those areas, whereas more than 40 percent worked in mining and the goods-producing sectors of the economy (*The Biography of a People,* 1974). In 1990 only 3 percent of the labor force worked in farming and subsidiary activities, whereas about 10 percent were found in the goods-producing sector (Statistics Sweden, 1990). At the same time, the tertiary (service) sector has increased. Thus, Sweden may be classified as a "postindustrial" society.

The rapid expansion of the service sector has opened up a new labor market, especially for women. Sweden has the highest rate of employment of women in the industrialized world. In 1988, over 80 percent of Swedish women of working age were in the labor force, compared with less than 60 percent for all countries in the Organization for Economic and Cultural Development (*OECD Employment Outlook,* 1990). The many women working outside their homes also create the need for more women in the caring professions, like child and elder care.

Until recently Sweden was an ethnically homogeneous country, but because of increased immigration, the number of foreign-born residents has increased to approximately 10 percent of the population (Statistics Sweden, 1990). Although this transition has been fairly smooth, in recent years there have been more signs of intolerance against foreign minority groups, something that may be of concern to social work.

Sweden has been called a "prototype of modern society," characterized by modern values and a rapid and tranquil transition from an agrarian to a highly industrialized society (Tomasson, 1970). This transition was the main impetus for the expansion of the welfare system in general and for social work in particular because it meant an uprooting of people that created problems at both ends. Many people who moved to the suburbs of the big cities had lost most of their social anchoring, and those who stayed in the rural areas were primarily elderly people, who were left without the social support they needed. This is, of course, a well-known pattern in most industrializing countries. What may have been different in Sweden was the societal response to these problems in the form of general social policy measures and, to a lesser extent, social work.

An important step in the development of social policy came with the introduction of the universal pension system in 1913, a step that has been followed by consecutive pension reforms. This result is a comprehensive and generous system of benefits that has almost eliminated the need for social assistance to senior citizens.

An important step in the development of social work in Sweden was the formation in 1903 of the Centralforbundet for Socialt Arbete (CSA), or the Central Association of Social Work. According to Olsson (1990, p. 64), "the association was launched by female philanthropists who missed a common forum for [the] exchange of ideas and experiences." (Swedish women were not granted suffrage until 1921.) CSA had a strong liberal and temperance stance and became a key organizer of many influential organizations in Sweden. The board members took an active part in organizing the Swedish Association of Poor Relief (Svenska Fattigvardsforbundet), in creating different associations of the municipalities, and in forming the National Board of Social Welfare (Socialstyrelsen) in 1913. It also took an active part in organizing the first courses in social work around 1909 and in initiating the first school of social work, which opened in Stockholm in 1921. Because the CSA was so successful in its efforts, it gradually lost its importance. The state took over, and social policy was developed by other forces, mainly the labor movement, which came into the government in 1932. The efforts of the Social Democratic Party, which was in power from 1932 to 1976 and from 1982 to 1991, were directed mainly toward the creation of general welfare measures, probably with the hope, expressed by its leader Hjalmar Branting, during the 1920s, that the abolition of poverty would eliminate such social problems as drinking (Olsson, 1990, p. 76).

In 1982, a new Social Services Act was implemented. This act is described in more detail in the section on Local Welfare Services.

Trends

Demographic Trends

A high proportion of Sweden's 8.6 million inhabitants are in the higher age brackets. Almost 18 percent are age 65 and over, and 10 percent are age 55–64 (Statistics Sweden, 1990).

The most common age of retirement in Sweden is 65, when people start collecting their pensions. About 1.5 million people are age 65, a figure that is expected to increase to 1.8 million in 2025. The greatest increase (38 percent) will take place among the very old—those age 80 and over—from 340,00 in 1990 to 483,000 in 2025, whereas Sweden's total population is predicted to remain almost constant. In addition, the number of young people is expected to continue to decrease, which will probably lead to lower unemployment in that age group than in earlier years, provided that there is a sufficient demand for labor, a somewhat dubious assumption at the present.

Economic, Political, and Social Trends

Some of the recent trends that are relevant for social work have already been touched on. Most of them have to do with the economic recession, which is expected to lead to increased unemployment. This situation should be a challenge for social work. However, it may not be seen as a challenge because the National Labour Board, with its Labour Exchange Offices, not the local social services (Socialtjansten), is expected to deal with unemployment, although almost half the clients of the departments for individual and family care are unemployed or in other ways marginal in the labor market.

Another effect of the economic decline is the need to cut back on welfare expenditures or at least to stop any further expansion. This trend is reinforced by the increasing conservatism in Sweden and the belief in the benevolence of market mechanisms. There is also a growing concern about the provision of services to elderly people when their numbers increase and the resources for their care decrease. The development of social policy and social services will be further affected by Sweden's wish to become a member of the European Common Market, because changes that will facilitate an adjustment to European norms will no doubt be favored.

Swedish society is preoccupied with alcohol abuse. This preoccupation is not an effect of high alcohol consumption by Swedes in general, given that Sweden ranks 27th in alcohol consumption among 35 countries (Statistics Sweden, 1990). In addition, alcohol-related diseases like cirrhosis of the liver are lower, particularly in comparison with wine-producing countries like France and Italy. However, the drinking pattern is such that alcohol abuse is visible. About 10 percent of the consumers of alcohol are responsible for most of the total consumption (*Trends in Alcohol and Drug Use,* 1989).

Another reason for the emphasis on alcohol abuse in Sweden is the traditionally strong temperance movement. Members of temperance organizations have always been overrepresented in the Swedish Parliament, which is one reason why Sweden has had legislation on the compulsory treatment of alcohol abusers since 1913. Today this legislation includes narcotic addicts, although they are a minority of the substance abusers in Sweden. It is estimated that of the several hundred thousand alcohol abusers, 50,000–

100,000 have severe drinking problems and about 50,000 are in contact with the local social services. The number of hard drug addicts is estimated to be about 15,000 (Statistics Sweden, 1990; *Trends in Alcohol and Drug Use,* 1989).

That alcohol abuse is considered such a severe problem in Sweden was demonstrated in an interview study of social workers and local politicians in four municipalities in Sweden in 1983 (Pettersson, 1986). When asked which social problem they thought was the most important, half the politicians and half the social workers mentioned alcohol abuse and unemployment, respectively. The social workers estimated that about one-third of their 650 clients had alcohol problems.

Social Work Roles and Functions

Social Work in Different Service Systems

The Swedish welfare system is almost entirely public, and benefits and services are provided on a universal basis. Thus, the roles of social workers differ in many ways from those in many other countries. Because pensions, child allowances, and sickness and parental insurances are universal programs, Swedish social workers are less involved in distributing economic support to elderly people and to families. Services for elderly people and day care for children are also universal and are provided by the local community without the involvement of traditional social workers.

Trained social workers in Sweden are found primarily within two sectors: 60–70 percent in the local social services and about 15 percent in the medical system. Others are engaged in personnel work (public or private), correctional services, and family service and child guidance agencies. Social work roles are determined by the fact that they are performed to such a great extent within statutory systems, whose most distinctive feature is bureaucratization.

In this context, social work methods and strategies vary from paperwork to the whole range of strategies aimed at promoting help and support to underprivileged groups. Traditional social work methods like casework, group work, and family therapy are used mostly in nonstatutory agencies, such as the family service and child guidance agencies, and in the medical sector. To understand social work roles and functions in Sweden, one must view them primarily in relation to the functions of the two major systems for social work: the local welfare services and the medical system.

Local Welfare Services

The Social Services Act of 1982 provides direction to the municipal social services and replaced three previous acts—the Public Assistance Act, the Child and Youth Welfare Act, and the Temperance Act. If differs from these earlier acts by being less detailed. The new act is a goal-oriented "framework" legislation, which its framers thought would make it easier for the local social welfare authorities to determine, in consultation with clients, the ways in which predefined objectives would be obtained. The new act encourages more professional social work, even if it was not explicitly mentioned by the committee that proposed the act. The objectives of the act are as follows:

> Public social services are to be established on a basis of democracy and solidarity, with a view to promoting economic and social security, equality of living conditions and active participation in the life of the community. With due consideration for the responsibility of the individual for his own social situation and that of others, social services are to be aimed at liberating and developing the innate resources of individuals and groups.
>
> Social service activities are to be based on respect for the self-determination and privacy of the individual. (*Social Services Act and Care of Young Persons,* 1981, p. 5)

The local social services are large municipal agencies with a board of local politicians and with thousands of employees. Their main functions are presented in Figure 1.

The largest function is to provide universal services for elderly people and day care facilities for children (home helpers, service houses, day nurseries, private-home day care, and so forth). These services take nearly 75 percent of the agencies' budgets. Trained social workers have only a few roles in this area, primarily as administrators. Social workers are found mostly within the departments for individual and family care, where economic benefits in the form of social assistance are provided for those who

STRUCTURALLY ORIENTED MEASURES	GENERALLY ORIENTED MEASURES	INDIVIDUALLY ORIENTED MEASURES
Participation in community planning	Services for children and youths	Social assistance
Community work	Services for aged people and handicapped people	Child welfare (including foster placement)
Case finding and outreach activities	Information	Treatment of alcohol and drug abusers
	Independent living	Family homes
	Emergency social work	Institutional treatment

FIGURE 1. The Main Functions of the Social Services in Sweden

fall through the universal welfare safety net. Those departments also handle child welfare cases and work with substance abusers. To a lesser extent, social workers may be involved in "structure-oriented measures," mainly community work, and a few are in community planning.

Even though the present legislation is different from the previous three acts, the client groups and the social work methods are about the same as before. To a great extent, the emphasis is on social control. The roles and functions of social workers in these settings may best by analyzed against the background of the clients' characteristics and the social work methods that are used.

Clients and Methods

A problem for all clients is inadequate financial resources. More than 90 percent of the clients need social assistance, the majority only temporarily or for brief periods. Nearly two-thirds of the clients are single men or women without children, and the remaining group consists primarily of single mothers. The composition of clients reflects the fact that universal social policy measures seem to be sufficient for families but are less sufficient for single people, with or without children (Pettersson, 1986).

Nearly half the clients are age 29 years or younger. The main reason for their problems is unemployment. Because unemployment insurance in Sweden is connected to unions, those who are not in the labor market usually lack support and therefore need social assistance. Social work with these groups may be described as "activating." Both individual- and group-oriented methods are used; the aim is to get the clients jobs as soon as possible. The roles of social workers in these cases are a combination of casework and brokerage-advocacy. For the great majority of these clients, however, the measures are primarily administrative (Pettersson, 1986).

About one-third of the clients in a local welfare agency are individuals and families with psychosocial problems (alcohol and drug abuse, psychiatric problems, and so on), and a minority of them are multiproblem families. It is in work with these clients that the social-control functions are more evident. Even though the Social Services Act is based on voluntary participation, and respect for the client's self-determination and integrity is emphasized, supplementary legislation on alcohol and drug abusers, as well as on children and youths, makes coercive measures possible (Pettersson, 1986).

Clients with alcohol problems belong to the lower social strata, and some of them have severe drinking problems. They are older than are other client groups, and most of them are single men, many of whom are divorced. For this category, more care than treatment is needed, primarily in the form of compulsory institutionalization. Social workers act as allocators of resources, as well as controllers, and may initiate a court procedure to get a client into a treatment home against his or her will. However, the great majority of alcohol abusers are treated on a voluntary basis through referrals to special agencies, mainly institutions.

Narcotic addicts are younger and are sometimes involved in criminal activities. If they are under age 18, they may be subject to the compulsory legislation for children and youths. As with the alcoholics, treatment is provided mainly outside the local welfare agencies.

Great attention is given to families in which small children are at risk. Social work with these families is similar to the practices of other countries. The placement of children in foster care with or without the consent of parents is generally avoided but sometimes is necessary. Equally important are psychological and other types of support to families, as in "home therapy." The aim of such support is to avoid separation or to maintain contact between the child and the biological parents during placement. The main social work roles in child welfare are counseling, psychological and material support, and the provision of supplementary resources outside the local agency. A strong element is social control.

Professional social work methods are less important in the local social services. As was discussed earlier, it is not possible to solve the clients' problems only through a relationship with a social worker. Additional resources are necessary, and treatment facilities are located elsewhere. To a great extent, therefore, social workers are links to other systems.

Because social workers have worked with all client groups and problems, their roles, until recently, have mainly been generic. However, specialization according to problem and client group is becoming more common. Thus, social workers now often specialize in social assistance, substance abuse, or the problems of children and youths (Pettersson, 1986). Specialization according to methods, on the other hand, has never been an issue in these services.

Community Work

Community work became increasingly popular in Sweden during the 1970s. According to a survey by the National Board of Health and Welfare (Wahlberg, Lundgren, Mattson, Ronnby, & Stridsman, 1978), the number of community projects grew from 7 in 1971 to 114 in 1976. This increase is a reflection of the more radical ideas of that time. Some projects were directed to the improvement of neighborhoods in older inner-city areas or in suburbs with poor and deteriorating housing, whereas others worked with groups of young people to prevent criminal behavior.

In the spirit of the time, social workers wanted to raise the consciousness of people in the neighborhoods and to mobilize them for change. These efforts were opposed by local politicians and others in the Establishment, and some of the projects ran into great difficulties. The parliamentary commission that prepared the new Social Services Act was anxious to stress the role of elected politicians in deciding about community action. It did not refer to community work but, rather, to "structural measures" that could take different forms, such as participation in community planning, which became a task for the social services, and working with social problems in the local community.

Since the 1982 act, little has happened in the area of community work. Planning for new housing or the improvement of existing housing has been transferred to public housing companies and architects (*Service i Samverkan,* 1990). Community work has also become more consensus oriented, with the goal of improving public services in the local community, a goal that may not always favor the most disadvantaged.

Health and Medical Care

Since the 1960s, the medical system in Sweden has undergone great changes. Organizationally, it has been restructured from mainly hospital care to a concentration on primary care. The number of local medical care centers has increased, and these centers are now available to people in all parts of the country. In 1983, a new Health and Medical Act went into effect. Like the Social Services Act, it is based on a holistic view and emphasizes health and prevention. Health risks, including those caused by adverse social conditions concerning the family, work, the economy, and so forth, are to be observed at an early stage. This emphasis makes expertise of social workers in the medical sector more important.

Social work roles and functions in the medical services vary according to sector. In hospital care (the traditional area for medical social work), social workers have more specialized tasks. As part of the medical team, they contribute to the complete assessment of the patients' situations. Increasingly, they also take part in the treatment process, with the aim of promoting the patients' social functioning. Often they play an important role in crisis intervention (in connection with death and dying, for example), not only with patients but with their families.

Because many people are treated in the open primary-care system, hospital care is mainly for severely ill people and those with complicated and long-term illnesses. This situation is expected to be even more pronounced in the future. Thus, social workers are using more intensive casework to provide patients support and to improve the quality of their lives.

In the few primary care centers that employ social workers, social workers play an active role on the medical team and often serve as coordinators in rehabilitation work. They provide social assessments and take part in the treatment process, which requires contacting relatives and other agencies in the community.

In Sweden, as in most other countries, psychiatric care has been deinstitutionalized. Psychiatric hospitals are rapidly disappearing, and decentralized open-care teams are providing most psychiatric care. Social workers have an important role on the psychiatric teams, where cooperation with the social services and other agencies is a central feature.

Because social workers also participate directly in psychiatric treatment, many social workers try to obtain further training as psychotherapists within the accredited psychotherapy education that is open to different professional groups. Those who complete their degrees may be licensed as psychotherapists and are allowed to practice independently. However, social workers are not licensed in Sweden.

The great emphasis on prevention in the Swedish medical system requires more active participation from all staff members to identify social-risk situations as early as possible. Therefore, social workers in hospitals, as well as in the open-care system, engage in teaching and supervising other groups of personnel. Such educational functions, as well as managerial positions, are new roles for social workers in the medical system.

Training for Social Work

When the first school of social work opened in Stockholm in 1921, its aim was to train those who were working in the administrations of the municipalities and local public welfare agencies. Originally, the local politicians worked with problems of poverty, child care, and alcohol abuse. As the municipalities grew larger, more personnel were required to handle such matters, as well as to do bookkeeping and administration. The degree of specialization varied, of course, with the size of the municipalities.

People who were recruited for this kind of work often lacked the formal education that was required for admission to universities. But they were admitted to the school of social work, or the "institute," as it was first called. It was not until 1964 that social work education became a responsibility of the national government and the educational standards were made comparable to those of a university.

The next reform took place in 1977, when the several schools of social work that had been started by then were integrated into the comprehensive university system. Social work was established as a new academic discipline, and the schools, of which four became university departments, were permitted to conduct research and to establish doctoral programs in social work.

Today, there are four social work departments at the universities of Göteborg, Lund, Stockholm, and Umeå; smaller schools in Örebro and Östersund that are not affiliated with universities; and another small school in Stockholm that is affiliated with the church. The total yearly admissions to social work degree programs are 500–600 students, according to information supplied by the schools. These programs take 3½ years of study, including two semesters of block field placement. Students who complete the requirements for study and pass an examination become *socionomer* (qualified professional social workers).

Continuing education programs in psychosocial treatment and, to some extent, structural social work, are conducted in most schools. These are usually one-year courses, but shorter and longer courses are also given, some of which are organized in cooperation with the local welfare services. The longer courses lead to a master's degree for those who have graduated from the basic program.

The introduction of research and of doctoral programs in social work will have significant effects on the recruitment of faculty and of qualified social work researchers at the larger welfare administrations and other organizations. In 1990, there were 178 doctoral students in social work (Lindholm, 1991), and the number is steadily increasing.

Challenges and Issues for Social Work

Challenge and Response

There is great concern about unemployment in Sweden. This concern may seem strange to outsiders, given that the level of unemployment in Sweden seldom rises above 3 percent of the labor force, a far lower rate than in most other nations. However, with the strong labor movement, the idea of full employment has become an essential part of national policy. Until 1991, this idea was accepted by almost all political parties—not only by the Social Democrats, who were in power for most of the years between 1932 and 1991 (Korpi, 1990). Despite this emphasis, Sweden has no general unemployment insurance. As was mentioned earlier, people receive unemployment insurance by belonging to a union. Those who do not belong to a union can get benefits through an alternative system, KAS, but these benefits are at a much lower rate and the recipients have to have worked for a certain amount of time to be entitled to this insurance. It is through this hole in the safety net of general social policy measures that many clients fall when they become unemployed. These clients are either not entitled to any benefits or are entitled only to the lower type of KAS benefits.

Why, then, is there no general unemployment insurance in Sweden? First, the unions have not been interested in giving up their prerogative to administer the unemployment insurance funds. This insurance helps them recruit members and has kept the number of members at a high level.

Second, Sweden has a strong work ethic. Earning a living is an important value, and it is thought that it is preferable to give people jobs, rather than cash benefits. "Workfare" is seen as a way of preventing people from becoming dependent on public transfers, and too generous and easily available unemployment benefits do not seem to be compatible with that view.

Whatever the reasons for the lack of general unemployment insurance, people without this insurance (especially young people who have not earned enough to be entitled to benefits) turn to the welfare office for economic help. According to the Social Services Act, "the municipality is ultimately responsible for ensuring that persons residing within its boundaries receive the support and assistance they need" (Section 3).

Many public welfare clients are not unemployed in a technical sense. To be classified as unemployed, a person not only has to be without a job but has to be looking for a job. Some clients should be classified instead as "unmotivated" or "unable" to work.

The social worker may send them to the employment exchange office, which often refers them back to the social welfare agency because they are seen as being in need of social rehabilitation. From a social work perspective, it may seem impossible to rehabilitate a person if he or she cannot find a job, but it is equally impossible to find a job for a person who does not function well enough socially. Thus, a "Catch-22" situation is created. The same may be the case with the housing market: Without a job, one cannot find housing, and without housing, one cannot obtain a job.

What, then, can social workers do to help these clients, other than provide social assistance benefits? So far, there have been some attempts to create better forms of cooperation among the welfare agencies, the labor-force offices, and the social security administrations. Sometimes representatives from these different administrations meet with the client together; sometimes they cooperate in creating job-seeker groups or other kinds of programs for their clients. But basically, such programs do not solve the problem of creating more jobs. Therefore, social workers must make the political establishment more aware of the detrimental effects of unemployment on their clients. It may not so much be a matter of advocating on behalf of individual clients as documenting the situation, especially of young people who are disadvantaged in a highly developed market economy.

Issues for Social Work

The two main issues that affect social work in Sweden today are decreasing resources and organizational changes. During the past decade, continuing budgetary cuts have been made in the public sector. In the welfare area, the cuts have primarily hit the social and medical services, whereas the vast social insurance system has been only marginally affected. Some programs, like child allowances and parental insurance, have even been expanded and improved.

During these years, the welfare system has been continuously reviewed to make it more efficient. Different solutions have been discussed. The Conservatives and the Liberals have been arguing for far-reaching privatization, whereas the Social Democrats favor changes in the public system. Because the Social Democrats were in power until 1991, the welfare system is still predominantly public, but there has been an increase in built-in market mechanisms.

This situation is particularly evident in the medical services, where decentralization has occurred. Hospital departments and primary-care units are responsible for their own budgets. A "buy-and-sell" system has been introduced, which means that departments buy services from each other but with public money. Social work departments in some hospitals are included in this system. One consequence is that social workers may have to advertise their services, employ their own staffs, and pay their own costs. Profit making is not allowed, but surpluses may be used for staff training or to lower the price of social work services.

In the present economic situation, evaluations of social workers' achievements in the local social services are encouraged. Computer systems have been introduced in many communities for use in follow-up studies and evaluations.

The decentralization and integration of different municipal bodies means that the social services are being split up into small departments that maintain close cooperation with other agencies. These departments often have few social workers or only one social worker who is responsible for working with all kinds of problems. It is feared that this decentralization and integration may lead to a weakening of professional roles and the loss of social work competence.

Future Directions

Sweden is in a state of transition. After having had strong political support for many years, the Social Democrats were replaced by a Conservative–Liberal government in 1991. This change reflects a conservative trend in the electorate, as well as a growing interest in religious values and a populist trend among some voters.

Because the situation is so new, it is difficult to predict what the future directions may be. The authors assume that, at least in the long run, social policy will become more restricted and benefits will be less generous. There may also be more means-tested benefits directed to marginal groups—the traditional clients of the public social services—which will be stigmatizing to those clients.

The privatization of services is certain to be an issue that the new government will consider. However, its effects will depend on how it is carried out. In the long run, changes in this direction will probably lead to unequal access to services and thereby contribute to increased inequality in the society as a whole.

There are also other signs that the most disadvantaged groups may have to suffer more in the future. If Sweden joins the European Common Market, as it is expected to do within a few years, one can expect that a higher level of unemployment will be accepted in Sweden, as it is in many other European countries. Furthermore, because most countries in Europe have lower taxes on alcohol than does Sweden, it is feared that an adjustment of the Swedish alcohol policy to European standards will lead to higher alcohol consumption and hence to more alcoholism.

The Social Services Act was planned during a time of prosperity, but it was implemented when economic problems were becoming more evident. It seems increasingly difficult to live up to the statements of its opening paragraph, quoted earlier. Therefore, a commission was set up in 1991 to revise the act.

It is not known which parts of the legislation will be revised, but it is probable that a new act will be less generous than the original one. Two issues that have been discussed are that the clients' "right" to assistance will be less imperative for the municipalities and that the local social services will be reorganized. A recent report by the National Board for Health and Welfare (*Behovssocialbyran?,* 1990) has even questioned whether individual and family care in its present form is justified. Some solutions that have been discussed are to transfer all or part of the social assistance program to local social insurance offices and to transfer other social work duties, such as counseling, support, and the provision of information, to agencies outside the social services.

Will organizational changes like these, in combination with drastic budgetary cuts, lead to reductions in social work services that are difficult to describe and evaluate? If so, what will remain are the functions of social control. Whatever the outcome, it is certain that social work in Sweden will soon face its greatest challenge.

References

Behovssocialbyran? [Is there a need for the welfare agency?]. (1990). Stockholm: Socialstyrelsen.

Berglind, H., & Hokenstad, M. C. (1981). Sweden's demogrants: A model for the U.S.? *Journal of Socioeconomic Studies, 6,* 75–84.

The biography of a people: Past and future population changes in Sweden, conditions and consequences (A contribution to the United Nations World Population Conference). (1974). Stockholm: Royal Ministry for Foreign Affairs.

The cost and financing of the social services in Sweden in 1988. (1990). Stockholm: Statistics Sweden.

Korpi, W. (1990). *The development of the Swedish welfare state in a comparative perspective.* Stockholm: Swedish Institute.

Lindholm, K. (1991). *Man och kvinnor i forskning i socialt abete* [Men and women in social work]. Stockholm: Allmanna Forlaget.

OECD employment outlook. (1990). Paris: Organization for Economic and Cultural Development.

Olsson, S. E. (1990). *Social policy and the welfare state in Sweden.* Lund, Sweden: Arkiv.

Pettersson, U. (1986). *Socialtjansten i praktiken: Fran mal till verklighet* [Social services in practice: From goals to reality]. Stockholm: Skeab.

Service i samverkan [Service in cooperation]: *Boendeservicedelegationens erfarenheter av utvecklingsarbete 1985–1990.* (1990). Stockholm: Bostadsdepartementet.

Social Services Act and care of young persons (Special Provisions Act/LVU). (1981, November). Stockholm: Ministry of Health and Social Affairs, International Secretariat.

Statistics Sweden. (1990). *Statistisk arsbok* [Statistical abstract]. Stockholm: Author.

Tomasson, R. F. (1970). *Sweden: Prototype of modern society.* New York: Random House.

Trends in alcohol and drug use in Sweden (Report No. 89). (1989). Stockholm: Swedish Council for Information on Alcohol and Other Drugs.

Wahlberg, S., Lundgren, K. E., Mattson, H., Ronnby, A., & Stridsman, K. (1978). *Samforstand eler konflict? Om samhallsarbete inom socialvarden.* Stockholm: Liber Forlag.

Recommended Reading

Erikson, R., & Aberg, R. (Eds.). (1986). *Welfare in transition.* Oxford, England: Clarendon Press.

Furniss, N., & Tilton, T. (1977). *The case for the welfare state: From social security to social equality.* Bloomington: Indiana University Press.

Lindholm, K. (1988). In search of an identity: Social work training in the Nordic countries. *Nordic Journal of Social Work, 8,* 4–14.

Marklund, S. (1988). *Paradise lost? The Nordic welfare states and the recession, 1975–1985.* Lund, Sweden: Arkiv.

Mishra, R. (1986). *The welfare state in crisis.* Brighton, England: Wheatsheaf Books.

Pettersson, U. (Ed.). (1990). *Etik och socialtjanst.* Stockholm: Gothia.

Sarnecki, J. (1989). *Juvenile delinquency in Sweden: An overview.* Stockholm: National Council for Crime Prevention.

Tengvald, K. (1982). Sweden. In M. C. Hokenstad & R. A. Ritvo (Eds.), *Social service delivery systems: An international annual.* Beverly Hills, CA: Sage Publications.

Wilson, D. (1979). *The welfare state in Sweden.* London: Heinemann.

11

Social Work in Uganda: Survival in the Midst of Turbulence

E. Maxine Ankrah

That social work is alive, well, and advancing in Uganda in 1992 is testimony to the adaptability and value of the profession as a fundamental response to human need. Uganda, unlike its closest East African neighbors—Tanzania and Kenya—contains a macrocosm of forces that have had a severe impact on both the people and the institutions of the country for more than two decades. This chapter examines the direction the profession has taken in the context of a developing nation struggling to survive, yet attempting to address the needs of its people.

Uganda gained its independence in 1962 and has since had 10 presidents; the former Idi Amin, Obote II, and Okello regimes, all between 1971 and 1986, were socioeconomically the most devastating. The ensuing instability led to the international notoriety of this landlocked African nation. As Jamal and Weeks (1988) noted:

> No other country in Africa has suffered from quite as many misfortunes as Uganda [did] between 1970 and 1985. On the general scene, it has shared with other African countries the negative repercussions of the recession in the West, the oil prices' shocks and disastrous weather conditions. But Uganda is unique in having had to adjust to the breakup of the East African Community, to a war with Tanzania, and to General Idi Amin Dada as supreme economic planner and political overlord. During the regime of regular economic mismanagement and political repression, he reduced a once prosperous and promising country to one of the poorest in the world.

The "economic war" that was launched against the Asian community in 1972 led to the subsequent collapse of the modern economic sector and brought ruin to all the social, health, and welfare systems of the country.

After almost 20 years of political unrest, tyranny, civil war, and social decay, the country is believed to be moving toward an era of restructuring

The author acknowledges the invaluable assistance of Samuel Wangalwa and Rose Kiggundu in preparing this chapter.

(Muranga, 1990). This change has been brought about by the regime of Yoweri Kaguta Museveni, who came to power in January 1986, through a people's revolutionary struggle against the former dictatorial governments. The National Resistance Movement (NRM), which currently holds power, issued the "Ten-Point Programme" (*National Resistance Movement,* 1986), a blueprint for fundamental change in Ugandan society (Holger & Twaddle, 1988).

The program stipulates the need to build a nation that is independent and integrated and that has a self-sustaining economy. One other intent is to reverse the trend toward massive poverty. A great concern for poor, weak, and vulnerable people (Camdessus, 1990) is implied by the aim of increasing the availability of such resources as food, employment, good shelter, clean drinking water, health services, education, and social security for all and the participation in decision making by the rural populations, women, and marginalized urban poor people (Burki, 1986; Walle, 1990). All these features already characterize the thrust of NRM's social development and welfare strategies.

Another important point in the program is the restoration of social services, which all but crumbled from 1972 to 1986. Efforts are being made to rehabilitate and expand rural health services; staff primary health care facilities for a community-based health care system; improve educational services; meet the needs of such vulnerable groups as aged, mentally handicapped, and other disabled persons; provide low-cost housing; establish employment schemes; and strengthen agricultural support facilities (Gupta & Nashashibi, 1990). The program further highlights the need to redress errors that have resulted in the dislocation of whole sections of the population, such as "internal" refugees, and to improve the welfare of ethnic minorities. A final theme of the program is the right of citizens to democracy and to the restoration of the security of persons and property.

The several aforementioned strategies hardly exhaust NRM's broad platform of reforms. Collectively, though, they provide vast opportunities for social work in Uganda. Among the NRM's specific social provisions that imply social work involvement are policies for rural development, participation of the masses in decision making by way of grassroots Resistance Committees, and multisectoral and interdisciplinary developmental programs. Despite the grounds for optimism, many challenging issues must be considered if social workers are to respond effectively to the openings that are being made available by the sociopolitical forces in Uganda.

Trends

Demographic Profile

According to the Ugandan Population Census ("Uganda Population Growth," 1991), the Ugandan population was 12.6 million in 1980 and 16.6

million in 1990, with a growth rate of 2.6 percent per year. This rate of growth represents a decline of .2 percent from 2.8 percent in 1980 ("Uganda Population Growth," 1991). Furthermore, only 7 percent of the population was classified as living in an urban center of 2,000 or more people in 1980 (Ssekamatte & Muwanga, 1988).

The consequence of the high birthrate and the reduction in infant mortality from 119 per 1,000 in 1980 to 108 per 1,000 in 1988 ("Uganda Population Growth," 1991) is a youthful population, 48 percent of which is under 15 years; only 3 percent is over age 65. Therefore, the dependency ratio is high. Because the population is overwhelmingly rural, every Ugandan farmer has to support at least an additional 1.5 other persons (Ssekamatte & Muwanga, 1988).

The social implications of this pyramidal structure for children and youths is an increase in child labor and the prolonged involvement of young people in agricultural production, which interferes with their formal education. The illiteracy rate in Uganda is 40–60 percent (*African Population Profile,* 1990). Furthermore, the high rate of growth of the population makes it difficult for the government to realize investments made for future development. An exacerbation of these trends could trap the country in a vicious circle of low levels of productivity, a low life expectancy of its citizens, continued high rates of dependence, massive illiteracy and poverty, and constant political instability.

Economic, Political, and Social Trends

With growing foreign assistance, the country is in the process of rebuilding. The Ten-Point Programme mentioned earlier outlines the other basic economic issues the government is trying to address. A growth of 6 percent in the real gross domestic product was registered in 1990 as a result of the remarkable recovery in major sectors of the economy, particularly in agriculture, transportation, and industries.

In 1987 Uganda decided to adopt the International Monetary Fund (IMF)–backed economic recovery program. As in many other developing countries that have attempted to implement IMF's structural adjustment program, too little attention has been given to its possible adverse effects on poor people (Ribe & Carvalho, 1990). One result has been the decrease in the prices of Uganda's agricultural products on the world markets, which has directly affected 85 percent of Uganda's population. IMF's requirements that the government's support and subsidization of such social services as health and education be reduced and that there be a large-scale retrenchment in the civil service further threatens the livelihood of millions. These terms may add to the socioeconomic hardships of Ugandans.

On the other hand, NRM, by restructuring the political and social organization of Ugandan society through locally based government structures called Resistance Committees (at the village and ward levels) and

Resistance Councils (at the district level), has started the process of democratization and change. The people's increased participation has thereby shown that the government itself is the prime mover, setting the pace in addressing basic needs, despite the constraints generated by past regimes and by the current international global economic order.

Uganda is one of the world's 36 least-developed nations, with an annual per capital income of U.S. $280. Therefore, social workers face the task of joining with the government and with nongovernmental organizations (NGOs) to challenge the poverty, backwardness, and needs of the majority. They must also persuade the apparently responsive regime to meet the new demands of the people in innovative ways.

Social Work Roles and Functions

From the foregoing perspective, it can be inferred that Uganda is a rich arena in which to provide relevant social work services. At the same time, constraints to more extensive involvement are evident. Social work practice in Uganda is largely defined by its introduction into Africa, which was determined more by the political economy of the colonies than by human need. It is determined, currently, by the structures in which social workers are employed. These two factors—local needs and the structures of employment—do not operate, synergistically, to ensure relevant practice.

Social work was introduced into Ugandan society by the British colonialists in the 1930s. The traditional, remedial, individualized approach dominated social welfare and social work, keeping both focused on marginal groups, such as orphans, juvenile offenders, and beggars, and basically ignoring the general population and the major issues and problems of concern to most Ugandans. That this model has proved woefully inadequate for addressing the vast needs of one section of the population, children, through one service, traditionally called "probation and welfare," is clear in this discussion by Parry-Williams (1991) of Save the Children, Uganda:

> Principally it is the scale of poverty which usually affects the greater majority of the population and results in their failure to access resources, e.g., medical, educational remunerative employment and the necessities for an adequate standard of living. In developing countries . . . it is the majority that face these social problems. . . . Also . . . half the population are children. . . . Consequently, children, who are . . . the most vulnerable group in respect of mortality, illness, exploitation, abuse and lack of rights as a group with the all pervading problem of poverty are at a much greater . . . risk.
>
> Traditional social work methods as taught in most developing countries do not address the seriousness of the social problems

> those countries have to cope with. Too often social work departments, and the social workers themselves are still espousing the traditional remedial approach with individuals; that is their inheritance from the colonial Western tradition of social work. The result [is] . . . that the [number] dealt with, as against the size of the social problem, is minute— . . . [and] . . . renders the actions of such a department so peripheral to the general issues as to be almost inconsequential. (p. 3)

With the independence of East African countries in the early 1960s, with professionalism introduced through social work education at the university level, and with the increased involvement of international NGOs, social welfare and social work began to change. In Uganda, that process, as was mentioned earlier, was interrupted from 1971 to 1986 by the turmoil generated by inept, repressive political regimes.

There is a dearth of systematic research and literature on contemporary social work in Uganda. Therefore, the author conducted unstructured interviews in 1990 and 1991 with a cross section of 36 qualified practitioners in some periurban communities and in Kampala and Entebbe, whose views inform the following perceptions of contemporary professional practice. It is also possible to discern new social work patterns that reflect promising attempts to formulate viable and appropriate direct and indirect practice roles to reduce deprivation and to accelerate development in Uganda.

Organizational Context

What social workers do in practice is largely defined by the structure and purposes of organizations in which they are employed. From the interviews just mentioned and a knowledge of rural employment patterns, the author determined that qualified social workers are employed in 47 organizations in the central region of Uganda alone. These organizations include governmental ministries; intergovernmental organizations and commissions; United Nations agencies; international and local NGOs that focus on women, children and youths, health, rural development, relief–material aid, and education; semigovernmental organizations; formal profit-making bodies; agencies that conduct research; and religious organizations that provide social services.

Social work education prepares prospective social workers for available jobs. An underlying objective is to equip professionals to influence organizations in the direction of the goals, values, and mandates of social work. The increasing range of organizations that are recruiting qualified social workers is testimony that the thrust of education and the subsequent impact of graduates on these organizations are reinforcing each other.

Qualified social workers choose to remain in the public sector a shorter part of their careers than do those without professional qualifications, primarily because public social work agencies have less prestige and hence provide low status and remuneration for all but a few highly qualified professionals.

Therefore, qualified professionals shy away from employment in the basically remedial service agencies that deal with juvenile delinquents and orphans, family conflicts, and the needs of handicapped and destitute people. In light of the acute poverty of the majority, such categories of the needy must, in effect, compete with all others in attracting professional attention. Unless agencies can provide adequate salaries, they fail to retain professional social workers. Thus, the profit-making agencies, the international NGOs, and the local semigovernmental agencies have had more success in recruiting qualified social workers.

Nevertheless, the ethic of social work service, together with the social policies formulated by the NRM government, has resulted in aggressive programs of multisectoral development through rural and social development and reorganization. Emphasis has been placed on the reordering of communities through the local Resistance Committees that ensure a central role for widespread participation, especially by women.

The Nature of Practice

The myriad practice settings require that social workers perform the functions inherent in the positions they occupy—for example, those of labor officers, district administrators, and trainers—in addition to structuring roles that constitute a social work response to the problems and needs inherent in the environment of practice. Some qualified social workers provide direct services to individuals, families, and small groups. Others engage in indirect practice in which the aim is to benefit the general population through preventive and developmental programs. Table 1 presents some of these two major types of activities in which social workers are involved, their client or target systems, and a cross-section of the organizations in which social workers practice.

Direct Services

Social workers at the microlevel work mainly as family and child welfare workers, counselors, juvenile and probation officers, and welfare social workers with destitute people, physically handicapped people, and orphans. The posts and functions in medical social work (as opposed to public health work with people with AIDS and their families), mental health, and school social work that were eliminated in the previous two decades of turbulence have yet to be revived as viable social work activities.

Work with small community-based groups, mainly programs directed toward rural women, youths, and villages, is an increasingly important facet of practice. Through branches of international bodies, such as the Boy Scouts, Girl Guides, the Young Men's and Young Women's Christian Associations, and Muslim Youth, women and children are reached through recreational social group work. Volunteers, rather than professional social workers, however, are usually the leaders of such programs.

An essential function of microlevel practice in Uganda is the mobilization of resources. Advocacy for resources is particularly important for children who have been orphaned by war and AIDS, widows, disabled people, and rural poor people. Moreover, the prevalence of poverty requires that the social work roles of enabler, broker, and advocate overlap and are reinforcing. Counselors must often function as brokers, and advocates must work as designers and implementers of projects at the community level or as managers of the resources they have succeeded in obtaining. In several organizations, social workers have had to assume the roles of planners, coordinators, and chief administrators—usually simultaneously.

Supportive networking is another distinguishable facet of direct practice. Several of the organizations surveyed have established programs that are concerned with community-based welfare and development activities. Such organizations as the Uganda Red Cross, Save the Children, and Community-based Health Care have attempted to create "safety nets" within communities to ensure that the most vulnerable children, aged poor people, and people with AIDS and their families are protected. Child care, material and financial assistance, and the provision of information and education are long-term services and involve multiple functions and roles. Social work professionals have demonstrated relevant skills and are therefore being routinely recruited by NGOs and governmental ministries that operate such programs. They function as researchers, educators, administrators, and community mobilizers, as well as implementors.

Indirect Services

Given the social policies of the NRM government, the rapid expansion of NGOs, and the creation of new ministries and new programs in existing ministries, professional social workers have become instrumental in shaping programs. For example, they have formulated policies for women, family planning, institution building, and social reform in the areas of child protection, welfare, and development. In the U.N. organizations, some social workers are recruited for top managerial and policy positions, whereas others head or coordinate affiliated bodies or NGOs. They also practice as local U.N. consultants, researchers, counselors, and implementers.

As was indicated earlier, the "marketplace" has attracted a large number of social workers, who work as managers and personnel officers or

Table 1.

Social Work Functions, Client Systems, Organizational Settings of Practice in Uganda

SOCIAL WORK FUNCTION AND CLIENT SYSTEM	ORGANIZATIONAL SETTING
Direct Services	
1. *Provision of Direct Services* Relief, material support, networking, resettlement, referrals, family counseling. *Client Systems* Families, widows, and orphans.	Ambassadors of AIDS (AOA), Church of Uganda (COU), Inter-Aid Uganda, Ministry of Rehabilitation, Save the Children Fund, (SCF), The AIDS Support Organization (TASO), Uganda Women's Effort to Save Orphans (UWESO), and World Vision International (WVI).
2. *Direct Support to Special Categories* Income-generation projects, funding of education and educational facilities, identification of resources for family support, sponsorship of children, referrals, rehabilitation (social and physical), adoptions, and child protection. *Client Systems* Windows, orphans, poor people, disabled people, and aged people in urban areas.	AOA, Centre for Basic Research (CBR), Ministry of Health, Ministry of Rehabilitation, National Commission for the Protection of Children, SCF, Voluntary Services Overseas, and WVI.
3. *Emergency Disaster Relief* Famine relief, rehabilitation of war-torn areas, drought relief, and employment. *Client Systems* Communities, families, orphans, and refugees.	COU, Food and Agriculture Organization (FAO), International Labor Organization, Ministry of Rehabilitation, National Social Security Fund, UNICEF, Resistance Councils, Uganda Red Cross, United Nations Development Programme (UNDP), United Nations High Commission for Refugees (UNHCR), and WVI.
4. *Health Care, Education, and Services* Care, treatment, and referrals of patients; AIDS counseling and testing; psychotherapy; information and educational services related to HIV and AIDS. *Client Systems* General populations (schoolchildren, women in the armed forces, youths, organizational groups), people infected with AIDS, families, individuals, and workers.	AIDS Control Program (ACP), AIDS Information Centre, CBR, Community-Based Health Care, Community Health Development Centre, Federation of Uganda Employers (FUE), Ministry of Health, TASO, Uganda Red Cross, UNICEF, and United Boys Brigade.

Table 1. Continued

SOCIAL WORK FUNCTION AND CLIENT SYSTEM	ORGANIZATIONAL SETTING
Indirect Services	
1. Services in AIDS research, policy development, and program development. *Systems* General population, governmental ministries, and NGOs.	ACP, African Medical Research Foundation (AMREF), FUE, Medical Research Council, Ministry of Health, SCF, TASO, Uganda Red Cross, Uganda Virus Research Institute, UNICEF, and USAID.
2. *Community Work* Community and rural development, mobilization of the community, cooperative movements, women's groups, yough clubs, community-based institution building, the identification and mobilization of resources, advocacy, labor development, administration, training, planning, and environmental protection projects. *Client systems* General populations, refugees, laborers, women's groups, youth clubs, other organizations.	Action for Development, COU, Experiment for International Living, FAO, FUE, International Development Agency (IDA), Ministry of Agriculture, Ministry of Cooperative Development, Ministry of the Environment, Ministry of Health, Ministry of Local Government, National Council of Women, Resistance Councils, UNDP, UNHCR, UNICEF, and USAID.
3. Planning of social programs, policy development, organizational management, communications, research, control of finances, public administration, and private-sector administration. *Target Systems* Community organizations, institutions, governmental organizations, and NGOS.	ACP, AMREF, COU, IDA, Inter-Aid Uganda, Makerere University, Ministry of Health, Ministry of Rehabilitation, Resistance Councils, private industries, and UNICEF.

as businesspersons, salespersons, and private entrepreneurs. In the semi-governmental and other governmental ministries, they work principally as personnel officers, executive (administrative) secretaries, program officers, and directors of finance. A few are educators in colleges and universities.

The major functions and roles in social work practice correspond to the three conceptually distinguishable emphases of social development, namely, the developmental, the preventive, and the remedial (Muzaale, 1988). Developmental social work includes roles in public administration, social support, the mobilization of resources, institution building, and community education. It also includes research on and planning and policy making for the development of human resources, mainly at the macrolevel. Preventive social work is particularly evident in rural communities and is conducted in nutritional education programs, AIDS-prevention programs, activities for youths, and the cooperative movement. Relief efforts to provide food, clothing, and medicine to people living in the war-torn northern and eastern regions and to ensure safe drinking water are aspects of preventive social work. Remedial social work, as discussed previously, deals with juvenile delinquents and orphans, family conflicts, and the needs of handicapped and destitute people.

Impact of Social Work on Different Service Systems

The structures of employment are a critical determinant of the expansion of social work into a broad range of activities and are instrumental in limiting practice in certain fields and encouraging it in others. Thus, few agencies deal exclusively with marital and family matters; marginal groups, such as disabled people; and individuals whose personal problems are not defined as public troubles.

Financial assistance programs, such as guaranteed social benefits to aid families and children or aged people, have not been started by the government. Most programs of financial assistance are tied to employment and do not cover the majority of the population. Still, the profession plays a highly significant role in guiding the direction of the leading organization, the National Social Security Fund, which caters to employees who are eligible for pensions and financial assistance, and many of the fund's policymaking, administrative, and top service positions are filled by social workers. Professionals also work as welfare and labor officers in personnel departments in industry—jobs that usually encompass the concerns of employees' families as well.

Social work's impact is most visible in the fields of social development, health, and public administration. Its participation has been influential in mobilizing sectors of the population. For example, social workers have been instrumental in the formation and programming of Action for Development, a national organization that champions the rights and welfare of women. In addition, through jobs as district administrators and in other district-level posts, social workers are making significant contributions to rural communities and to the development of the infrastructure. A heavy emphasis in social work education on research and the preparation of graduates to do field surveys has resulted in the deployment of social workers as research assistants, research officers, and staff members of anthropological research projects to conduct studies.

The most phenomenal growth in the number of social workers in recent years has been in the health field. Specifically, the AIDS epidemic, which threatens the welfare and lives of virtually millions of Africans, has spurred an interest by the general public in the special knowledge and skills of social workers. This interest has led to the rapid recruitment of professionals in roles as counselors, health educators, researchers, and policymakers in relation to AIDS in particular and health services in general.

Social Work Education

Beyond the context and structures of employment, the system of training has been a pivotal influence on the shape of social work's response to the needs of Uganda. The education of social workers is the responsibility of two institutions: the Department of Social Work and Social Administration, Faculty of Social Sciences, Makerere University in Kampala, and the Nsamizi Training Centre, an intermediate-level institution in Mpigi, 20 kilometers from the capital (Ankrah, 1980, 1984).

Social work and social administration at Makerere University is one of the three most competitive professional programs provided by the Faculties of Arts and Social Sciences at the university, ranking above law and business administration or commerce. According to the Makerere University Office of Admissions, more than 2,600 secondary students applied for the 55 openings in the 1990–91 academic year alone. Students are eligible to enter the university, following seven years of primary school, four years of ordinary-level studies, and two years of advanced-level studies. This model was introduced by the British colonial administration and was not substantially changed after independence. Thus, most of the students are young; only two or three older students enter the department on the basis of a competitive examination each year.

Since a two-year diploma program was inaugurated in 1963 and a bachelor's degree in social work and social administration was established in 1968, training has undergone continuous modifications. Social work educators have attempted to move away from a basically Western-biased social work curriculum to one that addresses the needs of Ugandans and that stresses a macrolevel approach to education and practice (Hall, 1990). The education of professional social workers has subsequently become more broad based, emphasizing preparation for social-development and community-based practice. This focus is made possible by a curriculum in which core courses include social policy and planning, research, organizational behavior, and management. Among the electives are such subjects as population studies, family law, and domestic relations. A revision of the bachelor's degree curriculum and the introduction of a master of social work degree are scheduled for the 1992–93 academic year. These new initiatives are intended to give a more decisive developmental and community orientation to social work education and practice.

The Nsamizi Training Centre was opened in 1959 to prepare East Africans for the social welfare and community development programs introduced by the British administration of that period. Following independence, public and civil servants continued to receive upgrading in these fields. The center was gradually transformed into an institution only for social work training as other institutions were established to train public-sector administrators. The courses offered at the center equip students to provide direct services in primary social work agencies, community-based programs, and correctional or criminal justice programs.

Social work is a relatively young profession in Uganda. The enrollment records for Makerere University indicate that since 1969, 734 undergraduates were admitted, 478 men and 256 women. Of these 734 undergraduates, 383 men and 202 women have completed the bachelor's degree in social work and social administration. In addition, an average of 120 students per year have been enrolled in the semiprofessional program of social administration. Combining the number of social workers trained at the Makerere University and the Nsamizi Training Centre with those trained abroad, it is estimated that 7,000 persons with degrees or diplomas are practicing in Uganda.

Challenges and Social Work's Response

Despite the intent of the NRM government to confront the backwardness, ignorance, divisions, and poverty of its people, the catalog of human needs and problems that Ugandans and professional social workers face remains formidable (Ankrah, 1986b). Among these challenges are crime and criminal justice, family instability, refugees, and ethnic-minority problems, as well as the abuse of children and women, marginalized groups in the society, illiteracy, alcoholism, and the unattended aged population. At the societal level, rampant corruption and the abuse of power in high places, mismanagement of public establishments, and urban social and physical decay have all affected the profession's capacity to bring about meaningful change.

Social workers have been limited in their response by their history, in which practice was concerned with the private troubles of a few, rather than with the large public issues that perplex policymakers. The low status of the profession is but one manifestation of this situation. Nevertheless, a new generation of social workers is emerging. These social workers are engaged as public and social administrators, policymakers, researchers, community mobilizers, and educators. They are practicing in the variety of structures listed earlier and function through interdisciplinary teams. These changes are gradually altering social work's response.

Nowhere are these changes more evident than in the field of public health, a new area for professional social work in Africa. Social workers' entrance into this field of practice was occasioned by the unanticipated AIDS pandemic, which has had a devastating impact on Africa. Close to 6.5 million of the World Health Organization's estimated 9 to 11 million persons who are infected by the human immunodeficiency virus (HIV) live in Africa ("By Year 2015," 1991). Thus, the immediate crisis of AIDS is perhaps most illustrative of the capacity of the profession to make a rapid and relevant response.

SOCIAL WORK AND THE AIDS CHALLENGE

Recently, government agencies, NGOs, and intergovernmental organizations have accelerated their efforts to check the spread of HIV and AIDS among the 16.6 million people in Uganda. The AIDS Control Programme of the Ministry of Health reported that by April 1991, the disease had struck an estimated 1.5 million people (*Expanded Programme,* 1991). In Rakai District, where the disease was first diagnosed, 25,000 orphans have been identified in a population of approximately 300,000 persons (Hunter, 1989). Urban and rural families are being impoverished by the expense of caring for AIDS patients or by the loss of the heads of their households. At the national level, the ranks of the educated elite, as well as the rural and urban labor forces, are being steadily reduced as the number of deaths mounts. No adequate security nets of the health, welfare, or economic systems are in place to ameliorate the onslaught of a disease that is adversely effecting all such systems.

In a purposive sample of all social workers who were known to be employed in AIDS-related organizations in Kampala and Entebbe, the headquarters of the Ministry of Health, Jackson (1991) found that 12 of the 16 listed persons are fully engaged in AIDS-related activities and that the remaining four are practitioners, such as professionals serving the Ministry of Rehabilitation and the Ministry of Health, whose responsibilities bring them into contact with people with AIDS and the broader social welfare concerns of the AIDS problem in Uganda. The Ministry of Rehabilitation indirectly addresses the consequences of HIV and AIDS, such as the needs of orphans, widows, and other survivors, whereas the activities of the Ministry of Health include health education, mobilization of communities, research, and program management.

The largest influx of professionals, though, has been in the nongovernmental, indigenous, and international humanitarian organizations. These organizations include the AIDS Information Centre, which provides testing and counseling, and the AIDS Support Organization, which provides counseling and relief. Church-related hospitals engage practitioners in mobile community outreach teams as well as in clinics. The Uganda Red Cross, World Vision, the Experiment in International Living, Save the Children, UNICEF, and USAID, in conjunction with the national AIDS Control Program and the multisectoral Uganda AIDS Commission, serve as the base for many social work activities. The Medical Research Council and Makerere University provide opportunities for research, institution building, mobilization of communities, and policymaking through interdisciplinary teams that include social workers (Development Network, 1990).

Supportive counseling is the most visible of the functions being undertaken by social workers. More than any others, it calls for direct professional intervention with AIDS sufferers and their families. A second area of critical involvement is the strengthening or building of social support networks among people with AIDS, their extended families, and the community.

The building of community-based support systems is being increasingly assigned to social workers. The needs addressed by this approach encompass more than treatment and health care for people with AIDS; they include the needs of families who have to pay school fees for orphaned children, villages whose agricultural production has been hit hard by the disease, and the committees that have been established to organize the response of entire communities to the problems of the remaining inhabitants of villages that have been devastated by AIDS. Women, in particular, are being mobilized in cooperative societies and churches, among other contexts, for income generation and emotional support. Indirectly, this mobilization is effecting greater social integration as rural and urban people organize themselves, collectively, to deal with the AIDS problem.

Research on the social, cultural, and behavioral aspects of AIDS has provided an important entry point for social work into policymaking, program development, and training (Ankrah, 1990a). Much of this activity has been spearheaded by the Department of Social Work and Social Administration, Makerere University, whose staff has conducted national social and behavioral surveys under the auspices of the World Health Organization (Ankrah, 1991; Ankrah & Ouma, 1989) and other international agencies (Ankrah, 1990b). At the headquarters of the AIDS Control Programme, social workers also provide educational programs for leaders of local Resistance Councils, religious groups, teachers, schoolchildren, and so forth. Social workers are also found in the labor sector, working with the Federation of Uganda Employers; others are involved through their positions as personnel officers and labor officers.

In a relatively short time, therefore, social work professionals have penetrated every sector of Uganda's social response to the AIDS epidemic. Participants in Jackson's (1991) survey and other informants indicate that social workers are making a decisive contribution to understanding and dealing with the AIDS problem. More rigorous and focused research is needed to delineate those activities that may sustain a social work presence in the many other major problems facing Uganda.

Other Critical Issues

Whether the momentum of social workers' response to AIDS will be carried over to other arenas may depend on a number of critical issues.

One issue is the preparation and deployment of a sufficient number of graduates who will remain in the social welfare system. A rapid increase in the number of graduates is being jeopardized by limited resources. Moreover, because of the inclusion of the field practicum and field research components, the social work education program is expensive. The requirements of the IMF and the NRM government's subsequent intent to reduce financial contributions to institutions of higher education while broadening the base of opportunity at the elementary and secondary levels, coupled with the withdrawal of students' allowances and research funds, means that prospective students are likely to be attracted to higher paying professions that serve the economic sector (Robinson, 1990).

A concern, voiced persistently by social workers, is the lack of recognition of the profession by the government and, perhaps consequently, by the public. The absence of governmental recognition is manifested particularly in the differentials in remuneration, positions, and prominence given to the policies and programs that emanate from social workers, compared with those of other professionals with similar qualifications. It is argued that without official recognition, social workers are being denied a platform from which to participate at appropriate levels of society and to demonstrate their relevance (Ankrah, 1990a). Thus, a major barrier to the more effective involvement of social workers in meeting human needs in Uganda is their exclusion or marginalization, rather than their reluctance to be engaged.

Many of the international humanitarian NGOs tend to be preoccupied with emergency, relief, and remedial programs (Development Network, 1990). This preoccupation is impeding progress toward developmental strategies. Direct service practices, rather than developmental roles, get entrenched, making it increasingly difficult for the profession to alter its "band-aid" image. However cognizant the local professionals are of the incongruence between their new orientation and their aspirations to move the profession beyond the individual case model to dealing with large-scale needs and problems, the reorientation of practice has been severely constrained by their limited power to influence the humanitarian NGO system to change. Yet, a decisively developmental stance would confer increased legitimacy from the government and the public on social work. Therefore, in Uganda, the profession appears to be in a no-win situation.

Future Directions

The foregoing discussion of the many debilitating problems that have become endemic in Ugandan society make it imperative that social workers learn to deal effectively with the major difficulties experienced by people in developing countries. These problems include increasing massive poverty, growing unemployment, poor housing, unsanitary and decaying environments, malnutrition, urban pressures, and heightened emotional stress and deaths from HIV and AIDS. The traditional family and social support networks will be inadequate systems for widespread coping (Ankrah, 1986a; Burki, 1986; Hall, 1990; Mallya, 1986; Siamwiza, 1986).

This array of problems—even without the AIDS epidemic—points to the need for the earlier mentioned broad-based, community approaches to practice. These approaches are required to empower people, to develop human resources, to increase institution building, and to strengthen social supports. The recruitment of social workers in the broad spectrum of community-based organizations and the array of evolving functions and roles strongly suggest that community work will be the direction of practice in the future.

The recent but highly impressive involvement of social work in the health field through activities to combat AIDS argues well for the continued strengthening of interdisciplinary collaboration with medical scientists. In addition, there will be a greater collaboration with other professions, both nationally and internationally, in research, curriculum development, exchanges of staffs, and the design of practice.

Both social work education and practice should become more radical and transforming through an approach that is holistic and concerned with the needs of the masses, emphasizes the proactive design of alternatives, brings about and sustains purposeful growth and change, has a futuristic orientation, and stresses the need for the political involvement of professionals in the arenas of power (Ankrah, 1987). This approach is being stressed in training at Makerere University. Although it is still evolving experientially through the close linkage of classroom teaching and the field practicum, the enthusiasm of the students and the increased employment of graduates has been encouraging.

Social work education will move toward awarding more higher degrees. The design of a master of social work degree is already under way. This degree should attract experienced professionals to renew their commitment to the profession. The bachelor of arts program will incorporate new options, including a strong emphasis on practice skills relevant to poverty, health, and women. Graduates who can function as social policy analysts, planners, and communicators, as well as researchers, will be needed to capitalize on the greater opportunities provided by the progressive governmental regime. Linkages with NGOs will be matched by measures to join educators and practitioners more effectively with the people through programs of empowerment. The government's increasing emphasis on the democratization of all segments of society will spur the profession to ensure such linkages.

Finally, there is growing recognition that professional education must be more autonomous if it is to produce the changes that are needed. The year 2000 will see the successful conclusion of efforts to establish a school of social work to replace the Department of Social Work and Social Administration at Makerere University. This change should further enhance the potential of educators and practitioners to determine the shape and future of social work in Uganda.

References

African population profile: A chartbook (2nd ed.). (1990). Addis Ababa, Ethiopia: Population Division, United Nations Economic Commission for Africa.

Ankrah, E. M. (1980). The contribution of social work education to social development: An African assessment. In *Discovery and development in social work education.* Vienna, Austria: International Association of Schools of Social Work.

Ankrah, E. M. (1984). *The contribution social work training institutions make to the rapid development of developing nations.* Unpublished manuscript, Nsamizi Training Centre, Entebbe, Uganda.

Ankrah, E. M. (1986a). The practicum after a decade (The Ugandan case). In J. Hampson & B. Willmore (Eds.), *Social development and rural fieldwork* (pp. 62–71). Harare, Zimbabwe: Journal of Social Development in Africa.

Ankrah, E. M. (1986b). Thinking globally and acting locally: The Africa region. In Y. Kojima & T. Hosaka (Eds.), *Peace and social work education* (p. 27). Vienna, Austria: International Association of Schools of Social Work.

Ankrah, E. M. (1987). Radicalising roles for Africa's development. *Journal of Social Development in Africa, 2*(2), 5–25.

Ankrah, E. M. (1990a, June). *AIDS in Uganda: An emerging social work response. AIDS '90: The social work response.* Paper presented at the Second International Conference on Social Work and AIDS, San Jose, CA.

Ankrah, E. M. (1990b). *AIDS: Screening Ugandan women.* Paper presented at the Bellagio Workshop of the AIDS and Reproductive Health Network, Bellagio, Italy.

Ankrah, E. M. (1991). Social analysis of AIDS in Uganda. *AIDS and Society, 2*(3), (insert), 3–4.

Ankrah, E. M., & Ouma, S. O. A. (1989). *AIDS in Uganda: Social and behavioral dimensions of the epidemic. Report of a pretest.* Kampala, Uganda: Makerere University–World Health Organization.

Burki, S. J. (1986). The African food crisis: Looking beyond the emergency. *Journal of Social Development in Africa, 1*(2), 5–22.

By year 2015 African projections: 70 million infected. The demographic impact of AIDS in Sub-Saharan Africa. (1991). *AIDS and Society, 2*(3), 1 (infold).

Camdessus, M. (1990). Arming for high-quality growth. *Finance Development Journal, 27*(3), 10–11.

Development Network of Indigenous Voluntary Associations. (1990). *A directory of non-governmental organizations (NGOs) in Uganda.* Kampala, Uganda: Author.

Expanded programme of communication for control of AIDS in Uganda: Plan of action, 1991–1992. (1991). Kampala, Uganda: Government of Uganda and UNICEF.

Gupta, S., & Nashashibi, K. (1990). Poverty concerns in fund-supported programmes. *Financial Development Journal, 27*(3), 12–14.

Hall, N. (1990). *Social work training in Africa: A fieldwork manual.* Harare, Zimbabwe: Journal of Social Work Development in Africa.

Holger, B. H., & Twaddle, M. (Eds.). (1988). *Uganda now: Between decay and development.* Nairobi, Kenya: Heinemann.

Hunter, S. (1989). *AIDS orphans in Uganda.* Paper presented at the International Conference on Mothers and Children, Paris.

Jackson, H. (1991). AIDS and social work in Africa. *Journal of Social Development in Africa, 6*(1), 47–62.

Jamal, V., & Weeks, J. (1988). The vanishing rural–urban gap in Sub-Saharan Africa. *International Labour Review Journal, 127,* 271–292.

Mallya, W. J. (1986). Successes and failures of rural social development. *Journal of Social Development in Africa, 1*(2), 23–34.

Muranga, L. B. (1990). *Counselling and HIV testing in Uganda.* Kampala, Uganda: AIDS Information Centre.

Muzaale, P. J. (1988). Social services to rural areas. *Journal of Social Development in Africa, 3*(2), 33–47.

National Resistance Movement Ten-Point Programme. (1986). Kampala, Uganda: NRM Government Press.

Parry-Williams, J. (1991, May). *The traditional definition of social work, its methods and principles: Problems of practicing traditional social work in developing countries.* Paper presented at the Child Law Review Commission Seminar, Kampala, Uganda.

Ribe, H., & Carvalho, S. (1990). Adjustment and the poor. *Finance Development Journal, 27*(3), 15–17.

Robinson, D. (1990). Civil service remuneration in Africa. *International Labour Review Journal, 129,* 371–386.

Siamwiza, R. (1986). Consequences of rural poverty in relation to the urban squatter problem in Lusaka. *Journal of Social Development in Africa, 1*(2), 35–52.

Ssekamatte, S. J. B., & Muwanga, E. S. (1988). *Population, food and agricultural development.* Paper presented at the Workshop on Population and Development, Uganda National Teachers Training College, Kampala, Uganda.

Uganda population growth on decline. (1991, June 25). *New Vision,* p. 2.

Walle, W. (1990). Policies for reducing poverty. *Finance Development Journal, 27*(3), 6–8.

12

SOCIAL WORK IN THE UNITED STATES: HISTORY, CONTEXT, AND ISSUES

JUNE GARY HOPPS AND ELAINE B. PINDERHUGHES

Social work in the United States emerged as a profession in the 20th century, largely in response to problems caused by industrialization and urbanization. With change its major constant, this era has been marked by the development of technology and the speed, if not depth, of communication; waves of immigration and in-migration; and the control and prevention of some diseases, as well as the appearance of new diseases yet to be understood, especially those involving deficiencies in the autoimmune system. The era also has included unprecedented violations of human and civil rights, periods of economic depression and instability, and two world wars. Technological advances have significantly outpaced ethical and moral understanding. Science and engineering have produced an unsurpassed nuclear defense system, and high-tech medicine is able to prevent, prolong, and terminate life. Despite superior agriculture that can feed the world, hunger continues even in a country such as the United States that can afford to eliminate it.

Although today social workers often talk in terms of global issues and see the interconnections among many of them, social work and social welfare programs are still carried out within national boundaries. Since its colonial beginnings, the United States has been confronted with the paradox of commonweal and individual ambition. Governor John Winthrop's sermon "A Model of Christian Charity," delivered to the settlers on the flagship *Arbella* just before it landed in Salem Habor in 1630, is perhaps the earliest example. Winthrop said, "We must delight in each other, make others' conditions our own, rejoice together, labour and suffer together, always having before our own eyes our community as members of the same body" (quoted in Morgan, 1965, p. 92). Governor Winthrop's sentiment found greater acceptance during some periods than it does today. Today there is an ambivalence about community, given that the commitment to this concept competes with individualism and the rationalizations common to a capitalistic society.

Historical and Social Context

American social welfare and social work have been influenced by societal forces throughout the country's history. The larger context today is shaped by fiscal constraints and related ills, including increases in poverty (especially as it affects children), changes in the character of urban neighborhoods, and the growth of both drug use and violence. Other societal forces include changes in the structure of families and the demographic transition that will result in a people-of-color majority in the next century. Fiscally, the call is for the curtailment of social welfare programs. This trend, which started in the late 1970s, will probably dominate the 1990s, with a concomitant need to establish "ins" and "outs."

Historically, social welfare in the United States was based largely on the English model and tradition. The Elizabethan Poor Laws, passed in the early 17th century, are still influential. Since the 19th century, social welfare policy in this country has been driven largely by two assumptions, namely, the value of competitive individualism and the validity of market-based economics. The free enterprise–market system has been supported and encouraged by the government's laissez-faire role. This residual, noninterventionist approach was at one time dominant in other Western countries but was challenged as societal conditions deteriorated. Correlative to the full development of the secular state and industrialization in both Europe (especially Western Europe) and this country, separate philosophies for and patterns of the government's role and responsibility became clearer. In the United States, there was the paradox of strong community concern at the local level but resistance to governmental involvement at the national level.

The Great Depression of the 1930s was the force that drastically altered this country's thinking about the necessity for a more active governmental role. Western European countries had moved to this more interventionist role and enacted national social welfare programs some 50 years earlier. In the United States the New Deal programs, initiated under the leadership of President Franklin D. Roosevelt to combat the joblessness and poverty of the depression, represented a new period in social welfare. The cornerstone of these legislative programs was the Social Security Act of 1935, which distinguished between people who were considered able and unable to work, and work continues to be the focus of debate in social welfare policy for poor, vulnerable citizens.

The debate and subsequent passage of the Social Security Act signified the increased recognition that poverty and other social ills were created by structural problems in the economy, not simply by individual problems and inadequacies (often perceived as sin and laziness). Similarly, it was recognized that the resolution of problems was beyond the scope of a volunteer-oriented charity system. The basic principle of governmental intervention to offset, moderate, or direct purely market-based economic forces and to reduce disparities in wealth and income became institutionalized and prevailed for 50 years. Although the philosophy has been challenged, particularly since the early 1980s, with the agenda of the Reagan administration, the public sector continues to dominate social welfare.

The philosophy of the Reagan administration in the 1980s was that the private sector, not the public sector, should carry the responsibility for planning, administering, and providing social welfare. President Reagan was a persuasive spokesperson, and under his leadership, conservative forces channeled the anxieties and dissatisfaction of middle- and working-class citizens into support for neoconservative ideals. Because of the shift in attitudes, political support for poor people declined, whereas it increased for the affluent (Edsall, 1984). The presidency of George Bush prolonged Republican control of the executive branch of government. For the first time since the depression, opponents of federal social responsibility have been able to replace top-level advocates of economic reform and to dismantle the layer of midlevel public servants who had ensured its implementation.

Poverty and Socioeconomic Ills

Changes in taxation policy and reductions in allocations for human services under the Reagan and Bush administrations have helped to increase poverty and related ills. These policies continue the historical trend of national ambivalence toward poor people. During the depression, at least a third of the population was poor. With the New Deal program of the 1930s and the war economy of the 1940s, poverty decreased; more Americans became middle class, and the gap between the rich and the poor classes became smaller. The 1950s were harsher economically, and by the 1960s slightly more than 22 percent of the population was poor. With the War on Poverty programs of Democratic administrations in the 1960s, the poverty rate reached its lowest point, of less than 11 percent, in 1973. That low point was not long lived, and since then, there has been an appreciable increase in poverty. By the late 1980s, the figure was up again to roughly 13 percent (Bloom, 1990).

The poverty of children seems particularly tenacious. The rate in the United States is approximately twice that of Canada and three times that of Switzerland and Sweden. During the 1980s, it increased appreciably, reaching 19.6 percent in 1989. Today, of the nation's 63 million children, over 12.5 million live in poverty. Although the poverty rates have fluctuated during recession and boom years, the rates peaked in 1983, when 22.2 percent of American children were in families whose incomes were below the poverty level. The net effect has been an increase of 2.5 million children in poverty since 1979. A more striking factor is the proportion of children who are deeply mired in poverty. In 1989, 41 percent of the children were in families with incomes of less than half the poverty level, compared with 34 percent in 1979. White children who live in poverty represent the largest numbers, but their number has grown by a rate that is half that of African American children. Both rates pale beside the 69.6 percent increase for Latino children (Children's Defense Fund, 1991).

Both urban and rural poverty have been well documented. Over the past 20 years, the highest growth rate in poverty actually has occurred in the suburbs of cities. Causative factors include both problems in the economy and deficits in human development for poor families that are due largely to the lack of supportive and nurturing programs. Earnings have dropped, especially for those who are not highly skilled or professionally educated. In many cities, manufacturing and low-skilled but high-paying jobs have declined (Mincy, 1989). However, the relative cause and effect of the economic change in the dynamics of poverty has not been absolutely demonstrated (Mead, 1989). Most poor people work. The minimum wage of $4.25 per hour leaves families with a single full-time minimum-wage earner with incomes that are below the poverty level.

Poverty is strongly associated with single-parent households, which are predominantly female. Today, 52 percent of poor families are headed by women (a sharp contrast to the 23 percent in 1959), 22 percent are headed by men, and 10 percent have both parents. The inadequate investment in human capital is yet another contributor to the persistence of poverty. Many poor people do not receive basic education and skills training: Roughly half the poor women who are household heads have not been able to complete high school, and 60 percent of the parents who received welfare checks for over 30 months from 1986 to 1991 had no high school diploma (Children's Defense Fund, 1991).

Today the concern is not just with poverty but with the multiple effects of poverty, especially on poor children (one in five children is poor, one in four children under age six is poor, and one in two African American children is poor). Among those who are in persistent poverty (defined as being in poverty at least eight of the past 10 years), two overlapping groups dominate: African American and female-headed households. The number of working poor people (full-time employees who cannot earn enough to pull themselves over the poverty threshold) in persistent poverty also has increased.

During the 1930s and the 1960s, when there was a major debate on poverty, the focus was on economic factors—on ways of opening the opportunity structure. In the current debate, the issues center on character and behavior to explain why some people break out of impoverished circumstances whereas others do not. Persistent poverty became an issue after the breakthrough in civil rights in the 1960s and 1970s. Structural, economic, and class-based views are now discredited increasingly by those who emphasize psychological and personal motivation, family structure, and lifestyle.

Shifts in taxation policy, reductions in allocations for the human services, and the increase in poverty are only the more obvious of several contextual concerns for American social work. A related problem is the downturn in the economy. The recession at the beginning of the 1990s has compounded the problems not only of poor people but of the cities in which many poor people live. (Although the majority of poor Americans reside in rural areas, they are not as concentrated and therefore not as visible.) Revenues are down, aid from the federal government has been severely curtailed, and all levels of government have been unwilling to raise taxes. Spending is outpacing revenues, and the results do not bode well for the immediate future. For fiscal 1990–91 there was roughly a $500 million budget gap in New York City, and the gap was projected to reach $2.1 billion in the 1991–92 fiscal year. In Philadelphia, the deficit was $229 million; in Chicago, $75 million; and in San Francisco, $27 million. Cities are downsizing, cutting payrolls and physical services, including the maintenance of such infrastructures as bridges, streets, and libraries, as well as human services programs like food and shelter for mentally ill people, drug addicts, and homeless people (Hinds, 1991). Despite great affluence, little money seems to be available for efforts to improve human capital. (The total gross national product for 1990 was $5,465.1 billion, or approximately $20,000 per person; *Economic Indicators,* 1991.)

Wealthy Americans are more able to escape the problems of cities and poor people by retreating to designated neighborhoods that are secured and protected by private forces. They also can purchase the private amenities—schools, day care, and social services—that are readily available to them. Decent public services are not essential to those who are most capable of demanding them. Therefore, the burden of impoverished neighborhoods and declining services is borne by those who are least able to effect change. Middle-class people leave cities; rich people, traditionally poor people, and new immigrants inhabit them. The absence of the middle class and of role models in cities is a troubling phenomenon, particularly for minority neighborhoods. The flight of the African American middle class and the social isolation of an underclass (a concentrated group of people who are left behind, cut off from social networks, organizations, and the government) should be the focus of debates on poverty policy (Wilson, 1987). The organization of underclass communities is changing, given that the former leadership, which exerted moral and social direction, has been replaced by young people, who are often affiliated with the drug trade. Gone are many surrogates who transmitted culture and socialized young people to the values of work, family, community, and respect for laws (Anderson, 1989).

Many Americans believe that in the absence of effective structures—capable families, civic organizations, and churches—a substitute force or authority is essential if young people are to be protected and given a chance to grow and develop. In Atlanta, Georgia, the city council passed an

11:00 p.m. curfew on November 5, 1990, for youths under age 17 (personal communication with Ms. Woods, Mayor's Office, Atlanta, Georgia, January 28, 1992). The city obviously thought that it must function *in loco parentis,* given the breakdown of important structures and, primarily, the urban family. Other cities have taken or are considering similar actions. The loss of authentic authority is serious—a cause of societal atomization and the fragmentation of communities, resulting in disrespect for due process, privacy, and individual rights (Nisbet, 1975).

Demographic Changes

Yet another contextual issue is the demographic changes that have occurred from the settlement of displaced people (immigrants and refugees). This cohort has nearly doubled since 1970 (Weiss, 1990). The Center for Immigration Studies (1988) reported that the greatest immigration in U.S. history occurred between 1980 and 1990. Three acts were largely responsible for this growth and shift. They were the National Immigration Act of 1965, which facilitated the change from predominantly European to largely Third World populations; the Refugee Act of 1980, which identified a quota for refugees who could not return to their own countries because of potential persecution; and the Immigration Reform and Control Act of 1986, which gave legal status to formerly undocumented aliens and controls the flow of new "illegal" aliens through penalties on employers. Despite their increasing number, displaced people have not been universally well received. Different regions of the country have been forced to absorb new cultures, languages, value systems, and—perhaps what is most significant—interact with new peoples of color.

These new Americans are often viewed as siphoning off jobs, depressing wages, and consuming public assistance and social services. Actually, these attitudes are ill founded. Displaced people are not as reliant on the welfare system as are native-born people. They use kinship and informal help more than formal supports, and when they do resort to public assistance, they tend to use it to become self-sufficient, which they usually become within five years of their arrival (Ross-Sheriff, 1990). These facts not withstanding, some new immigrant groups have been the recipients of violence from others who, for various reasons, feel alienated and deprived. Ethnoviolence, which has its origins in bigotry, is increasing not only because of the number of new immigrants but because of institutionalized discrimination, economic bifurcation, and the presentation of violence in the media (Weiss, 1990).

Ethnoviolence is not new in this country. It dates back to the European settlers' treatment of Native Americans (Atteave, 1983). Still, it has recently become a more widely acknowledged phenomenon. As a result, the Hate Crimes Statistics Act was passed in 1990 to collect more accurate data on the extent of the problem and the nature of related crimes. Already the National Institute Against Prejudice and Violence has reported that roughly 7 percent of the population had been exposed to intimidation or violence because of race, ethnic-group status, sexual orientation, or religion (Weiss, 1990). Many victims are minorities. As new population groups become acculturated, they most likely will experience more ambiguous barriers and become participants in the political system in which their votes will be solicited and counted.

Changes in the Family

Finally, that most basic social institution, the family, has changed significantly. The two-parent family with two children, in which the husband is the breadwinner and the wife is the homemaker, is no longer the normative family form. "Alternative" styles dominate, including the two-parent, two-earner family; the single-parent family (because of divorce or out-of-wedlock births); and blended families, as well as unrelated adults forming a household with or without children.

The role and functions of the family have also changed, and many families have less time for nurturing and caregiving. The formal social welfare system was developed in the expectation that strong informal systems, such as the family and the neighborhood, would provide primary supports while they would compensate for shortfalls. The reality is that the family, in whatever form, is becoming increasingly unable both to give the traditional range of nurturing and care and to provide for economic necessities. Compounding the situation is a government that has become less willing and less able to provide financial supports and services that many contemporary families need (Humphreys, 1989). Minority families have experienced a particularly extensive transition from the two-parent to the single-parent family. Poverty is a major factor for these families (Davis & Proctor, 1989).

The Boundary Nature of American Social Work

How is social work in the United States adjusting to these contextual changes? Given the ever-shifting context in which it is practiced, boundary maintenance of the social structure and its identity becomes a major task of social work as the "practice arm" of social welfare programs that deliver "services devised through social policy to the citizen-consumer-client-patient" (Meyer, 1976, p. 1). Like a suspension bridge, social work is sustained by its cables of respect for human dignity and the right of every individual to self-realization. It is anchored in service and in the goal of empowering those in acute human need on one side and in the "dominant segment of society that controls the resources and sharing of power essential to meeting that need" on the other side (Hopps & Pinderhughes, 1987, p. 353).

The consequences of this dual accountability have been compounded by the ambivalence of society toward social work. In its more expansive cycles, society tends to view social work benignly as a mirror of its own openhandedness and optimism. However, when times are hard and when shortages exist or conflict abounds, society tends to resent social work as an unwelcome reflection of its own priorities and injustices.

Even in its most benign cycle, this ambivalence is characterized by a residual approach to the delivery of services. As a result of this noninterventionist base to service delivery, people receive help not to ensure mastery and competence in the execution of life tasks and functions but only to cope with situations in which failure has occurred. Many of those whom social work has traditionally been called on to help have been trapped in poverty, racism, sexism, and powerless roles that breed helplessness and alienation. For them, laissez-faire and individualism have meant only abandonment and more victimization, particularly when the economy is on the downside. Thus, dual accountability and societal ambivalence, together with the constraining philosophy and the lack of a clear mandate for publically funded services to people, have been major systemic dynamics that have hampered social work's fulfillment of its mission.

The most damaging consequence of social work's boundary role is the way in which the societal inconsistency that is embodied in these dynamics has been mirrored in the function and process of social work. It is evident in the duality that has plagued the profession from the beginning. Because social work always has been responsive to the prevailing milieu, shifts in the climate of society have caused it to vacillate in its emphasis on one or the other side of this duality. Throughout its history, its vulnerability to the tenor of the times has been seen in its fluctuating focus on cause or function, environmental reform or individual change, social treatment or direct service. For example, during the progressive era of the 1900s, the desperate depression of the 1930s, and the tumultuous social unrest of the 1960s, social work was preoccupied with cause, and "new" social work methods were seen as addressing noxious institutional influences, whereas the "old" methods were accused of adjusting people to them (Meyer, 1976). When times have been conservative, as in the 1920s, the 1950s, and the current period since the 1980s, the profession has emphasized function and direct service and has retreated from a focus on cause.

This context has made it difficult for social work to define itself clearly and to hone an identity that is integrated and valued. Because of its state of flux and scope of practice, it has been attacked as being devoid of a theory that it can claim as its own and accused of constructing eclectic approaches that draw on theories from other disciplines. It has been criticized as being semiautonomous practice that is performed mainly in formal agencies or host institutions. In responding to these charges, social work has fought hard to define its purpose, build its knowledge base, establish high standards through self-regulation, and achieve the degree of autonomous practice that would justify its identity as a profession.

Social work's striving for professionalization and the battle to gain respect for its work, its clients, and those who help them have created yet another dilemma. The demand for the empirically based knowledge, autonomy, self-regulation, and other attributes of a traditional profession can lead to a certain narrowing of social work's broad but unique commitment. However, as Meyer (1976) suggested, the critical issues about "the state of social work practice do not derive essentially from the drive toward professionalism, but rather from the preoccupation with it" (p. 20).

Yet another factor in the dilemmas inherent in the profession's boundary role has been the growth in diversity and complexity of the programs in which social workers work. This growth has occurred as a result of society's efforts to meet the proliferating needs and realities emanating from urbanization, industrialization, and changes in the economy. It was the effort to meet these needs and realities that led to the Great Society initiatives in the 1960s and the 1962 amendments to the Social Security Act that expanded services. The battles waged to obtain these programs were regrettably waged mainly by activists, clients, social work students, and others—not by professional social workers (Ehrenreich, 1985). Although social workers were swept up in the rapidly growing welfare departments, poverty agencies, community mental health centers, preschools, and other programs, at least a substantial part of the profession did not support such changes. In the battles about necessary reforms in the delivery of social services and social work education that ensued, "for the first time, the social work profession itself was the target rather than the ally, of a movement for social justice" (Ehrenreich, 1985, p. 205). Nevertheless, expanded roles produced a gigantic leap in the depth and breadth of the knowledge and skills that social workers needed, and the profession found itself confronted with the specters of differentiation and specialization in its various systems.

SPECIALIZATION

The type, scope, and depth of knowledge and skills that social workers need is unquestionably vast because they deal with the countless variables in human life and the multiple causes of human stress. "Whereas other professional specialists become expert by narrowing their knowledge parameters, social workers have had to increase theirs" (Meyer, 1976, p. 21). The need to broaden the horizons of knowledge to cope with the range of problems that exist and to develop the strategies for dealing with them has made specialization inevitable.

Specialization, in and of itself, has posed a threat to the unity of the profession because the variety of perspectives that were generated have created tension, conflict, and fragmentation within its ranks. In addition, the specializations evolved in such diverse directions that there has been no coherent, orderly scheme to classify and order the categories. The lack of a scheme is evident in the following sample of a typology (Minahan & Pincus, 1977, p. 351):

- Method: casework, group work, community organization
- Field of practice: schools, health care, occupational social work
- Problem areas: mental health, alcohol and drug abuse, corrections, mental retardation
- Population groups: children, adolescents, and elderly people
- Methodological function: clinical social work; social planning, development, and research; social work administration; social work education
- Geographic areas: urban, rural, neighborhoods
- Size of target: individual, family, group, organization, micro, mezzo, macro
- Specific treatment modalities: behavior modification, ego psychology, gestalt therapy, cognitive therapy
- "Advanced generalist."

The many conflicts inherent in these categories of specialization have fueled disagreements in both practice and education. There has been conflict not only over which method should be the primary one (for example, casework versus community organization) but over the saliency of one classification over another (for instance, methods versus problem areas). These struggles have threatened the effectiveness of the profession, forcing social work yet again to expend enormous energy on activities to resolve conflicts and to broaden its definition to obtain some cohesion and unity. And again, social work's critics, viewing the time, energy, and talent diverted from service to debating professionalism have questioned the profession's ability to deal with its own "ostensible concerns" (Ehrenreich, 1985, p. 206) and fulfill its mission.

Yet another serious threat to the cohesion and unity of the profession has grown out of the effort to meet human needs in a fast-changing, complex society. Numerous workers from a variety of educational backgrounds were recruited to the multiplying positions (especially those in the public sector) that were created by the new Great Society programs. These new social workers were performing tasks that required them to function at various levels of difficulty and with a wide range of expertise. They were identified equally in the public mind as social workers, and their inclusion in the profession meant that the profession was differentiated not only into higher levels of education and skill beyond the professional master of social work (MSW) degree but into lower levels. In an effort to provide some order to the reigning confusion about functional parameters and to meet the demand for accountability in relation to them, the National Association of Social Workers (NASW, 1981) came up with the following classification:

Preprofessional level:
- Social work aide (high school diploma)
- Social services technician (associate degree)

Professional level:
- Social worker (BSW accredited)
- Social worker (MSW accredited)
- Certified social worker or member of the Academy of Certified Social Workers (ACSW; two years of post-MSW experience and passage of the ACSW examination)
- Social work fellow (advanced practice).

Social Work Education

Social work's response to its increasing differentiation and specialization again moved professionalism to the fore. There were debates about whether undergraduate education could be sufficiently "professional," as distinct from "preprofessional," in its character and whether it warranted the assumption of the responsibilities, as well as the privileges and the prerequisites, of professional status. Concerns have been raised about the preoccupation with credentialing and the monitoring of education and services at the end of the continuum and whether practice at these lower levels has had a negative impact on the profession.

The massive cutbacks mandated by Reaganomics in the 1980s undermined support for social services, while the growing demand for social workers, accompanied by rapidly rising personnel costs and budgetary constraints, led to declassification. This trend downgrades requirements for specific social work positions, so people with lesser degrees and professional training can fill them and be paid lower salaries. Thus today, the majority of those who are delivering social services have not been trained as social workers and do not belong to the major professional association. There are twice as many "social workers" in the labor force without a professional degree as there are those with one (Hopps, 1989).

American social workers and social work educators who seek to unify the profession, consolidate its identity, and facilitate cohesion have most recently turned to generic practice as a solution. This solution, of course, has added another category to the classification scheme and mobilized more opposition and conflict. Resisted intensely by those who specialize in methods, generic practice has been criticized by some as simplistic and unrealistic, while considered by others to be the most complex form of practice yet devised.

The Council on Social Work Education (CSWE), the central accrediting body since 1946, monitors the response of training institutions to these dynamics and ensures the standardization of the social work curriculum. Through its curriculum policy, which serves as the basis for the development and accreditation of educational programs, CSWE permits schools and programs to design curricula but mandates that careful attention be given to the levels of social work education and the relationship among them. At the bachelor's degree (BSW) level, the curricula are expected to prepare students for beginning social work practice and for generalist practice and to provide the professional foundation for practice. Five areas must be covered: human behavior and the social environment, social welfare policy and services, social work practice, research, and the field practicum. Although it is not required that the content of the professional foundation be taught in discrete courses, it should be integrated. Although there is some variation in format, a typical program may require two years of liberal arts study, followed by two years in the social work major, and 400 hours in a field practicum.

At the master's degree level, which prepares students for advanced practice, the curricula must include the professional foundation, along with one or more concentrations. Schools may design and organize their own advanced social work curricula; concentrations may be structured by fields of practice (such as mental health or child welfare), problem areas (such as alcoholism and drug abuse), population groups (such as children or elderly people), or practice roles (such as practice with individuals, families, or groups; Lloyd, 1987). The newest concentration category is that of advanced generalist. For this category, content in every concentration must include social policy and legislation, practice theories, and practice strategies along a continuum from prevention to treatment. Values must be emphasized, and content on populations who are victimized as a result of race, ethnicity, gender, age, religion, disability, and sexual orientation must be included. The typical format requires two years of study, along with at least 900 hours of the field practicum.

In 1990 it was reported that 97.7 percent of all master's degree students were in programs organized around social work methods (macro, or indirect, practice involving social welfare policy, administration, and planning and micro, or direct, practice involving clinical work with individuals, families, and groups). Sixty-three percent of those in a methods concentration combined it with a field-of-practice or problem-area concentration. Direct practice was the most prominent methods concentration, followed by generic practice. Mental health was the most prominent field of practice, or social problem concentration, followed by family services, health, and child welfare (Lloyd, 1987).

Programs at the doctoral level that grant a Ph.D. or a doctor of social work (DSW) degree offer advanced preparation for research and teaching. Recently, there has been increasing interest in "clinical doctorate" programs that prepare post-master's students for advanced clinical social work practice (Lloyd, 1987). CSWE has directed a great deal of attention to questions related to the interrelationship between these levels of social work education; to specification of the linkage between them; and to assessments of the degree to which there is a true educational continuum, integration in the levels, and congruence in the content at the master's and baccalaureate levels.

As of November 1990, 366 BSW programs used over 1,200 faculty and enrolled over 33,000 full- and part-time students, not including those who take social work courses. Ninety-nine MSW programs involved over 3,357 faculty members and over 17,000 full-time and nearly 10,000 part-time students, and 48 doctoral programs enrolled 838 full-time students (Spaulding, 1991).

The U.S. Department of Labor estimates that 600,000 persons in the labor force are called social workers (U.S. Department of Labor, 1992), whereas NASW generally estimates that 250,000 to 300,000 persons have received a social work degree. However, as far back as 1985, 440,000 to 460,000 persons were called social workers, not including administrators and aides (M. Johnson, personal communication, January 17, 1985, quoted in Hopps & Pinderhughes, 1987, p. 356; Williams & Hopps, 1990).

Changes and Issues in Social Work Practice

In the next decade, people who are now identified as minorities will outnumber those who are now considered the majority in some states; by the year 2000, 42 percent of new entrants to the labor force will be native nonwhites and immigrants, and 40 percent of the clients in the service delivery system will be members of minority groups (Cross, Bazron, Dennis, & Isaacs, 1989; U.S. Department of Labor, 1988). Thus, training for work with multicultural populations will be a priority in the preparation of social workers. Preparation for the needed cultural competence should be directed toward producing workers who are comfortable with culturally different clients; are able to appreciate others' different values, beliefs, and cultural practices; are flexible in their thinking and behavior; and are able to engage in the extra steps that are required to understand and manage the complexities involved in cross-cultural work.

A pivotal element in the development of these skills is comfort with oneself and one's cultural identity. Students need training not only to understand and respect their clients' cultures and the personal sense of meaning that derives from these cultures but to identify elements of their own cultural identity and meaning because the culturally competent behaviors that are necessary in work with diverse populations can be demonstrated only when one is clear and positive about oneself culturally. Only then will social workers be able to manage any related troublesome responses to their own cultural identities and meaning that automatically get mobilized in work with clients who are culturally different. The awareness of personal identity and meaning on all levels, including the cultural, should therefore be mandatory in social work training in the future.

Another anticipated change in social work practice will be the application of an eclectic framework in clinical social work. In the context of an ecological approach, workers will be trained to use a variety of theories. No longer exclusively psychodynamic, the armamentarium of helping strategies will be based on cognitive, behavioral, humanistic, and other theoretical approaches that inform practice models, such as crisis intervention, time-limited social learning, and problem solving. These approaches are significant to success in work with severely dysfunctional clients, including severely emotionally disturbed people and those who are trapped in multigenerational poverty and victimization. Home-based services, intensive family preservation services, and assistance that is structured to enhance life skills and coping strategies are promising developments.

A critical although elusive issue is the need for the profession to come to grips with its dual obligation to social justice and the amelioration of individual problems. Social work will not maintain its identity and focus unless it clearly addresses this dual focus. To build on an ethos of justice, schools of social work must help students integrate political-economic dynamics, along with policy, research, and practice skills. Doing so may lead to the increased use of the fields-of-practice model and curricular design. Such a model will help students expand their perspectives, foster their appreciation of the fuller dimensions of the problems that clients bring, and give them a greater sense of advocacy.

Changes in the Employment of Social Workers

American social workers have been historically identified with the provision of public social services, such as income maintenance, child welfare, family planning, and other welfare activities. From the early 1920s, social workers also have constituted the primary group of providers of mental health services. Because social workers are trained to intervene when the fit between the individual and the environment is poor and when there is a need for social restructuring (Manderscheid & Sonnenschein, 1990), they are found in virtually every human services setting. In the public sector, they are in public and child welfare agencies, publicly funded health and mental health clinics, public housing, and public schools. In the private sector, they are in family agencies, hospitals, clinics, and private practice. Other settings for social workers are the workplace, where they deliver services in employee assistance programs and in alcohol and chemical dependence programs, and church agencies, where they work for outreach programs and in pastoral counseling. Finally, social workers are in planning and policy-analysis positions for both government and voluntary agencies. About 116,800 social workers who have master's or doctoral-level training are estimated to be practicing in the United States.

Data from the NASW member data bank were analyzed for 71,634 master's-level social workers whose job definition was consistent with mental health (social workers in community organization–planning, corrections–criminal justice, and public assistance–welfare were excluded). It was found that these workers are shifting from agency practice to private practice and that the salaries of male workers are higher than those of female workers (Gibelman & Schervish, 1991).

Eighty-one percent of these workers work full time, and 19 percent work part time. Two-thirds of the clinical social workers practice in clinics, hospitals, and social agencies; 19 percent are in private or group practice; and 4 percent are in academia. Thirty percent have a second job, 49 percent of such second jobs are in individual or group practice, and 8 percent are in university settings. This finding suggests that practitioners are well used as adjunct faculty members in social work education programs, whether as classroom instructors or fieldwork faculty (Gibelman & Schervish, 1991).

Despite historical patterns and the fact that the not-for-profit sector ranks first as the primary employer of full-time social workers, the for-profit sector is fast becoming a major employer, accounting for 25 percent of full-time and 46 percent of part-time employment. More of those who earn higher salaries (over $50,000) have a doctorate (35 percent) than have a master's degree (9 percent). More of those with doctorates (32 percent) than with master's degrees (21 percent) are in private practice.

In the future, because the profession will be challenged to provide services to changing populations, collaboration between practitioners and educators will be imperative. Schools of social work will need to work more closely and creatively with public-sector agencies. New collaborative efforts between schools of social work and 58 directors of public welfare agencies led to the development of the California Social Welfare Education Center, which is designed to attract students to public and nonprofit social services. The center is funded by grants from the Ford Foundation and a consortium of California Foundations ("Public Agency Work Urged," 1991). This is a positive example that other states may wish to explore.

In Closing

All people have a human obligation to care, and social workers have a professional obligation to care effectively. All over the world, social workers are becoming more and more aware of the connection between public policy and the welfare of human beings, especially those who are needy and become clients. Unfortunately, this is a time when the body politic considers that concern to be misplaced and not considerate enough of its own struggles and fears. In a shifting world economy, those fears are real. The mood invites demagoguery and simplistic solutions. In the United States and much of the industrially developed world, the excesses of the 1980s echoed those of the 1920s. The response in the 1930s was to gravitate to the extremes on both the Left and the Right. The world cannot afford a repetition in the 1990s. Social work has a responsibility to encourage a just global village.

References

Anderson, E. (1989, May 25). *Hearing before the Joint Economic Committee, Congress of the United States.* Washington, DC: U.S. Government Printing Office.

Atteave, C. (1983). American Indians and Alaska Native families: Emigrants in their own homeland. In M. McGoldrick, J. Pearce, & J. Giordiano (Eds.), *Ethnicity and family therapy* (pp. 55–83). New York: Guilford Press.

Bloom, M. (1990). *The drama of social work.* Itasca, IL: F. E. Peacock.

Center for Immigration Studies. (1988, May 17). *CIS announcement series.* Washington, DC: Author.

Children's Defense Fund. (1991). *The state of America's children.* Washington, DC: Author.

Cross, T., Bazron, B., Dennis, K., & Isaacs, M. (1989). *Toward a culturally competent system of care.* Washington, DC: CASSP Technical Assistance Center.

Davis, L., & Proctor, E. (1989). *Race, gender and class: Guidelines for practice with individuals, families and groups.* Englewood Cliffs, NJ: Prentice Hall.

Economic indicators (prepared for the Joint Committee by the Council of Economic Advisers). (1991, April). Washington, DC: U.S. Government Printing Office.

Edsall, T. B. (1984). *The new politics of inequality.* New York: W. W. Norton.

Ehrenreich, J. (1985). *The altruistic imagination: A history of social work and social policy in the United States.* Ithaca, NY: Cornell University Press.

Gibelman, M., & Schervish, P. (1991). *Social worker professional activities survey: Report and analysis of findings.* Silver Spring, MD: National Association of Social Workers.

Hinds, M. (1991, January 6). Cities take painful steps. *New York Times,* p. 14.

Hopps, J. G. (1989). Services to and by real people. *Social Work, 34,* 193–288.

Hopps, J. G., & Pinderhughes, E. B. (1987). Profession of social work: Contemporary characteristics. In A. Minahan (Ed.-in-Chief), *Encyclopedia of social work* (18th ed., Vol. 2, pp. 351–366). Silver Spring, MD: National Association of Social Workers.

Humphreys, N. (1989). The new demographic reality. In L. Healy & B. Pine (Eds.), *Social work leadership for human service management in the 1990s: The challenge of the new demographic reality* (pp. 8–15). West Hartford: University of Connecticut School of Social Work.

Lloyd, G. A. (1987). Social work education. In A. Minahan (Ed.-in-Chief), *Encyclopedia of social work* (18th ed., Vol. 2, pp. 695–705). Silver Spring, MD: National Association of Social Workers.

Manderscheid, R. W., & Sonnenschein, M. A. (1990). *Mental health, United States, 1990.* Washington, DC: U.S. Government Printing Office.

Mead, L. (1989, May 25). *Hearing before the Joint Economic Committee, Congress of the United States.* Washington, DC: U.S. Government Printing Office.

Meyer, C. (1976). *Social work practice.* New York: Free Press.

Minahan, A., & Pincus, A. (1977). Conceptual frameworks for social work practice. *Social Work, 22,* 347–352.

Mincy, R. (1989, May 25). *Hearing before the Joint Economic Committee, Congress of the United States.* Washington, DC: U.S. Government Printing Office.

Morgan, E. S. (Ed.). (1965). *Puritan political ideas, 1558–1794.* Indianapolis, IN: Bobbs-Merrill.

National Association of Social Workers. (1981). *NASW standards for the classification of social work practice.* Silver Spring, MD: Author.

Nisbet, R. (1975). *The twilight of authority.* Oxford, England: Oxford University Press.

Pinderhughes, E. B. (1983). Empowerment for our clients and for ourselves. *Social Casework, 64,* 312–338.

Public agency work urged. (1991, February). *NASW News,* p. 16.

Ross-Sheriff, F. (1990). Displaced populations. In L. Ginsberg et al. (Eds.), *Encyclopedia of social work* (18th ed., 1990 suppl., pp. 78–93). Silver Spring, MD: National Association of Social Workers.

Spaulding, E. (1991). *Statistics on social work education in the United States: 1990.* Alexandria, VA: Council on Social Work Education.

U.S. Department of Labor. (1988). *Opportunity 2000.* Indianapolis, IN: Hudson Institute.

U.S. Department of Labor, Bureau of Labor Statistics. (1992). *Employment and earnings, 39*(1), 185.

Weiss, J. C. (1990). Violence motivated by bigotry: Ethnoviolence. In L. Ginsberg et al. (Eds.), *Encyclopedia of social work* (18th ed., 1990 suppl., pp. 307–319). Silver Spring, MD: National Association of Social Workers.

Williams, L., & Hopps, J. G. (1990). The social work labor force: Current perspectives and future trends. In L. Ginsberg et al. (Eds.), *Encyclopedia of social work* (18th ed., 1990 suppl., pp. 256–288). Silver Spring, MD: National Association of Social Workers.

Wilson, W. J. (1987). *The truly disadvantaged.* Chicago: University of Chicago Press.

13

Social Work Today and Tomorrow: An International Perspective

M. C. Hokenstad, S. K. Khinduka, and James Midgley

Today social work is truly an international profession. In one form or another, it is practiced in all regions and countries of the world. Rich nations and poor, countries that are predominantly rural and those that are primarily urban, societies with population explosions and those with low reproduction rates, capitalist and socialist countries, countries under democratic or authoritarian governments, traditional and emerging nations, post-industrial and industrialized and industrializing nations, countries under conservative and liberal governments—all have social work in common. Nations that have not yet established social work services or mechanisms to train social workers are taking steps to do so, often with aid and consultation from abroad.

The universality of social work does not mean that the pattern of social work's organization, roles, and fields of service; modes of educational preparation; or degree of social recognition are uniform throughout the world. As the previous chapters have shown, there is cross-national diversity in the models and methods of social work practice and in the political, cultural, economic, and social context within which social work is practiced. Also, the theoretical and ideological underpinnings of the profession, the level of its involvement in making public policy, and the priorities given to social services differ from country to country and region to region. Yet there are impressive commonalities in the profession's roles and functions. This chapter explores these similarities and differences in the context of a rapidly changing world. It also analyzes selected common issues and offers projections and speculations about the future direction of social work.

Roles and Functions of Social Workers

Social workers everywhere have a broad and diverse set of roles and responsibilities. They work with people throughout their life cycles: with children, youths, adults, and elderly people. Their fields of practice embrace health, mental health, community development, criminal justice, school systems, family planning, income security, labor welfare, and employee assistance. They provide individual and group counseling; engage in case management; organize support networks; and plan, coordinate, administer, and evaluate social services. They deal with traditional clientele, such as children and elderly people, and new clientele, such as AIDS patients and their families, recent immigrants and refugees, victims of crime, and homeless people.

In all countries, social workers see themselves as agents of social change and institutional reform. In emerging nations, the social work role is cast in terms of the challenge of nation building; in divided communities social workers are expected to be agents of reconciliation. Everywhere, they serve as educators, catalysts, and coalition builders with other professionals, using their skills in group work, communication, networking, and program planning. They organize at the grassroots level and engage in advocacy and community action. In almost all countries they work with poor people. Whether social workers are employed by the government or by the voluntary sector, they share a commitment to the values of promoting human dignity and social justice, empowering poor and vulnerable people, and encouraging intergroup harmony and goodwill.

Shared Challenges in Diverse Contexts

There are appreciable differences in the way social work originated in various countries and in the way it is organized and has matured. These differences include the mechanisms for delivering social services, the degree of public recognition given to social work as a profession, and the immediate tasks assigned to social workers. Yet certain key issues and challenges are international in scope and confront social workers throughout the world.

The conservative attack on the welfare state and the associated shortage of resources is a dominant issue for social workers in many nations. Educational qualifications for social workers and standards for programs of social work education are also of considerable importance. Another challenge is the search for models of intervention that provide an optimum mix of social change and direct service approaches to practice. The low status and poor working conditions of social workers require attention in many countries. And finally, the role of social work in increasingly diverse, multiethnic and multicultural societies is a fundamental challenge. Each of these issues deserves careful attention.

Retreat of the Welfare State?

The shortage of resources is a common challenge that social workers face throughout the world. In one country it may be due to a recession and in another, to a negative trade balance or foreign debt. However, this shortage of resources is far from being only a short-term concession to economic realities. The diminishing allocation of resources to social welfare clearly is part of an ideological shift that is taking place in many countries.

The single most important trend in social welfare during the past decade and a half has been the conservative onslaught on the welfare state (Glennerster & Midgley, 1991). The New Right blames poor people for their plight, accusing them of lethargy and lack of thrift and discipline. Its ideological gurus assert that expenditures for all but the most "deserving" poor individuals deplete the public exchequer and compound public bureaucracies, thus centralizing decision making in the hands of the government. Furthermore, they contend, such expenditures encourage recipients' dependence on governmental "handouts."

Even in countries with a more egalitarian ideological base for social welfare, there has been a rethinking of the criteria for the provision of social welfare benefits and services. In Sweden, often regarded as the prototype of the welfare state, the combination of budgetary problems and an already high level of taxation has lent attractiveness to the development of programs that are limited to segments of the population with special needs. Such targeted benefits and services mark a shift from a system of universal provision. For example, the targeting of services for frail and single elderly people represents a significant departure from the principle that care should be provided to all citizens on equal terms (Hokenstad & Thorslund, 1991).

This ideological and political shift, evident in other parts of the world as well, has negative consequences for social work, given that most social workers are employed by the public sector, and in some countries, as many as 90 percent of them are. Thus, an attack on the welfare state is also an attack on the profession and its role in modern society, and it continues today, even though in the United States it has supposedly given way to a "kinder and gentler" version. This attack and its implications for a constricted and remedial role for the government pose a grave threat to social workers and their clientele.

In most nations, poor people are the principal clientele of social workers, and the problems they face often are derived from their poverty. The acceptance of the conservative explanation that poverty is a product of individual failings, rather than a consequence of structural arrangements, is tantamount to settling for a residual approach to social welfare. Social workers recognize that neoconservatism is only revamped residualism and that it is incompatible with the notion of community and citizenship (Mishra, 1989; Stoesz & Midgley, 1991).

The failure of command economies and the success of market-based economies, those in the Pacific Rim, for example, show that economic development is impeded by a cumbersome bureaucracy working under massive central control. But it would be an unwarranted leap of logic to conclude that the retrenchment of governmentally provided social services will do for the public weal what the free market is supposed to do under certain circumstances for economic growth.

The disturbing trend of an increasing gap between the rich and the poor classes is already evident in countries that have experimented with neoconservative policies. Many of the hard-won victories of the post–World War II social welfare state have been undermined. In the name of privatization and voluntarism, the state is in danger of abdicating its responsibilities to its citizens. As Mishra (1989) noted, in addition to offending social work's commitment to compassion, social justice, and the dignity and autonomy of individuals, the conservative attack on the welfare state presents a technical and intellectual challenge to social workers—a challenge "to demonstrate that there are other ways of integrating economic and social welfare" (p. 180).

The good news is that social work has survived even in the face of antagonistic governments and, as in Chile, even under hostile military dictatorships. In Britain more people are employed as social workers than ever before, and in the United States more students are applying for admission to schools of social work. The profession's resilience, in our view, is only partly attributable to the adaptability of social work organizations. We suspect, rather, that social work has survived because it meets some fundamental needs of people in a modern society—needs that other institutions are unable to fulfill. In this sense, one may argue that if there was no profession of social work, modern societies would have to invent it.

Issues in Social Work Education

Internationally, there is no uniform set of standards for the educational preparation and certification of social workers. Some countries have clearly delineated curricular standards that are enforced by a process of peer review or through statutory regulations, whereas other countries have no formal standard-setting or accreditation mechanisms. Also, there is considerable diversity in the level at which social work education is offered. In some countries, social work is taught primarily in universities at the baccalaureate, master's, and doctoral levels; in others, it is taught primarily outside universities and is rarely offered at the graduate level; and in still others, it is taught at the secondary school level.

In most countries one does not have to have a formal social work degree to be employed as a social worker. South Africa is a notable exception. In that country, the training of social workers is regulated by a statutory body, and one can become a social worker only after obtaining four years of training at an institution of higher education. The practice of social work without registration is a punishable offense.

Although the approaches to and auspices of social work education vary considerably from country to country, the curricula usually include elements of field or practical training, concepts from social and behavioral sciences about human behavior and the social environment, information about social services policies and provisions in the country, and methods of social work intervention. Depending on the level of training, some information on methods of evaluating programs and practice is also included.

The lack of an agreed-on curriculum and its enforcement is only one problem for social work education in many countries. The paucity of financial aid to students and shortages of qualified faculty are other concerns. Some practitioners criticize the undue "academization" of social work education, which they say widens the gap between the practitioners and those who teach in social work education programs.

The Western, primarily the North American, model of social work education has had a major influence on training in most countries. Many educators resent this influence, characterize it as hegemonistic, and question its applicability to countries in which the cultural traditions, social structure, and economic conditions are radically different from those in the West (Harris, 1990; Midgley, 1981). Efforts have been made to "indigenize" social work education in many countries. Some countries have attempted to do so by orienting their social work training programs toward social development, whereas others have introduced the study of local laws and local economics. However, the amount of Western, particularly U.S., influence on social work education in developing nations continues to evoke much debate and controversy.

Search for Appropriate Models of Intervention

Social workers in the Third World have expressed growing dissatisfaction with the ascendancy of a model of social work that focuses more on those who are misfits and maladjusted than on those who are disadvantaged and disenfranchised. It is now generally recognized that the traditional individual-centered model of social work practice is of only limited relevance in countries that must grapple with problems of mass poverty and the associated ills of inadequate housing, malnutrition, and poor health. It is argued by many authors that the macro-oriented developmental approach would be more appropriate in such countries. Essentially, a social development–oriented approach would stress social change, social policy, planning, social action, and community development rather than individual counseling or casework (Khinduka, 1971; Meinert & Kohn, 1987; Midgley, 1981; Paiva, 1977).

Several factors should be considered in determining the appropriate model of social work practice, some of which clearly support a social development model. First, because social work is a contextual profession, its strategies of intervention should be relevant to the environment in which they are applied. Second, a commitment to social and economic justice and to the amelioration of poverty and poverty-related problems must inform all social work practice. Third, the defense of human rights, the empowerment of people, universal access to services, and a fair distribution of resources must remain priorities for social workers wherever they practice.

Nevertheless, one must recognize that macro social work is practiced in a highly politicized context. Prudence and common sense would suggest that social workers have to moderate their maximalist goals. Except in a rhetorical sense, social workers as professionals are simply not in a position to engineer the fundamental transformation of the social structure (Khinduka & Coughlin, 1975). Also, they have a distinct comparative advantage in delivering individual- and group-level services that it would be unwise to overlook (Horowitz, 1991). It may be argued that there is a false dichotomy between the micro and the macro tracks of intervention that must be replaced by the recognition of the complementarity of these approaches and of the need for a simultaneous dual focus on the individual and on his or her surrounding environment (Billups, 1990; Gordon, 1965). The important point, it seems to us, is not to be distracted by the presumed superiority of either the developmental or the therapeutic approach to social work but to apply both of them differentially as the situation warrants.

Yet it is important to note that social work knowledge has so far been dispersed predominantly from developed to developing countries. Many of the innovative approaches to dealing with community conflicts, housing shortages, or family tensions that have been tried with some success in the industrially less advanced countries have not yet been adapted in the economically developed countries. Clearly, the latter have much to lose if they fail to take advantage of learning from the experiences of developing countries (Midgley, 1990).

Uncertain Professional Status

Social work's relatively low status in the hierarchy of professions is a challenge to social workers in every country. The lack of recognition of the profession and the resulting poor working conditions leave much to be desired; salaries are low and workloads are generally heavy. In many countries there is no clear ladder for promotion or professional advancement, and most of the work is carried on in bureaucratic settings, where the regulations often hinder good professional practice. In some countries the public image of the profession is far from flattering. These conditions, coupled with the demanding and sometimes overwhelming problems presented by the clients and communities that social workers serve, produce a high rate of burnout. They make the recruitment and retention of requisite talent a constant challenge.

Although much headway has been made in recent years, the relatively weak knowledge base of social work nevertheless contributes to the status problems of the profession. Largely derived from other disciplines, social work's practice knowledge is at times internally inconsistent and incoherent. Furthermore, the profession lacks systematic empirical validation of its practice strategies. Ongoing evaluation of social work interventions seems to be a desperate need all over the world.

As long as social work fails to provide strong empirical evidence that social work practice makes a difference in the lives of clients, its credibility and professional standing will remain precarious. In the absence of persuasive research to corroborate their many achievements, social workers have difficulty defending their profession against the frequently voiced skepticism about the effectiveness of their interventions. Although social work research is more advanced in some countries than in others, the development of scientific research and evaluation as an integral part of social work practice remains one of the urgent tasks for the profession in the years ahead (Task Force on Social Work Research, 1991).

Social Work in an Ethnically Diverse World

A review of social conditions in every continent shows that few problems are going to be as persistent, pervasive, or daunting as are the relations among different racial and ethnic groups (Nash, 1989). Even the hitherto homogeneous societies are experiencing the tensions resulting from recent immigration. Ethnic heterogeneity in the modern world is the norm, not the exception; it is ubiquitous (Wyzan, 1990).

Ethnic heterogeneity has been caused by historical events, military conquests, immigration, colonialism, and boundaries drawn by foreign powers. It often has been accompanied by differences in the demographic, human-capital, labor market, and economic characteristics of the population (Rupesinghe, 1988; Stavenhagen, 1990). Governments are inevitably drawn into interethnic or interracial conflicts. In some countries, these tensions develop around religious, linguistic, or national allegiances. The recent conflicts in Yugoslavia, India, Sri Lanka, and many parts of the former Soviet Union and the continuing problems of race relations in Great Britain, South Africa, and the United States, to cite only a few obvious examples, illustrate the highly explosive nature of interethnic and interracial conflicts.

The issue of dominance and distribution further complicates the phenomenon of heterogeneity. The more income distribution is skewed, the greater potential there is for conflict based on ethnicity, race, religion, and nationality. The role of government in ethnic conflicts itself is the subject of impassioned controversy and contention. When the issue becomes politicized, violence often follows.

Regrettably, not much attention has been given to the role social workers can play in resolving and managing conflicts in diverse societies. While sympathizing with the underdog and the have-nots, social workers must act as honest brokers and mediators in intergroup conflicts. They must also play a key role in peace-building activities (Paiva, 1991).

Violence is only an extreme consequence of intergroup conflicts in a multiracial or multicultural society. In the day-to-day world of direct practice where violent conflict is not an issue, social workers must still learn how to work with clients who are different. The Council on Social Work Education (1988) in the United States requires each graduate and baccalaureate program of social work education to incorporate subject matter dealing with ethnic and cultural minorities in its curriculum. As Davis and Proctor (1989) suggested, the social worker's ability to work with clients who are ethnically or racially different from him or her requires that clients consider the social worker to be a person of goodwill and expertise. But more than anything else, clients should regard the social worker as credible, that is, as a person who understands their reality and is in a position to offer helpful advice. Therefore, cultural sensitivity and cultural competence will be required more and more of all social workers in this increasingly heterogeneous world (Lum, 1992; Schlesinger & Devore, 1988).

Recognition of the value of diversity within as well as among societies must be part of this cultural competence. Diversity in the modern world should not be regarded as a liability but as a strength. However, social workers should also look beyond diversity and emphasize the common human connectedness, the shared human destiny. The challenge for social workers is to recognize cultural and ethnic differences while transcending narrow cultural and ethnic affinities. If the world is to live in peace and harmony, all people will have to learn to convert the clash of cultures into the confluence of cultures. Will social workers play a role in this process?

The Future of Social Work

The breakneck pace of change in the modern world is shattering old assumptions and arrangements. The collapse of communism in the former Soviet Union and Eastern Europe is opening new opportunities for the profession of social work. The communist ideology never recognized the need for a social work profession. According to the communist doctrine, socialist societies, by definition, were supposed to be free of the human problems that social workers typically address. Now many of the former communist countries are assiduously seeking international assistance to develop both social work education and practice.

The end of the Cold War has created a historic opportunity for the transition to a peacetime economy. If this opportunity is wisely used, the decreasing international tensions may make enormous new resources available for improving the quality of human life—resources that hitherto had been appropriated for defense and military purposes. This opportunity could be translated into an expansion of social work education and improved human services in many societies.

These developments, coupled with other encouraging trends, including the gradual elimination of apartheid in South Africa and increased international cooperation in human services programs through the United Nations and international nongovernmental organizations, are causes for optimism. Still other world trends, such as the increasing disparity between both rich and poor nations and individuals and the aforementioned conservative attack on the welfare state, require a tempering of this optimism.

Given this context, what can one say about the future of social work internationally? Although we do not intend to make any predictions, we do offer a few speculations and some projections based on current trends. First, it seems axiomatic that social work practice will continue to be shaped by its proximate historical, cultural, social, economic, and political contexts. In some cases (for example, the European Community), these contexts will broaden and change, but social work practice will continue to reflect national boundaries more than international interaction. International standards of social work practice and education are not imminent.

Still, it is likely that the social work perspective on both education and practice will gradually become more international, largely because of the increasing internationalization of the context in which it is practiced. No nation can now remain isolated from the international impact of human problems any more than it can remain isolated from the international impact of political or economic problems. Policies on migrant labor and refugee programs already have worldwide implications. Social security policies and social services delivery systems are often better understood in a cross-national context. Thus, it will be necessary for social workers to extend beyond the boundaries of their own nation and into the international arena (Hokenstad, 1988b).

Internationally, as well as in individual countries, demographic and social changes will play a decisive role in determining the priorities of practice. Work with elderly people, new immigrants, and refugees will assume greater importance, and work with women and children, particularly those in single-parent families, will demand increasing attention. As was previously mentioned, diversity among people also will be a key factor in determining the nature of practice. Social workers will increasingly be called on to promote intergroup tolerance in a world that is rapidly becoming more heterogeneous, multicultural, and pluralistic.

The availability of resources will obviously continue to be a major influence on the possibilities and priorities for social work roles and functions. Governmental funding for social programs will depend on economic growth, as well as on political ideology. Although, as the experience of industrialized and newly industrialized countries demonstrates, economic growth per se does not automatically bring about improved social conditions and social benefits for all people in the society, it is still a necessary base for funding social welfare programs.

Balancing economic development with social equity will continue to be the paramount concern of social workers and other human services providers, planners, and advocates. An intellectual challenge for social work educators and practitioners will be to demonstrate the reciprocal relation between economic growth and social welfare. The political challenge will be to persuade policymakers to see this relationship and to fashion public policies accordingly.

The service delivery system in which social work is practiced will diversify in many nations and continue to diversify in others. The economy of the system for delivering social services will continue to be mixed, with voluntary agencies under religious or secular auspices and, to a lesser extent, for-profit agencies coexisting with governmental agencies and state-subsidized agencies. Some privatization of services is likely to occur in such countries as Japan, Sweden, and the former communist countries that have not had this tradition. Certainly, societies that are shifting from command to market economies will expand their personal social services to complement already existing income-support and social-benefit programs. It is likely that the expansion of social work will be most apparent in those countries as well.

Changes in the vehicles for providing services that will have an impact on social work will also occur internationally. For example, such trends as the use of primary health structures to provide mental health services are apparent throughout the world. In this regard, deinstitutionalization and the resulting focus on the availability, accessibility, and effectiveness of community-based care are of equal concern to both developing and developed nations. The organization of services and the division of responsibilities between social workers and members of other disciplines for providing health care and social services, although affecting countries differentially, also are of international interest. These and other trends, such as the decentralization of the provision of services, will clearly influence social work roles and functions in many countries (Holmes & Hokenstad, 1991).

Within this environmental and service-delivery context, social work roles will continue to include an uneasy mix of social-control and social change functions. Social workers will continue to act as regulators and rationers of services, as well as champions and advocates of increased services, improved services, and universally accessible services (Harris, 1990). The creative use of the humane social-control function will be as important as social change if social workers are to contribute to improvements in the quality of the lives of both individuals and communities.

Social work roles in different countries have many similarities, but the place of the social worker in the provision of services differs sharply from nation to nation. As Hokenstad (1988a) explained, the position of social workers in the service delivery system is determined largely by two factors: (1) the stage of development of the profession and the corresponding roles and responsibilities of social workers in a specific country and (2) the amount and level of training that social workers receive. Some of the countries discussed in the previous chapters accord trained social workers the primary role in the provision of social services, whereas others give it a limited or even peripheral role. It is likely that this situation will change in the future, but only as the profession becomes better established and social work education becomes more integral to university education throughout the world.

In view of the depletion of natural resources and the rapid deterioration of the physical resources in all countries—industrially advanced as well as those still struggling to become industrialized—environmental problems that were formerly regarded as being mainly of interest to the middle class will become a major concern of social workers throughout the world. Social workers are beginning to draw increasingly pointed attention to the interrelation between the physical and the social environment, as well as to the international character of environmental problems. Thus, the discussion of the toxic effects of deteriorating rural and urban environments on the health and well-being of individuals, families, and communities in different parts of the world is likely to become a major theme for international social work in the years ahead (Khinduka, 1977; Krauss, 1988; Rogge, 1992; Singh, 1991; Soine, 1987).

Social workers all over the world share common values yet operate within a specific context. All social work practice, like all politics, is local. There is much wisdom in the adage "Global in outlook, local in action." There is only a superficial contradiction between "indigenization" and internationalism. However, both indigenization and internationalism are easier preached than practiced. Developing the most appropriate synthesis of the universal and the unique, the global and the local, is perhaps the most formidable professional challenge that practitioners must confront.

Yet it is not an impossible task. Despite the obvious political, cultural, demographic, and economic differences among nations, the extraordinary similarity of issues that social workers face all over the world is probably the most salient conclusion one can draw from a review of social work in different countries. As social work becomes more internationally focused, there will be increased opportunities for shared understanding and collaborative action on these issues.

References

Billups, J. (1990). Toward social development as an organizing concept for social work and related social professions and movements. *Social Development Issues, 12,* 14–26.

Council on Social Work Education, Commission on Accreditation. (1988). *Handbook of accreditation standards and procedures.* Alexandria, VA: Author.

Davis, L. E., & Proctor, E. K. (1989). *Race, gender, and class: Guidelines for practice with individuals, families, and groups.* Englewood Cliffs, NJ: Prentice Hall.

Glennerster, H., & Midgley, J. (Eds.). (1991). *The radical Right and the welfare state: An international assessment.* Savage, MD: Barnes & Noble.

Gordon, W. E. (1965). Toward a social work frame of reference. *Journal of Education for Social Work, 1,* 19–26.

Harris, R. (1990). Beyond rhetoric: A challenge for international social work. *International Social Work, 33,* 203–212.

Hokenstad, M. C. (1988a). Cross-national trends and issues in social service provision and social work practice for the elderly. In M. C. Hokenstad & K. Kendall (Eds.), *Gerontological social work: International perspectives* (pp. 1–15). New York: Haworth Press.

Hokenstad, M. C. (1988b). Internationalizing social work education. *Council on Social Work Education Reporter, 36,* 1–2.

Hokenstad, M. C., & Thorslund, M. (1991, July–September). Old age care in Sweden: Policy directions and program limitations. *Perspective on Aging* (journal of the National Council on Aging), 17–21.

Holmes, T. R., & Hokenstad, M. C. (1991). Mental health services: An international perspective. *Journal of Sociology and Social Welfare, 18,* 5–23.

Horowitz, D. L. (1991, November 7–8). *The helping professions and the hurting conflicts.* Paper presented at the symposium on Ethnicity, Social Justice and Development: Implications for the Social Professions in Working with Diverse Populations, Michigan State University, Lansing.

Khinduka, S. (1971). Social work and the Third World. *Social Service Review, 45,* 62–73.

Khinduka, S. (1977). Environments. In *People and places: Social work education and human settlements* (pp. 36–50). New York: International Association of Schools of Social Work.

Khinduka, S., & Coughlin, B. (1975). A conceptualization of social action. *Social Service Review, 49,* 1–14.

Krauss, C. (1988). Grass-roots consumer protests and toxic wastes: Developing a critical political view. *Community Development Journal, 23,* 258–265.

Lum, D. (1992). *Social work practice and people of color: A process-stage approach* (2nd ed.). Pacific Grove, CA: Brooks/Cole.

Meinert, R., & Kohn, E. (1987). Toward operationalization of social development concepts. *Social Development Issues, 10,* 4–18.

Midgley, J. (1981). *Professional imperialism: Social work in the Third World.* London: Heinemann Educational Books.

Midgley, J. (1990). International social work: Learning from the Third World. *Social Work, 35,* 295–301.

Mishra, R. (1989). Riding the new wave: Social work and the neo-conservative challenge. *International Social Work, 32,* 171–182.

Nash, M. (1989). *The cauldron of ethnicity in the modern world.* Chicago: University of Chicago Press.

Paiva, J. F. (1977). A conception of social development. *Social Service Review, 51,* 327–336.

Paiva, J. F. (1991, November). *Ethnicity, social justice, and development: The role of the social professions.* Paper presented at the Symposium on Ethnicity, Social Justice and Development: Implications for the Social Professions in Working with Diverse Populations, Michigan State University, Lansing.

Rogge, M. (1992). *Toxic waste, social welfare, social justice and community involvement.* Paper presented at the Annual Program Meeting of the Council on Social Work Education, Kansas City, MO.

Rupesinghe, K. (Ed.). (1988). *Ethnic conflict and human rights.* Oslo, Norway: United Nations University and Norwegian University.

Schlesinger, E., & Devore, W. (1988). Educational strategies for ethnic sensitive responses to social development and social rights. In C. Guzetta & E. Mittwoch (Eds.), *Social development and social rights* (pp. 52–60). Vienna, Austria: International Association of Schools of Social Work.

Singh, S. (1991). Social work and environment. *Lucknow University Journal of Social Work, 8,* 11–23.

Soine, L. (1987). Expanding the environment in social work: The case for including environmental hazard content. *Journal of Social Work Education, 23,* 40–46.

Stavenhagen, R. (1990). *The ethnic question: Conflicts, development, and human rights.* Tokyo: United Nations University.

Stoesz, D., & Midgley, J. (1991). Society, politics and the radical Right. In H. Glennerster & J. Midgley (Eds.), *The radical Right and the welfare state: An international assessment* (pp. 3–23). Savage, MD: Barnes & Noble.

Task Force on Social Work Research. (1991). *Building social work knowledge for effective services and policies: A plan for research development.* Austin, TX: Author.

Wyzan, M. L. (Ed.). (1990). *The political economy of ethnic discrimination and affirmative action.* New York: Praeger.

INDEX

S

T

THE EDITORS

M. C. Hokenstad, PhD, is the Ralph S. and Dorothy P. Schmitt Professor and Chair of the PhD Program at the Mandel School of Applied Social Sciences, Case Western Reserve University. His prior positions include those of Dean at Case Western Reserve University and Director of the School of Social Work at Western Michigan University. He has long been active in international organizations and has been on the Board of Directors of the International Association of Schools of Social Work (IASSW), the Council of International Programs, and the Cleveland International Program. He is currently President of the North American and Caribbean region of IASSW. His publications include several articles and three books in the areas of international social welfare, social work, and social work education. The books are *Gerontological Social Work: International Perspectives* (with Katherine Kendall, 1988), *Linking Health Care and Social Services: International Perspectives* (with Roger Ritvo, 1982), and *Participation in Teaching and Learning: An Idea Book for Social Work Educators* (with Barry Rigby, 1977). Dr. Hokenstad has served as editor-in-chief of *International Social Work* and has co-edited a special international mental health issue of the *Journal of Sociology and Social Welfare.* He also serves on the editorial board of the *Journal of Applied Social Sciences.* He has been the recipient of two senior Fulbright Awards for teaching and research in Scandinavia and has been a visiting professor and lecturer at several European universities.

S. K. Khinduka, PhD, is Dean and Professor at the George Warren Brown School of Social Work, Washington University. He previously taught at Lucknow University in India and, for a brief period, worked at the United Nations Secretariat in New York City. He is a founding member of the

Inter-University Consortium on Social Development. Dr. Khinduka has published extensively in U.S. and foreign journals on technical assistance, community and social development, and international social welfare. He is a former chair of the NASW Publications Committee and currently serves as a member of the NASW International Activities Committee and the U.S. Committee of the International Council on Social Welfare. He is also the editor of two books, an editorial consultant for the *Journal of International and Comparative Social Welfare,* a member of the editorial review board of *Social Development Issues,* and the founding chairman of the editorial board of the *Journal of Social Service Research.*

James Midgley, PhD, is Professor and Dean of the School of Social Work at Louisiana State University. He previously taught at the London School of Economics where he directed an international program for social planners from developing countries. His books have focused largely on social welfare issues in the developing countries and include *Professional Imperialism: Social Work in the Third World* (1981); *Social Security, Inequality and the Third World* (1984); *Community Participation, Social Development and the State* (1986); *Comparative Social Policy and the Third World* (with Stewart MacPherson, 1987); and *The Radical Right and the Welfare State: An International Assessment* (with Howard Glennerster, 1991). He has published articles on social development issues in leading journals and is co-editor of the series *Studies in International Social Policy and Welfare,* which is published by Simon and Schuster in England.

CONTRIBUTORS

E. Maxine Ankrah, PhD, is Associate Professor in the Department of Social Work and Social Administration at Makerere University in Kampala, Uganda. She is also a Research Affiliate with the Uganda Virus Research Institute at Entebbe. She has served as a social work practitioner, administrator, and educator in North America, Europe, and West and East Africa, as well as a researcher and consultant with numerous national and international organizations.

Nidia Aylwin, MSW, is Professor and former Director of the School of Social Work at the Pontifical Catholic University of Chile in Santiago. She is currently a member of the Coordinating Committee of the Program for Post-Graduate Studies on the Family at the Catholic University of Chile. Ms. Aylwin is a renowned academician and is the author of numerous articles. She also serves as editor of the university's social work magazine.

Hans Berglind, PhD, is Professor of Social Work at Stockholm University in Sweden and has chaired its PhD program in social work for about 10 years. He is currently doing research in social problems connected to the labor market and in theories and methods for social work practice.

A. B. Bose, PhD, is a Professor at Indira Gandhi National Open University in New Delhi, India. He began his career in the Department of Social Work in the University of Lucknow in India. He has subsequently worked in senior positions in the field of social policy and development in the Ministry of Social Welfare and the Planning Commission. He has also worked as a United Nations Adviser and Consultant on Social Development with the Economic and Social Commission for Asia and the Pacific and the Asian Development Institute and with the governments of Cyprus and the Republic of Korea.

Gabor Hegyesi, MS, is Assistant Professor in the Department of Social Policy at the University of Eötvös Lóránd in Budapest, Hungary. He is active as a trainer and officer in various nonprofit and professional associations. He has worked in the human services arena for more than 20 years and has published articles on social work education and nonprofit human services.

June Gary Hopps, PhD, is Professor and Dean of the Graduate School of Social Work at Boston College in Massachusetts. She is also former Editor-in-Chief of *Social Work;* current Associate Editor-in-Chief of the *Encyclopedia of Social Work, 19th Edition;* and former President of the National Association of Deans and Directors of Schools of Social Work. She has published numerous articles and edited books in the field of social services and is currently coprincipal investigator of a study on clients in transgenerational poverty sponsored by the Boston Foundation.

Monica Jimenez, MSW, is Professor and former Director of the School of Social Work at the Pontifical Catholic University of Chile in Santiago. She is also Executive Director of PARTICIPA, an international consultant in the fields of social development and education, and a member of several foundation boards.

Chris Jones, PhD, CQSW, is currently head of the Department of Social Work and Community Studies at the University of Central Lancashire, Preston, England. He has worked in social work education for 14 years and has been actively involved with a range of working-class community action projects in England and Scotland.

Peter Ching-Yung Lee, DSW, is Professor at the College of Social Work and Director of the Center for Human Services Research and Development at San Jose State University in California. He is External Examiner for social work programs at the Chinese University of Hong Kong and served as Dean at Tunghai University School of Social Work while on sabbatical between 1986 and 1988. Dr. Lee is also on the U.S. Board of Directors of the International Council on Social Welfare and now serves as Secretary-General for the Inter-University Consortium for International Social Development.

Yasuo Matsubara, Master of Sociology, is Associate Professor at the Department of Social Work at Meiji Gakuin University in Tokyo, Japan. He has 12 years of a distinguished career in university teaching and research. He also serves as chairperson on several child welfare projects.

Fikile Mazibuko, MSW, is a national social work consultant for the South African National Council for the Blind.

Brian McKendrick, PhD, is Professor and Head of the School of Social Work at the University of the Witwatersrand in Johannesburg, South Africa. He has 25 years of experience as a social work practitioner, researcher, and educator and is a frequent contributor to the South African and international professional literature.

Leila Patel, PhD, was formerly a social work lecturer in the School of Social Work at the University of the Witwatersrand in Johannesburg, South Africa. She is currently a research fellow at Yale University.

Ulla Pettersson, PhD, is Professor of Social Work at Stockholm University in Sweden. She has been a researcher and teacher in social work for 25 years. Her research area is the local social services. Currently, she is co-coordinator for research and development within the medical services.

Elaine B. Pinderhughes, BcD, ACSW, is Professor and Chair of the Clinical Sequence of the Graduate School of Social Work at Boston College in Massachusetts. She is also in private practice and serves as a diversity training consultant to medical and service delivery systems, educational institutions, and corporations. She is immediate Past-President of the American Orthopsychiatric Association and has authored numerous publications, including *Understanding Race, Ethnicity, and Power: The Key to Efficacy in Clinical Practice*.

Katalin Talyigas, MS, is a lecturer in the Department of Social Policy at the University of Eötvös Lóránd in Budapest, Hungary.

(order form on back)

Profiles in International Social Work, *edited by M. C. Hokenstad, S. K. Khinduka, and James Midgley*. Sixteen authors from around the world provide a glimpse into the social work profession, addressing the societal and historical context of social work and social work education and training in their respective countries. They also describe the challenges faced by social workers worldwide. An important book that is sure to stimulate research and discussion in both the international social work community and the global community-at-large. **$24.95**

Organizing (Revised Edition), *by Si Kahn*. A step-by-step guide on how to unite people to effect change. Tells readers how to become successful organizers and fundraisers and how to bring about social change through grassroots organization and mobilization. **$22.95**

Perspectives on the Small Community, *by Emilia Martinez-Brawley*. Helps human services students and practitioners understand small towns and rural communities. Focuses on both the positive aspects, such as community pride and the sharing of traditional values, and the negative aspects, such as lack of anonymity and confidentiality. **$18.95**

Social Work Almanac, *by Leon Ginsberg*. The most comprehensive compilation of statistical social welfare data available in one source. Provides clear, succinct information on virtually every human services category. Topics include families, income, children, crime and delinquency, health, mental health, aging, and more. **$29.95**

(order form on back)

ORDER FORM

Send me the NASW Press publications checked below.

Title	Item #	Price	Total
☐ *Profiles in International Social Work*	2154	$24.95	______
☐ *Organizing*	1972	$22.95	______
☐ *Perspectives on the Small Community*	1832	$18.95	______
☐ *Social Work Almanac*	1964	$29.95	______
	+ 10% postage and handling		______
		Total	______

☐ I've enclosed my check or money order for $ ______________.

☐ Please charge my credit card. ☐ NASW Visa ☐ Other Visa ☐ MasterCard

Credit Card No. ______________________ Exp. Date ______________

Signature ______________________________________

Name ______________________________________

Address ______________________________________

City ________________ State ______________ Zip ________

(Payment must accompany this order. Make checks payable to NASW Press.)

Send to—
NASW Distribution Center
P.O. Box 431
Annapolis Junction, MD 20701

NASW PRESS

Or call toll free—
1-800-227-3590

INS4

ORDER FORM

Send me the NASW Press publications checked below.

Title	Item #	Price	Total
☐ *Profiles in International Social Work*	2154	$24.95	______
☐ *Organizing*	1972	$22.95	______
☐ *Perspectives on the Small Community*	1832	$18.95	______
☐ *Social Work Almanac*	1964	$29.95	______
	+ 10% postage and handling		______
		Total	______

☐ I've enclosed my check or money order for $ ______________.

☐ Please charge my credit card. ☐ NASW Visa ☐ Other Visa ☐ MasterCard

Credit Card No. ______________________ Exp. Date ______________

Signature ______________________________________

Name ______________________________________

Address ______________________________________

City ________________ State ______________ Zip ________

(Payment must accompany this order. Make checks payable to NASW Press.)

Send to—
NASW Distribution Center
P.O. Box 431
Annapolis Junction, MD 20701

NASW PRESS

Or call toll free—
1-800-227-3590

INS4